Windows™ VisiRef

Trudi Reisner
with
Michael Watson

que

Windows VisiRef

Library of Congress Catalog No: 94-66542

ISBN: 1-56529-805-5

96 95 94 6 5 4 3 2 1

Interpretation of the printing code: the rightmost double-digit number is the year of the book's printing; the rightmost single-digit number, the number of the book's printing. For example, a printing code of 94-1 shows that the first printing of the book occurred in 1994.

Screen reproductions in this book were created with Collage Plus from Inner Media, Inc., Hollis, NH.

Windows VisiRef is based on Microsoft Windows versions 3.1, 3.11 and Windows for Workgroups 3.11.

Publisher: David P. Ewing

Associate Publisher: Michael Miller

Publishing Director: Joseph B. Wikert

Managing Editor: Michael Cunningham

Product Marketing Manager: Greg Wiegand

Credits

Publishing Manager
Brad R. Koch

Acquisitions Editor
Angela J. Lee

Product Director
Robin Drake

Technical Editor
Wendy Arnold

Acquisitions Coordinator
Patricia J. Brooks

Novice Reviewer
Michael Stanley

Book Designer
Amy Peppler-Adams

Cover Designers
Dan Armstrong
Amy Peppler-Adams

Production Team
Stephen Adams
Angela Bannan
Claudia Bell
Anne Dickerson
Karen Dodson
Carla Hall
Andrea Marcum
Nanci Sears Perry
Amy Steed
Michael Thomas
Tina Trettin
Lillian Yates

Indexer
Michael Hughes

Composed in *Stone* and *MCPdigital* by Que Corporation

Dedication

To Ellie Sulston, with special thanks for her encouragement and support.

About the Authors

Trudi Reisner is a computer consultant specializing in training users of IBM PCs, PC compatibles, and Apple Macintoshes in the use of applications software. She is the owner of Computer Training Solutions, a Boston, Massachusetts company that offers training, technical writing, curriculum development, and consulting services in software programs. Trudi has written many books on Windows and other software, including Que's *Ami Pro 3 Quick Reference; Easy 1-2-3 Release 4 for Windows; Easy Excel 5 for Windows; Easy Word 6 for Windows,* Second Edition; *Easy WordPerfect 6 for Windows,* Second Edition; *Excel VisiRef;* and *Word for Windows 2 Quick Reference.*

Formerly an engineer and designer of computer-controlled machine tools, **Michael Watson** is principal of Archetype Communications, a firm offering professional services to the computer publishing trade. He is revision author of *Easy DOS 6.2* and has performed technical editing on more than 25 titles from Que.

Acknowledgments

I owe thanks to many others who helped complete this book. At Que, foremost is Robin Drake, Product Development Specialist, who developed and edited the manuscript. Also, thanks to Joe Wikert, Publishing Director, and Brad Koch, Publishing Manager, for their guidance in the structure and design for this book. Special recognition must go to Angela Lee, Acquisitions Editor, for her outstanding management skills, who suggested the project and gave support and encouragement throughout the project. Thanks also to Patty Brooks, Acquisitions Coordinator, for her assistance in obtaining software needed to write this book.

Also, many thanks to technical editor Wendy Arnold, whose timely proofing helped maintain the accuracy of the text from cover to cover. Special thanks to the production staff, who turned the final draft on disk into this printed copy in record time—a monumental task.

Finally, thanks to Microsoft Corporation, who developed and produced a fine operating environment for MS-DOS.

Trademark Acknowledgments

Contents

How To Use This Book

Welcome to a revolutionary concept in quick references! Unlike traditional pocket references, which usually pack a lot of text on the page but few, if any, illustrations, the *VisiRef* series presents nearly all of its "how-to" information *visually*. You'll find all the essential tasks here, color-coded and organized alphabetically by larger task category. Use the color-coded sections to quickly locate the task you need to find, follow the full-color screen shots to see each step in the process, and then complete the task yourself. If you prefer to learn or recall information by being *shown* how a task is accomplished, Que's *VisiRef* series is well matched to your needs. The *VisiRef* books are the perfect complement to today's graphical software. You don't have to read a lot of text to find the reference information you need.

Each page provides the following information:

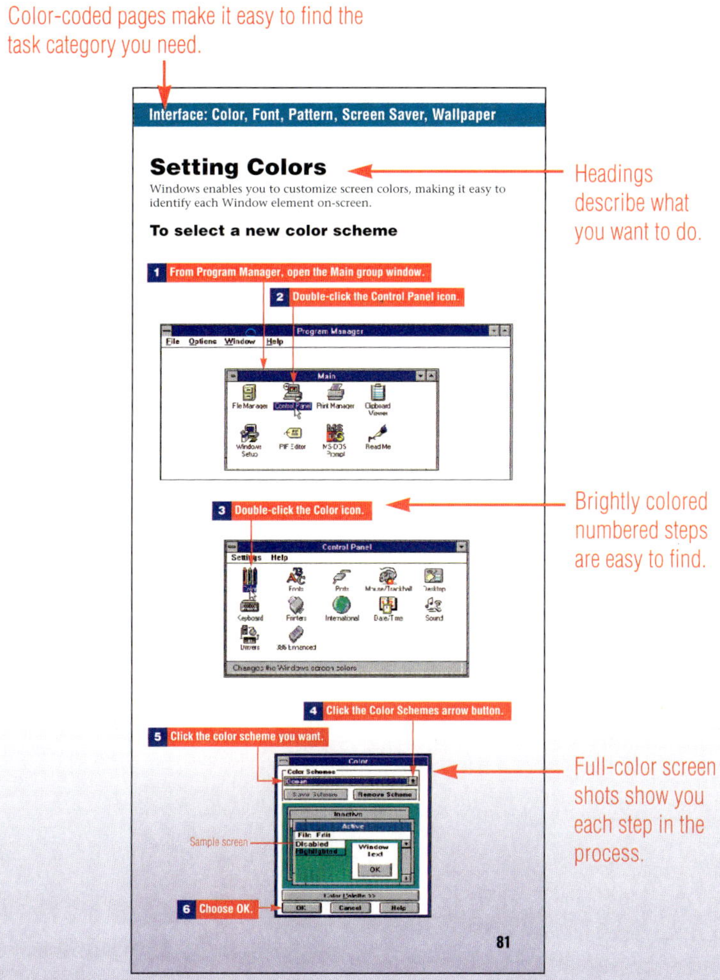

Starting and Exiting Windows

Most users start Windows from the C:\WINDOWS directory. But if Windows is in your computer's path, you can start the program from any directory. When you exit Windows, you return to the DOS prompt in the directory where you started the program.

You should always exit Windows before turning off your computer.

To start Windows

1 At the DOS prompt, type win and press Enter.

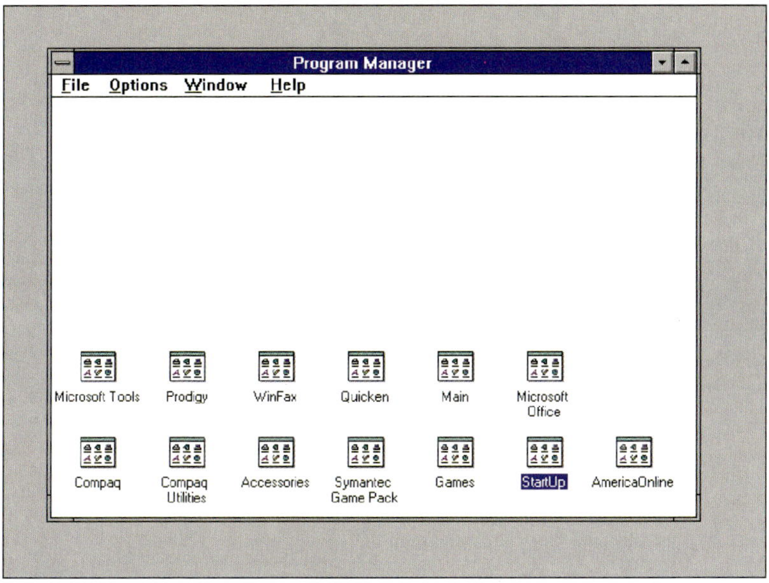

Depending on your setup, Windows generally opens to the Program Manager window

To exit Windows

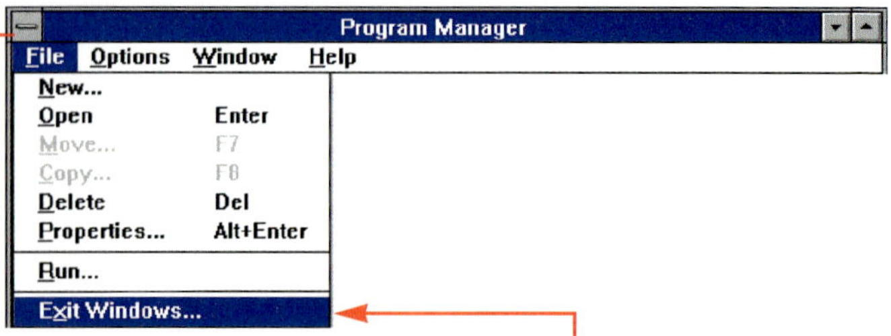

You can also double-click Program Manager's Control menu box or press Alt+F4

1 Choose File, Exit Windows.

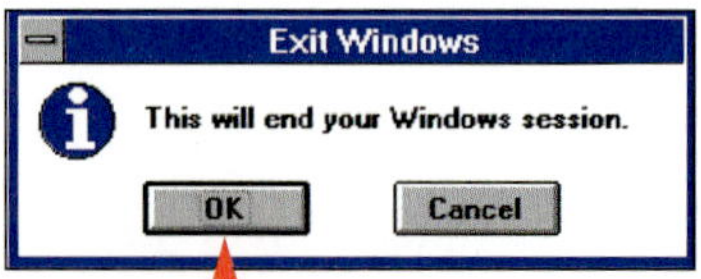

2 Choose OK.

Parts of the Windows screen

The Windows desktop is the screen background on which windows and minimized program and window icons are displayed. Desktop activities originate from Program Manager. Other windows have the same basic elements as Program Manager.

Control menu box

Title bar

Minimize button

Maximize button

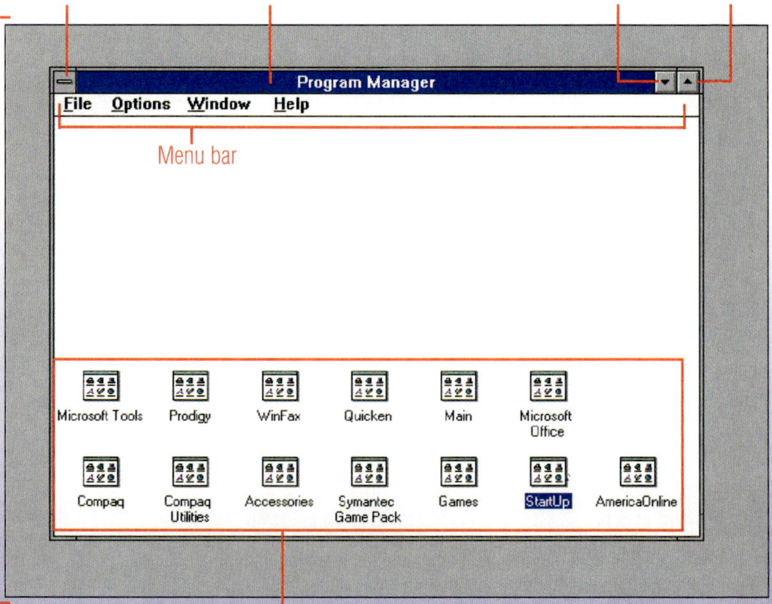

Menu bar

Desktop

Icons

Mouse Actions

Using the mouse is the easiest and most natural way to open and close windows, open menus, select menu commands, and select text and graphics.

To point and click

1 Position the mouse pointer on the item (point).

2 Press and quickly release the left mouse button (click).

To close a pop-up menu, press Esc

To double-click

1 Position the mouse pointer on the item.

2 Quickly press and release the left mouse button twice (double-click).

To move or size an item by dragging

1 Position the mouse pointer on the item.

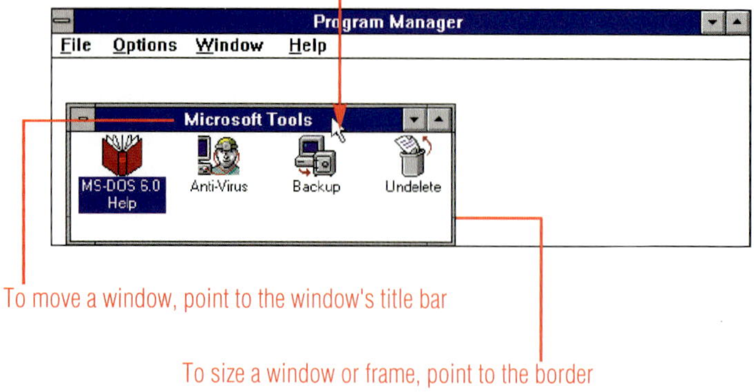

2 Press and hold down the left mouse button.

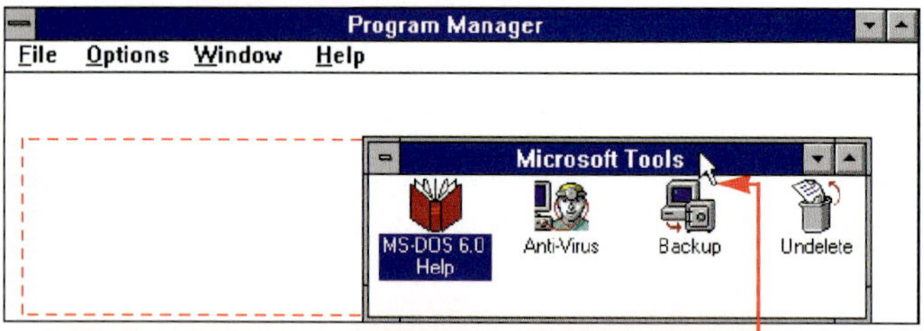

3 Drag the mouse until the item is how you want it.

4 Release the mouse button.

Arranging Icons

You can arrange icons in a window so the icons are in the order you prefer (for example, programs you use most at the top of the window). You can also let Windows arrange icons for you automatically.

To move an icon

1 Point to the icon you want to move.

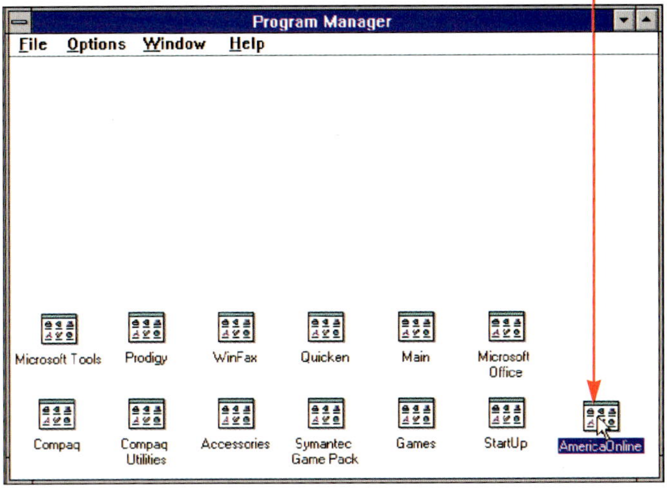

2 Hold down the left mouse button.

3 Drag the mouse until the icon is in the desired location.

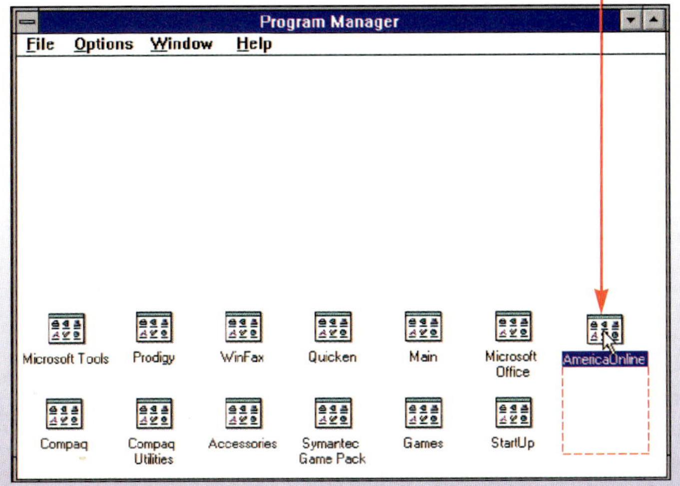

4 Release the mouse button.

If icons seem to move on their own, see the section "To arrange icons automatically"

To arrange all icons in a window

1 Click the title bar of the window with icons you want to arrange.

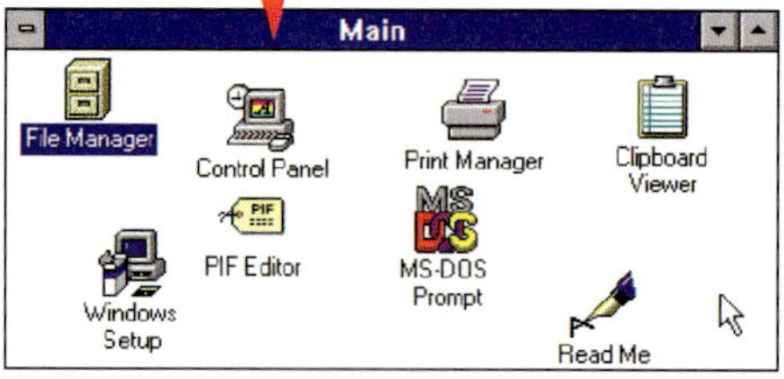

2 Choose Window, Arrange Icons.

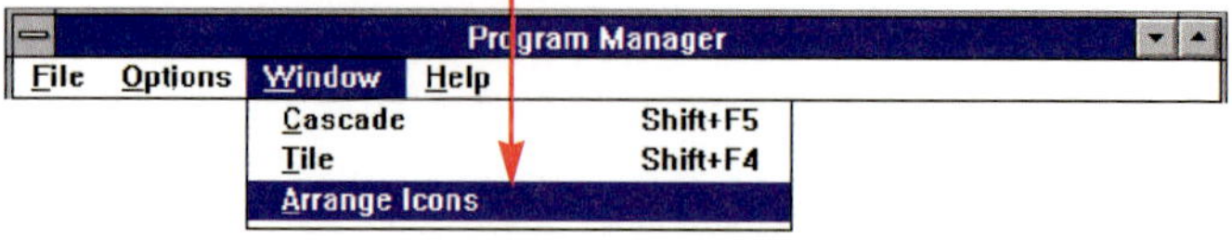

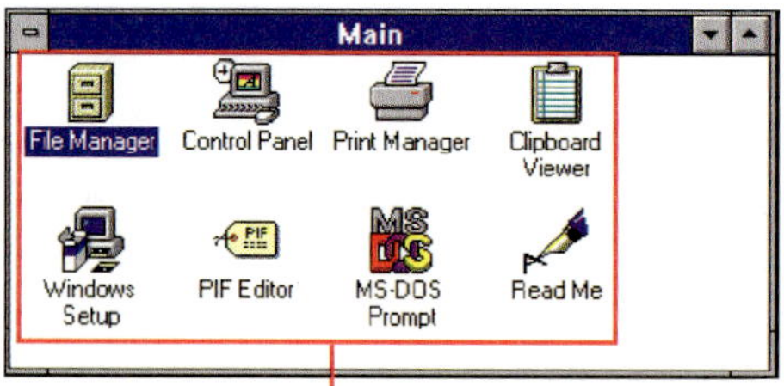

The icons are rearranged

To arrange icons automatically

1 Choose Options, Auto Arrange.

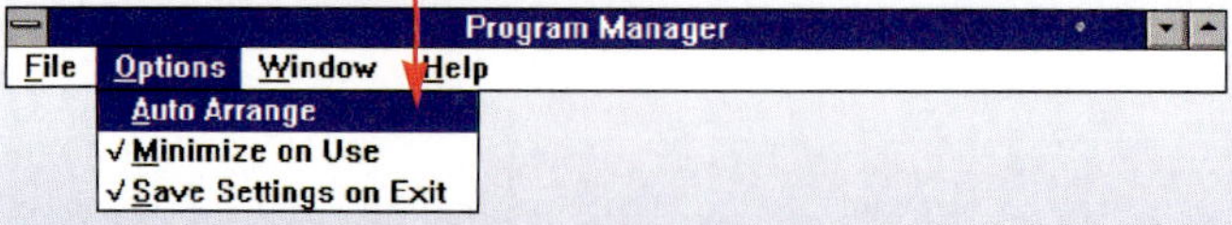

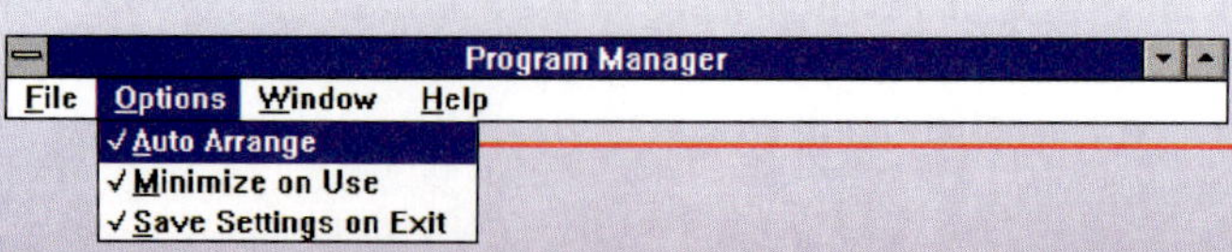

2 To turn off auto-arranging, choose Options, Auto Arrange again.

A check mark appears next to the option when it's selected

Opening Windows

A window is a rectangular area on-screen in which you view applications, files, or icons. All programs are stored in program group windows. A group window is indicated by a group icon.

1 Click the icon of the window you want to open.

2 Choose Restore or press Enter.

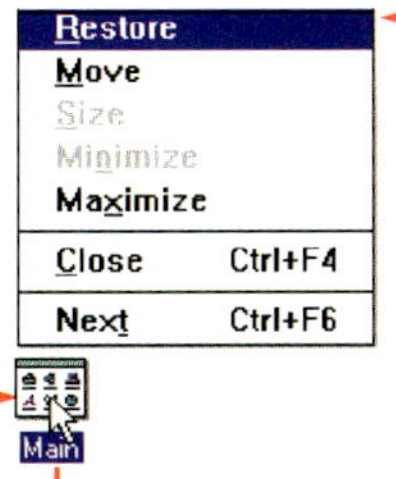

The name of the window appears below the group icon

Open a window quickly by double-clicking the icon

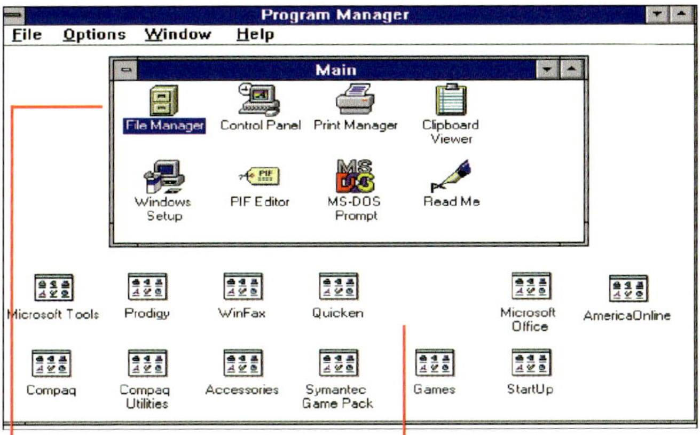

The icon disappears when the window is open

The open group window

Closing Windows

Your desktop can get confusing with different windows open in different sizes. You can close the windows you don't need and reopen them later when you need them again.

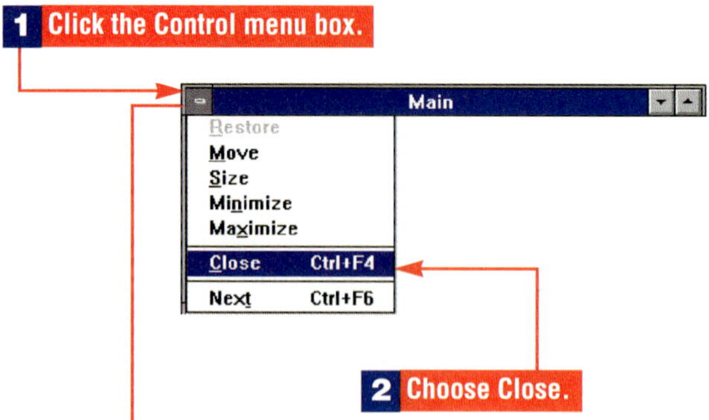

Close a window quickly by double-clicking its Control menu box or pressing Ctrl+F4

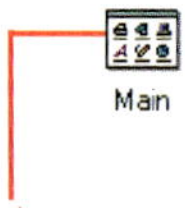

The closed window appears as an icon

Selecting Windows

Only one window at a time is active. You can select which window is currently active—so that you can quickly switch from application to application.

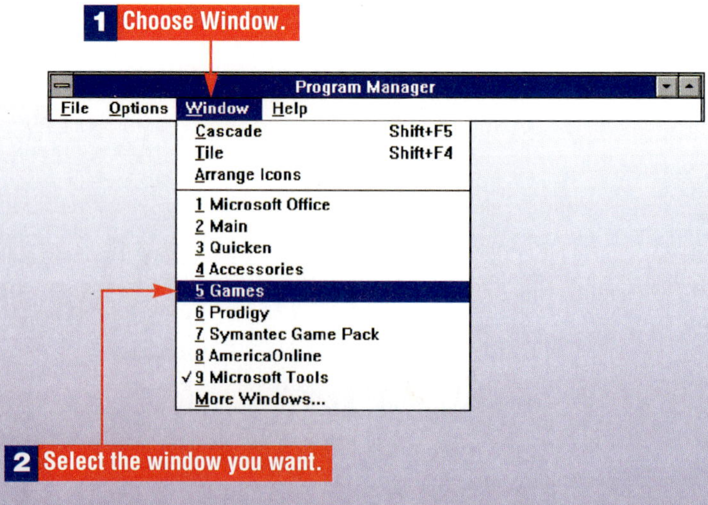

Select a window quickly by clicking it

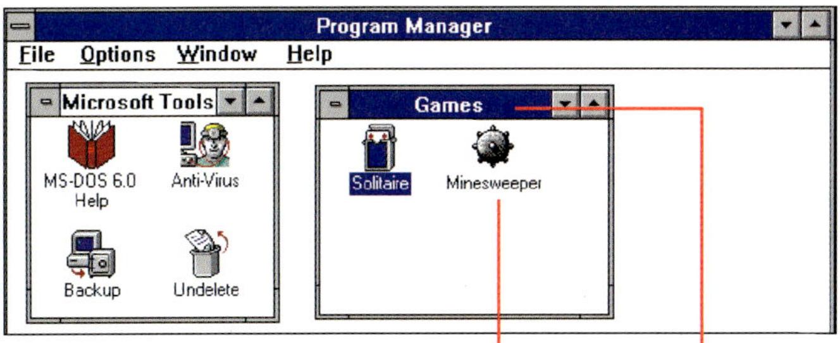

The active window is moved to the foreground of the desktop

The border and title bar of the active window appear in a different color or shade

Minimizing, Maximizing, and Restoring Windows

You can reduce a window to an icon (minimize it) or enlarge a window so that it takes up the entire screen (maximize it). If you minimize or maximize a window, you can restore the window to its previous size very easily.

To minimize a window

1 Click the Minimize button.

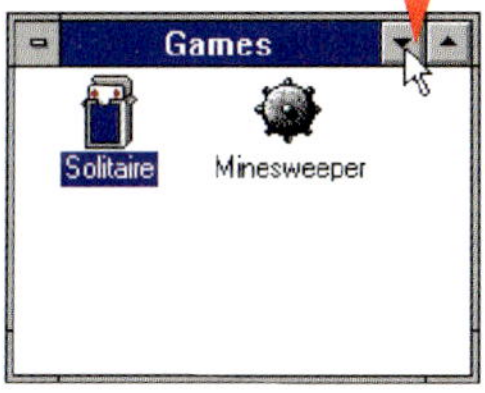

The window is minimized to an icon

To maximize a window

1 Click the Maximize button.

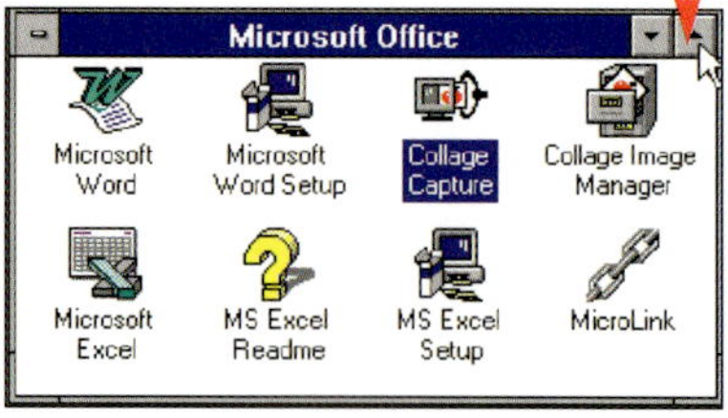

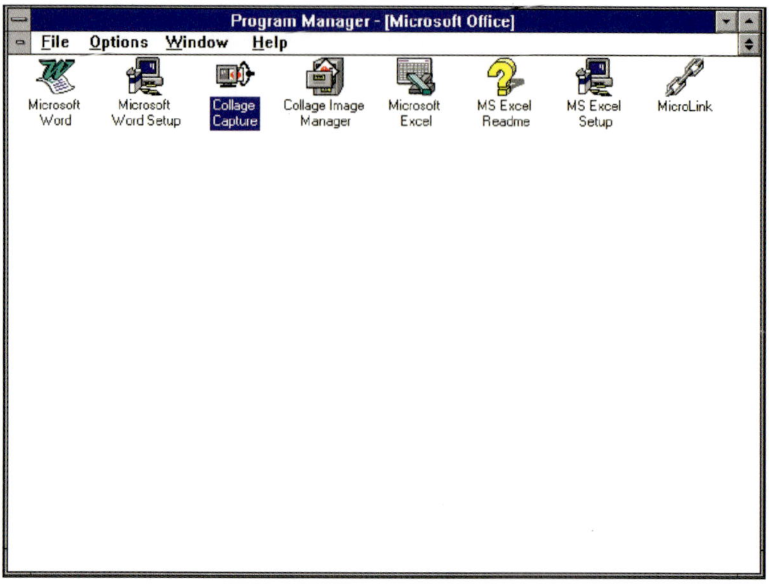

A maximized window fills the entire Program Manager screen; maximizing Program Manager fills the entire desktop screen

To restore a window

1 Click the Restore button.

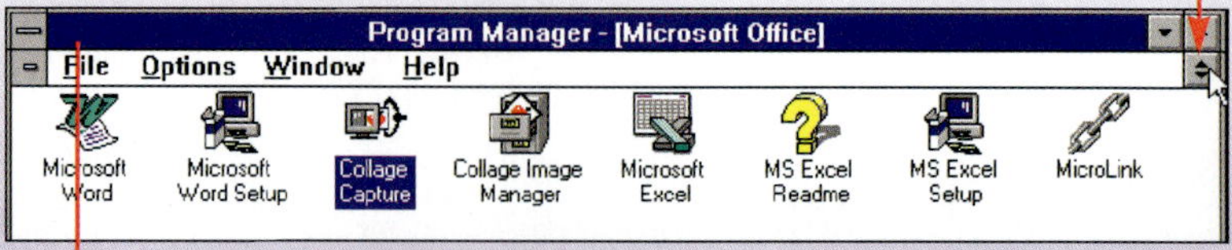

Another fast method is to double-click the title bar

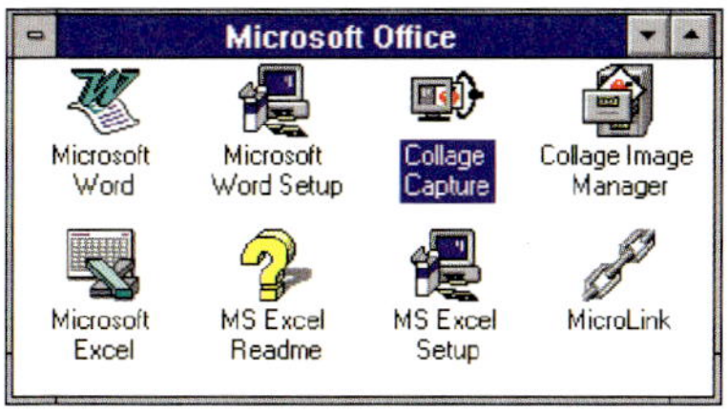

The window is restored to its previous size and location

Moving Windows

You can move open windows so that each window is accessible or to achieve a more pleasing or useful arrangement of windows.

1 Select the window you want to move.

2 Point to the window's title bar.

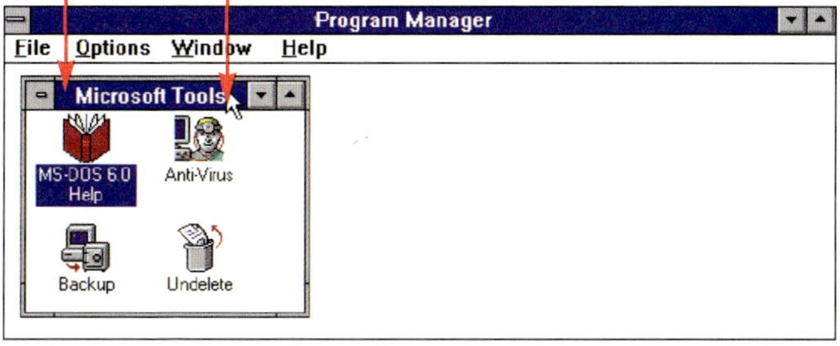

3 Hold down the mouse button and drag the window where you want it.

4 Release the mouse button.

The window appears in the new location

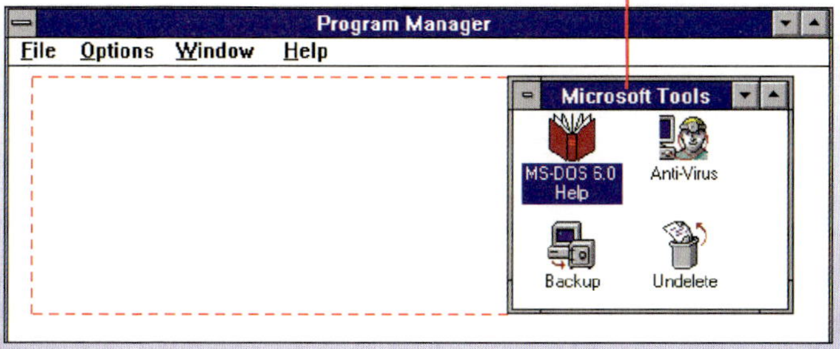

Resizing a Window

You can change the size of a window from the left or right side, top, bottom, or a corner. Resizing is useful, for example, when you want to be able to see more icons in the window.

1 Select the window you want to size.

2 Point to any side of the window's border.

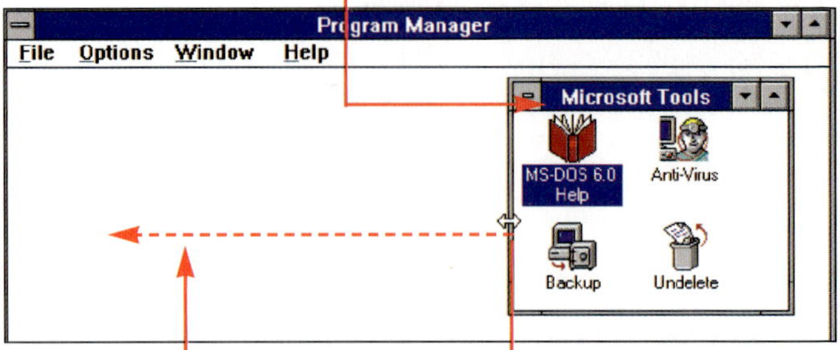

A two-headed arrow appears when you point to a border

3 Hold down the left mouse button.

4 Drag the border to shrink or stretch the window.

5 Release the mouse button.

The window is resized

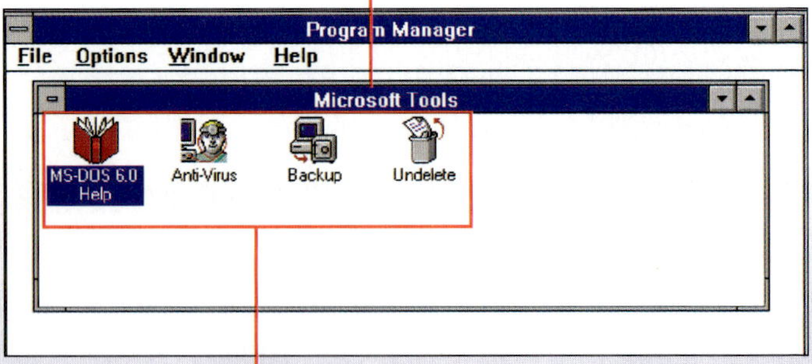

Rearrange the icons to fit the new window size

Arranging the Desktop

You can arrange the windows in Program Manager in many ways. Tiling keeps windows small and places them side by side. Cascading keeps all windows the same size, but stair-steps the windows so you can see all their title bars.

To tile windows

1 Choose Window, Tile.

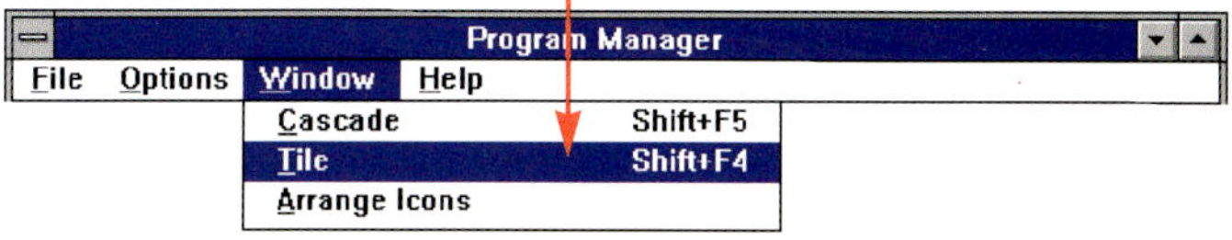

Another fast method is to press Shift+F4

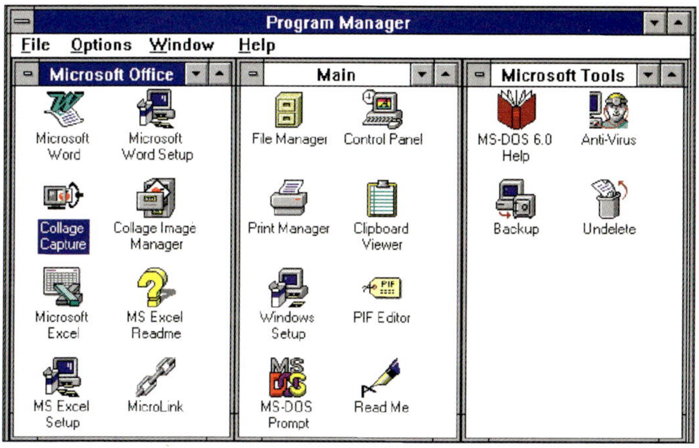

Program Manager tiles the open windows

To cascade windows

1 Choose Window, Cascade.

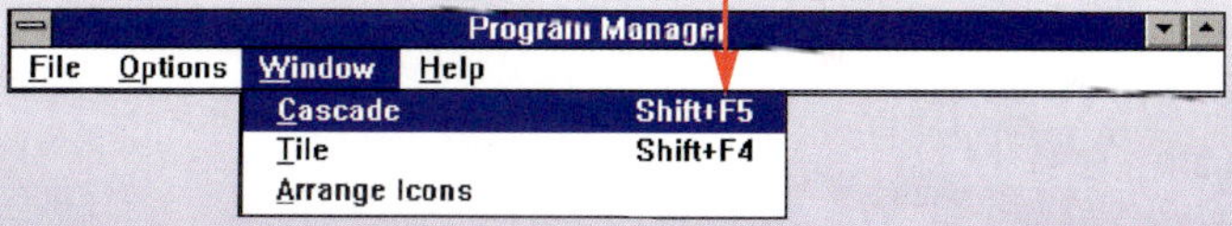

Press Shift+F5 for another quick method

more ▶

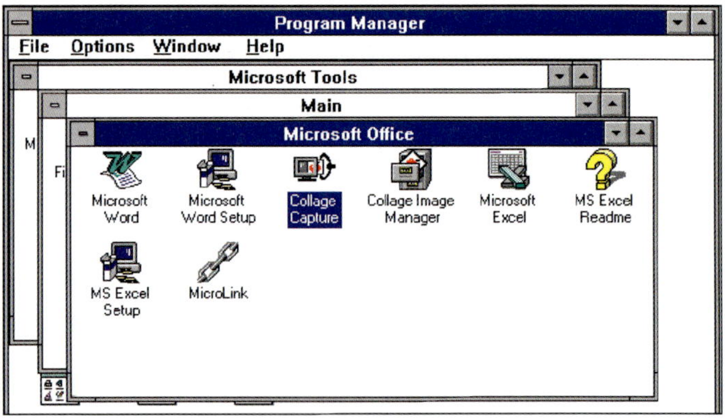

Program Manager cascades the open windows

Saving Desktop Settings

You can save your desktop arrangements at any time, or when you exit Windows. Periodic saving can prevent you from having to start over if you lose power while changing your desktop arrangement.

1 Press and hold down the Shift key.

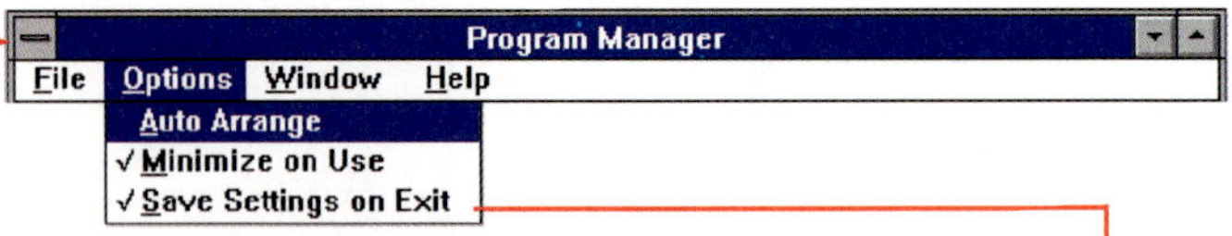

2 Double-click the Program Manager Control menu box.

To save your changes every time you exit, select Options, Save Settings on Exit

Changing the Driver Settings

After you set up equipment to run in Windows, you can change the driver settings. For example, if you play WAV files, you may want to lengthen the playing time so that you can hear the whole recording.

1 In the Main window, double-click the Control Panel icon.

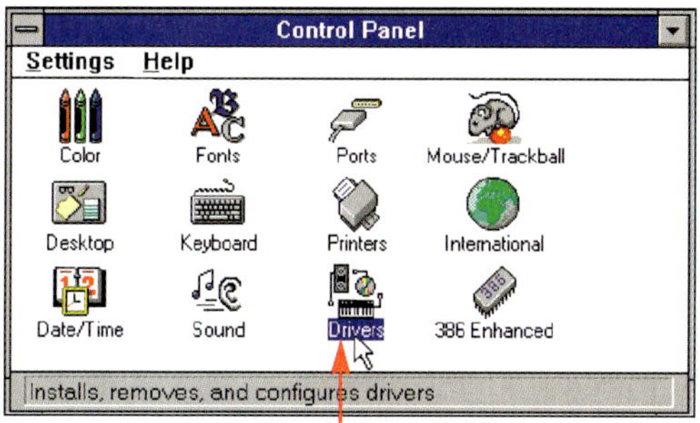

2 Double-click the Drivers icon.

3 Select the driver you want to change.

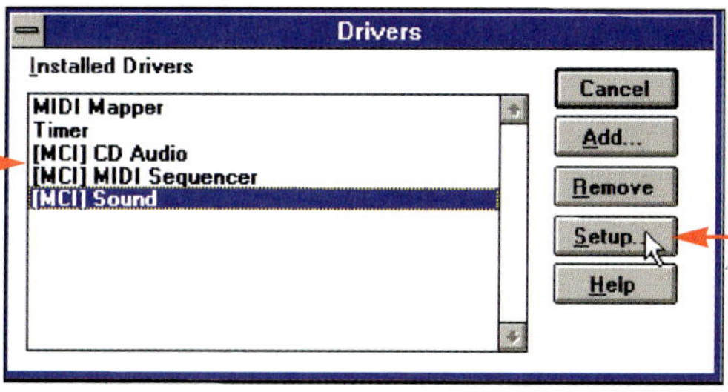

4 Choose Setup.

The Setup button is dimmed if the driver requires no settings

5 Change setup options as desired.

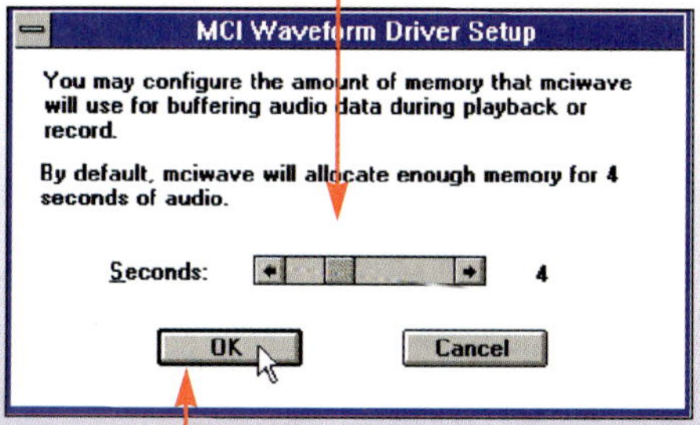

6 Choose OK.

more ▶

7 Respond to any additional dialog box(es) and choose OK.

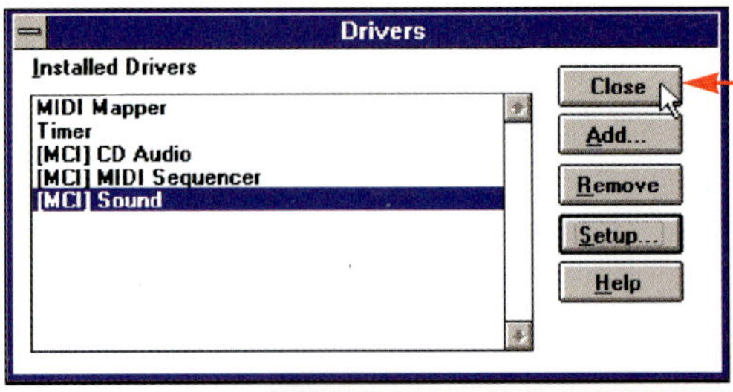

8 Choose Close to close the dialog box.

Changing the International Settings

The International feature controls several settings for Windows operation, based on the selected country. For example, you can change how dates and keyboard characters appear by changing the country setting.

To access the International settings

1 In the Main window, double-click the Control Panel icon.

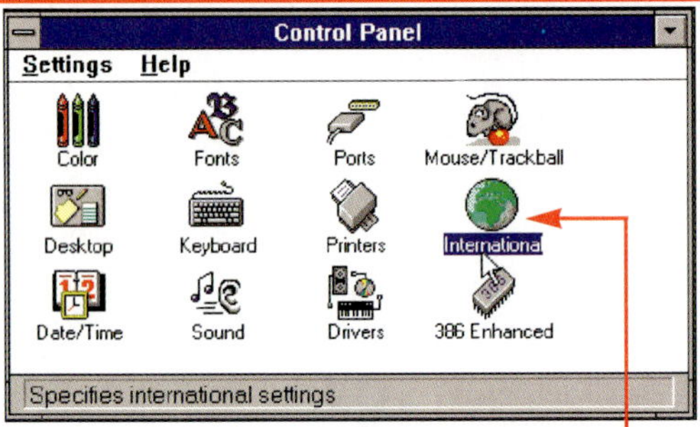

2 Double-click the International icon.

To change the country

1 Click the Country arrow button.

2 Scroll the list and select the desired country.

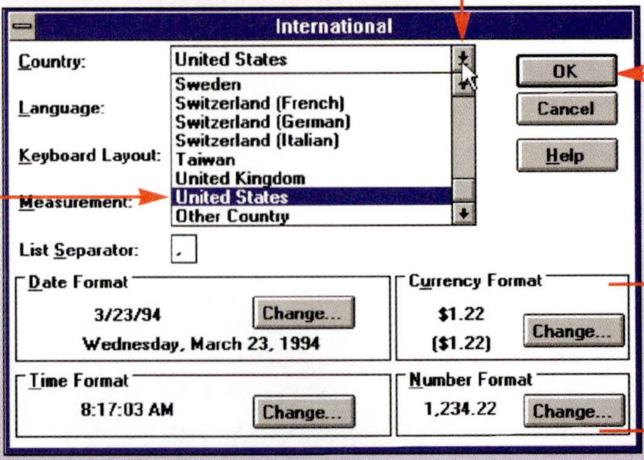

3 Choose OK.

The Format options change automatically when you change countries

To change the language

1 Click the Language arrow button.

2 Scroll the list and select the desired language.

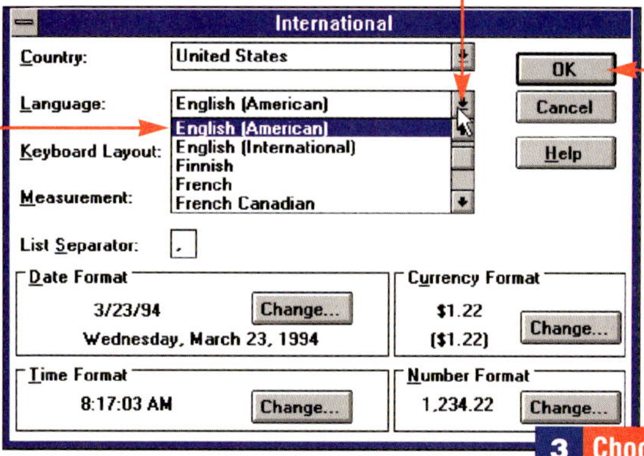

3 Choose OK.

To change the keyboard layout

1 Click the Keyboard Layout arrow button.

2 Scroll the list and select the desired keyboard layout.

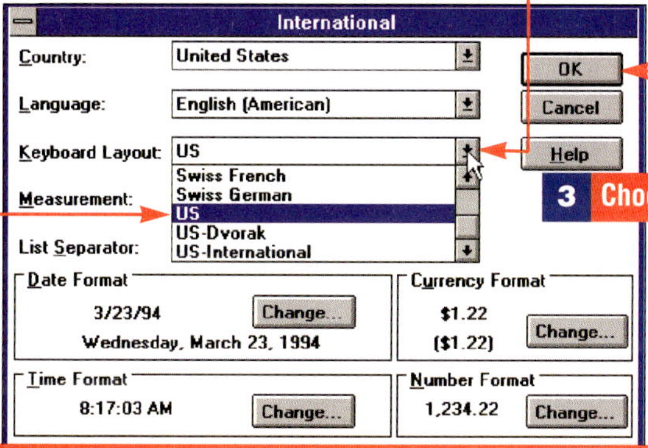

3 Choose OK.

4 If necessary, specify the location of the keyboard driver.

To change the unit of measure

1 Click the Measurement arrow button.

2 Select the desired measurement.

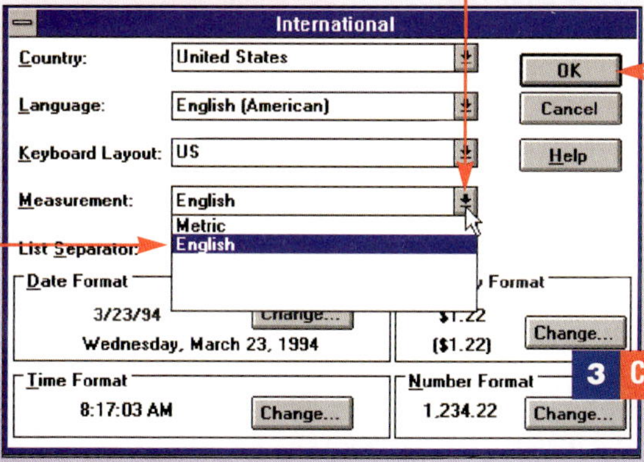

3 Choose OK.

To change the date, time, currency, or number format

1 Click the Change button for the format you want to change.

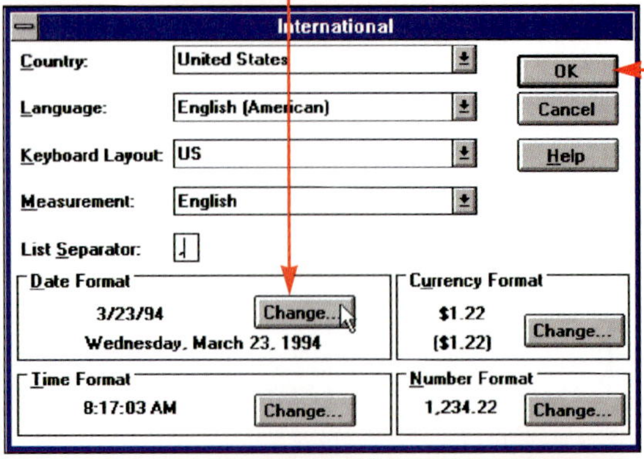

2 Specify the format you want in the dialog box that appears.

3 Choose OK twice.

Changing Keyboard Speed

Keyboard settings control the key repeat rate of your keyboard, increasing or decreasing the speed that your cursor moves on-screen.

1 In the Main window, double-click the Control Panel icon.

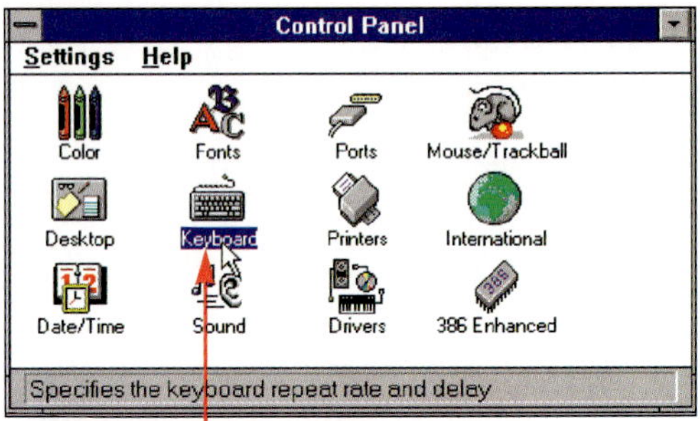

2 Double-click the Keyboard icon.

3 Change the keyboard options as desired.

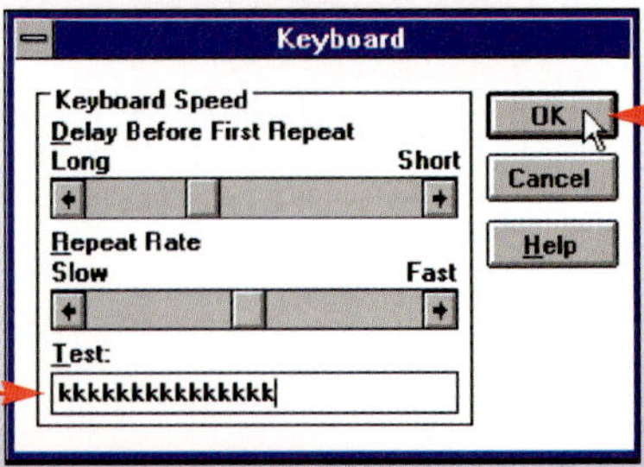

4 Click Test.

5 Hold down any key on the keyboard.

6 Repeat steps 3-5 until you get the desired repeat rate.

7 Choose OK.

Changing the Mouse Settings

The Mouse or Mouse/Trackball settings enable you to change the sensitivity of the mouse and swap the mouse buttons (for left-handed usage).

1 In the Main window, double-click the Control Panel icon.

2 Double-click the Mouse or Mouse/Trackball icon.

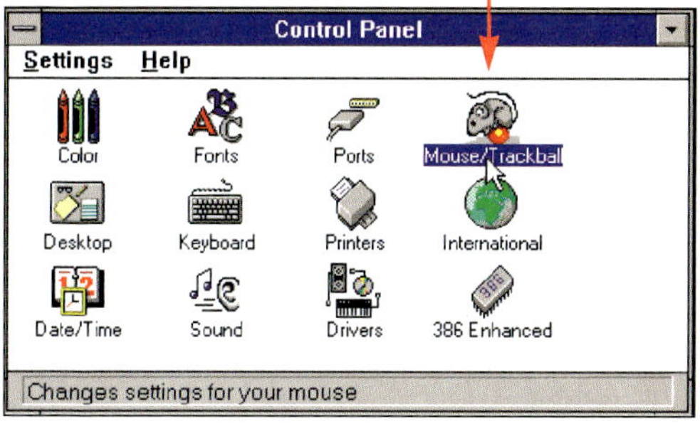

3 Change options as desired.

4 Choose OK.

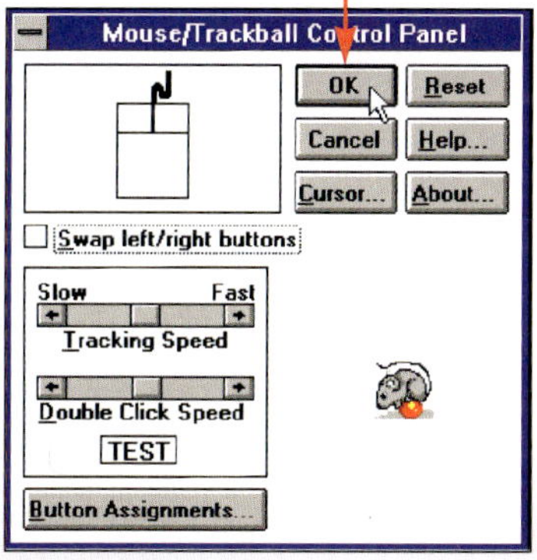

Changing the Network Settings

You can change network options, such as the ability to send and receive messages to/from other network users, and controlling the printer from your system.

Exact steps in this section depend on your network setup.

1 In the Main program group, double-click the Control Panel icon.

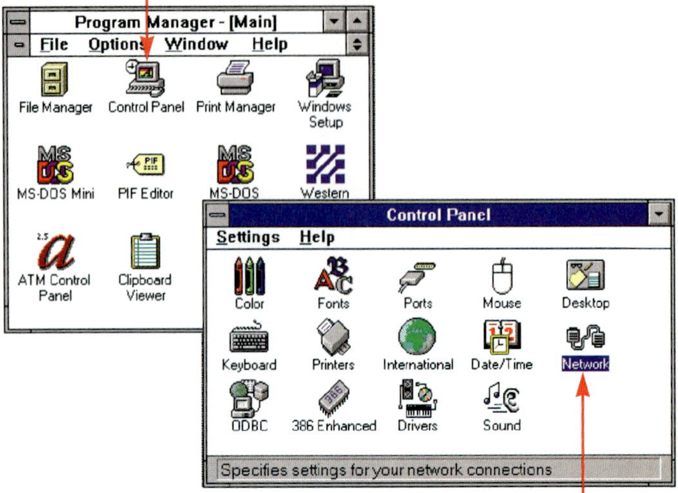

2 Double-click the Network icon.

3 Change network options as desired.

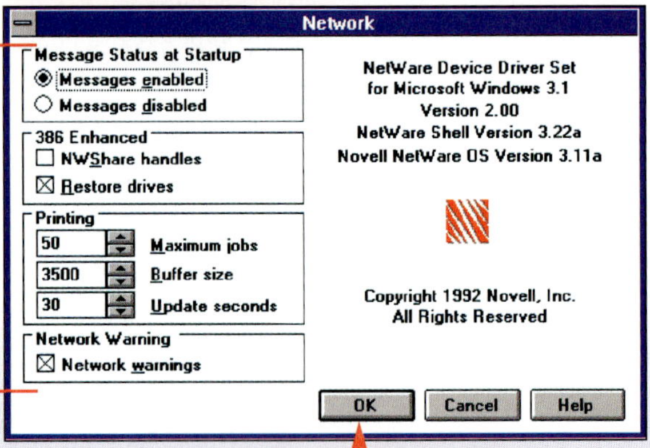

4 Choose OK.

Menus and options vary, depending on the network setup

Changing the Printer Settings

Printer settings tell Windows about your printer—paper size, ports, fonts supported by the printer, and other features.

To access the printer settings

1 In the Main window, double-click the Control Panel icon.

2 Double-click the Printers icon.

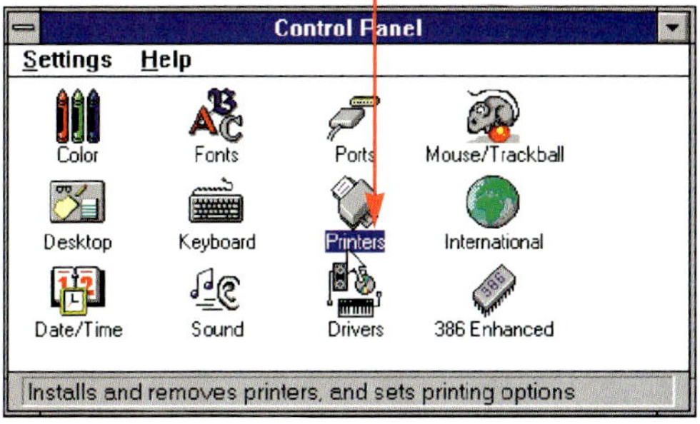

3 Select the printer you want to configure.

To use the selected printer as the default, choose this option

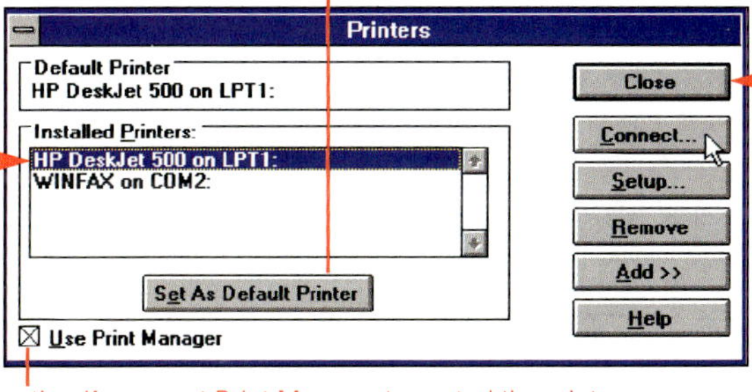

Select this option if you want Print Manager to control the printer

4 Change settings as described in the following sections.

5 Choose Close.

To change the printer setup

1 Choose Connect.

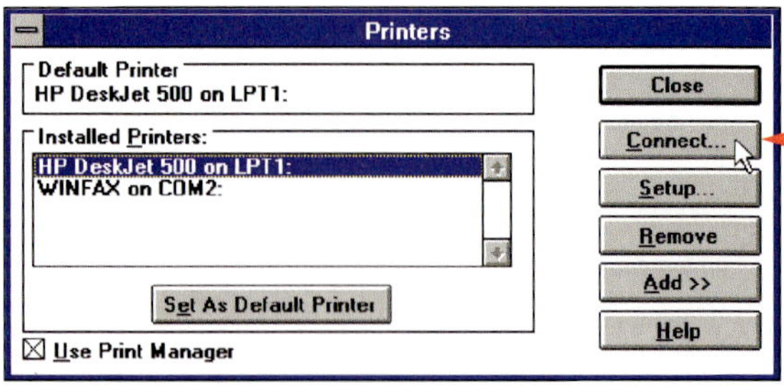

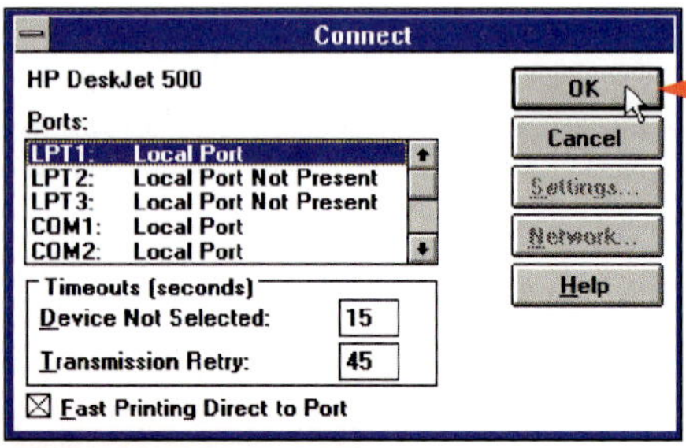

2 Change settings as desired.

Connect settings vary, depending on the installed printer

3 Choose OK.

1 Choose Setup.

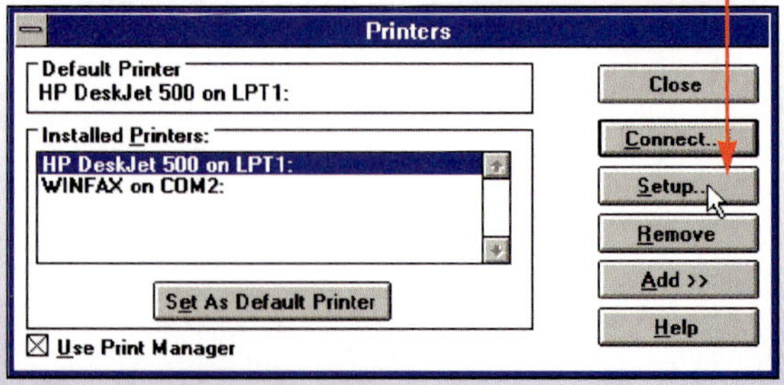

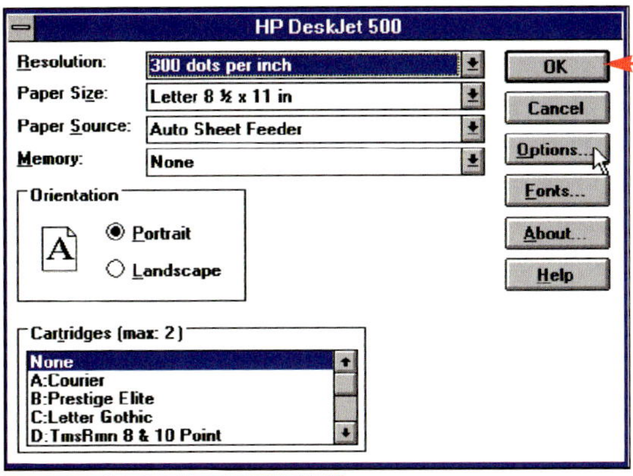

2 **Change the settings as desired.**

Setup options vary, depending on the installed printer

3 **Choose OK.**

Changing the Serial Port Settings

You can configure any serial port so that a Windows application can communicate with a device, such as a printer or modem, atttached to that port. Use this option if the device requires a special parity setting, baud rate, and so on.

1 **In the Main window, double-click the Control Panel icon.**

2 **Double-click the Ports icon.**

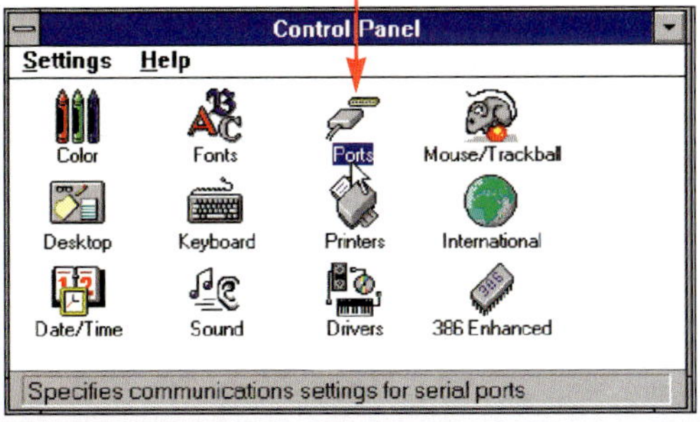

3 **Click the port you want to change.**

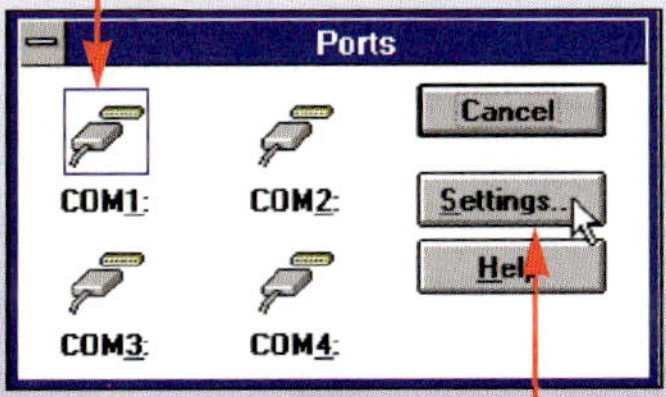

4 **Choose Settings.**

more ▶

5 Change the settings as desired.

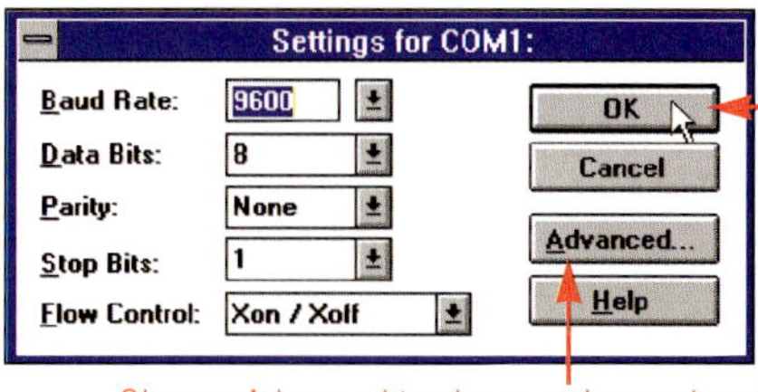

6 Choose OK.

Choose Advanced to change advanced port settings

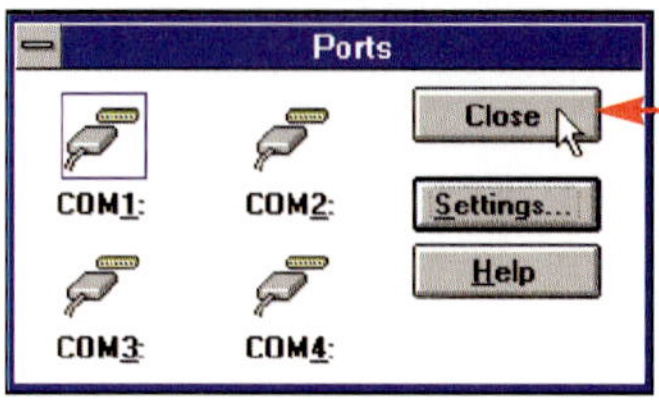

7 Choose Close.

Changing the Sound Settings

You can change the sound of an alarm for different Windows events. For example, you can use a special sound when you start or exit Windows, or when an operation ends in an error. You can even turn the sound completely off.

This feature requires a sound card or the Windows speaker driver, SPEAKER.DRV. To get the speaker driver, contact Microsoft or see Que's Killer Windows Utilities.

1 In the Main window, double-click the Control Panel icon.

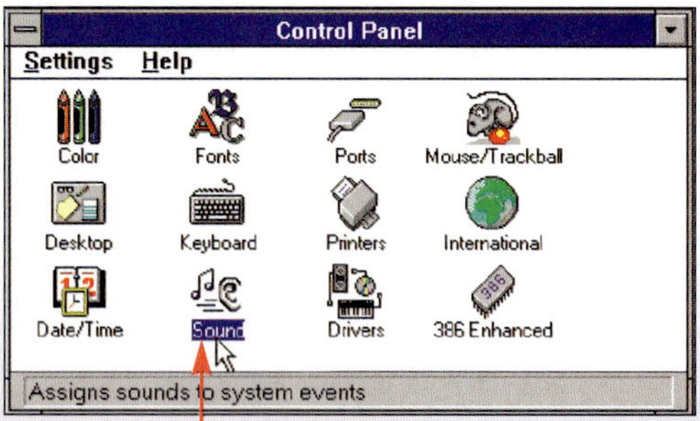

2 Double-click the Sound icon.

3 Select Enable System Sounds (deselect to turn off sound).

4 Select the event for which you want to assign a different sound.

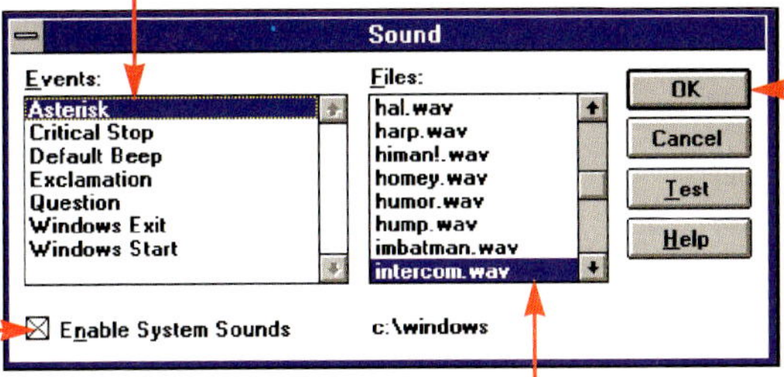

5 Select the sound file you want to use.

Choose Test if you want to listen to the selected sound

6 Repeat steps 4 and 5 until you have selected all the sounds you want.

7 Choose OK.

Changing the Swap File Settings

Windows uses a swap file to swap data between RAM and the hard disk—making the most of system memory. You can change the size, location, and kind of swap file Windows uses.

1 In the Main window, double-click the Control Panel icon.

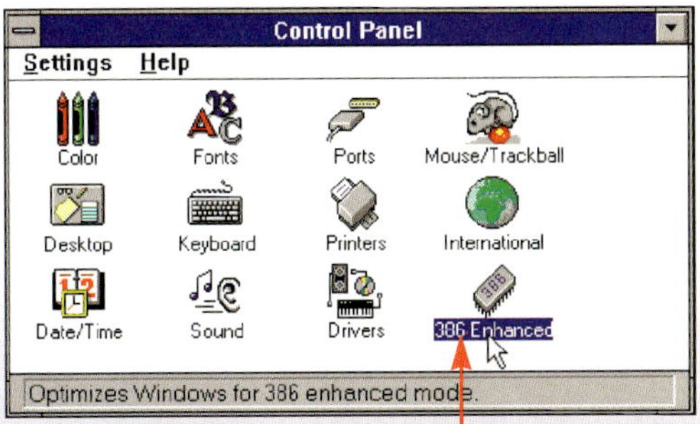

2 Double-click the 386 Enhanced icon.

more ▶

3 Choose Virtual Memory.

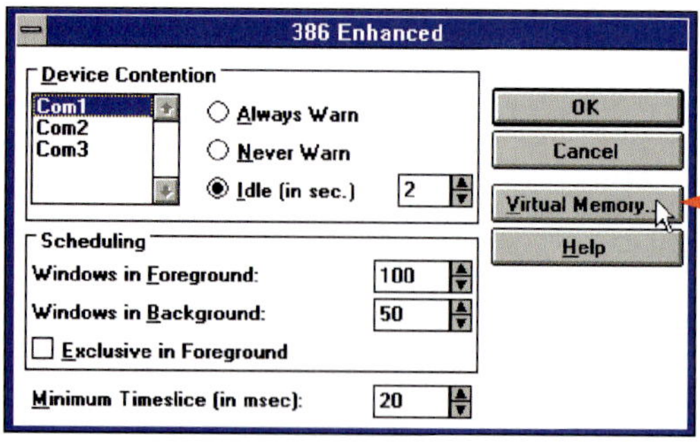

4 Choose Change.

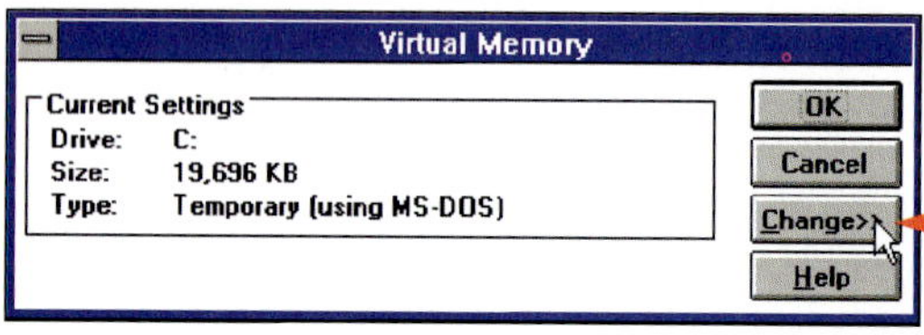

5 Change the settings as desired.

6 Choose OK.

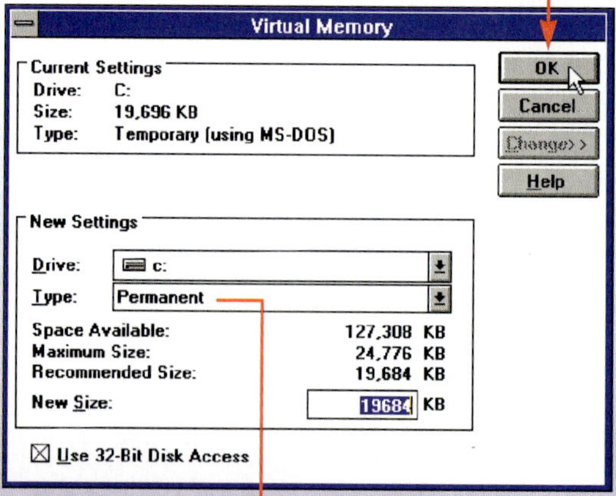

Consult your documentation before making changes if you use DoubleSpace

7 Choose Yes.

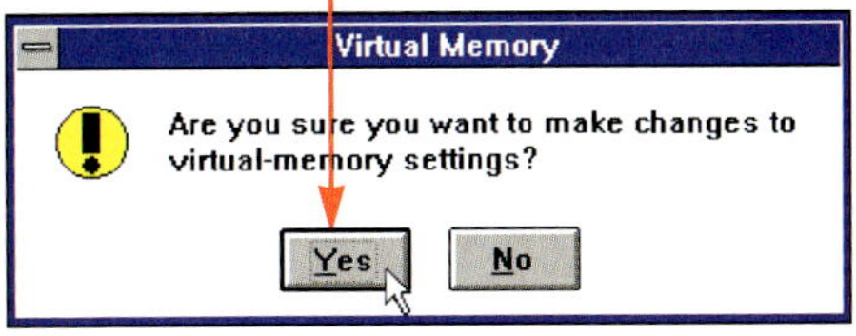

8 Choose Restart Windows for changes to take effect.

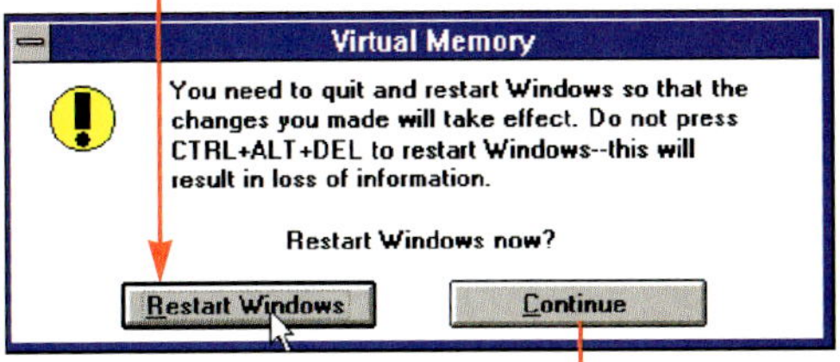

Choose Continue if you want the changes to start with the next session

Changing the Date and Time Settings

The Date/Time settings enable you to change the date and time of your computer's clock.

1 In the Main window, double-click the Control Panel icon.

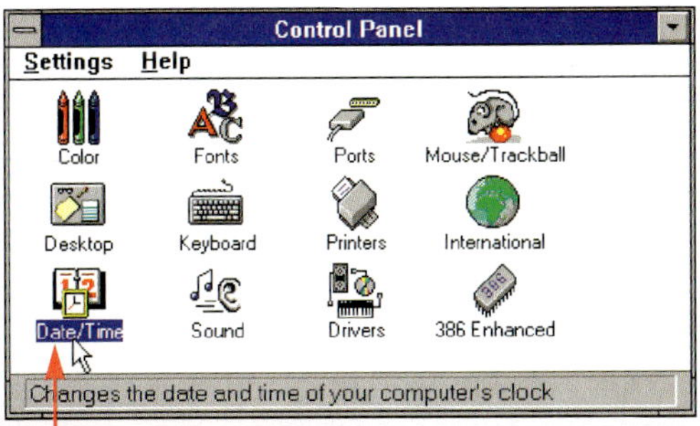

2 Double-click the Date/Time icon.

3 Type the correct date.

4 Type the correct time.

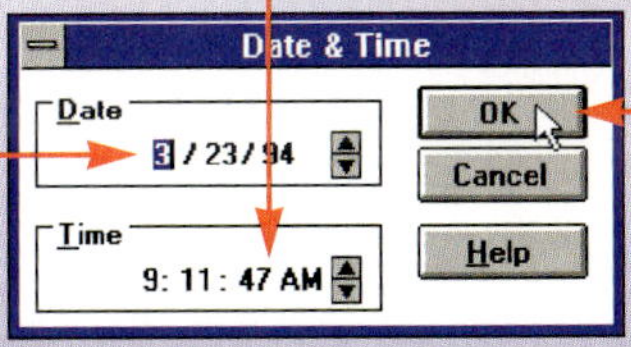

5 Choose OK.

Copying a Disk

File Manager's Disk Copy feature lets you duplicate an entire disk—for example, to make backup copies of program disks or work disks. When duplicating a disk, you must use disks of like capacity. If the disk you want to duplicate is 3 1/2-inch high density, for example, the disk you copy to must be 3 1/2-inch high density.

To copy a disk with a single disk drive

1 In the Main program group, double-click the File Manager icon.

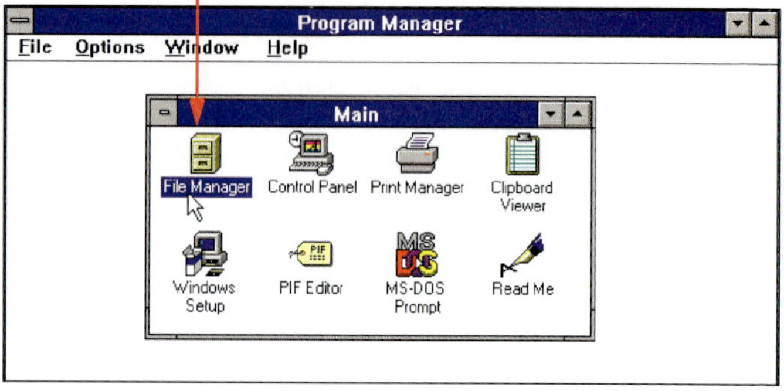

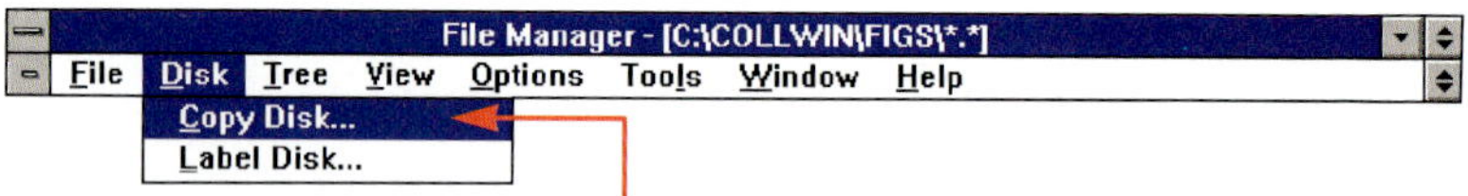

2 Choose Disk, Copy Disk.

Change the source drive, if necessary

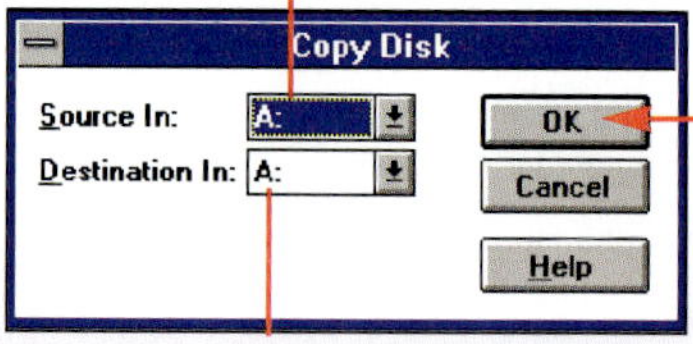

3 Choose OK.

Change the destination drive, if necessary

Be careful—this procedure deletes all data on the destination disk

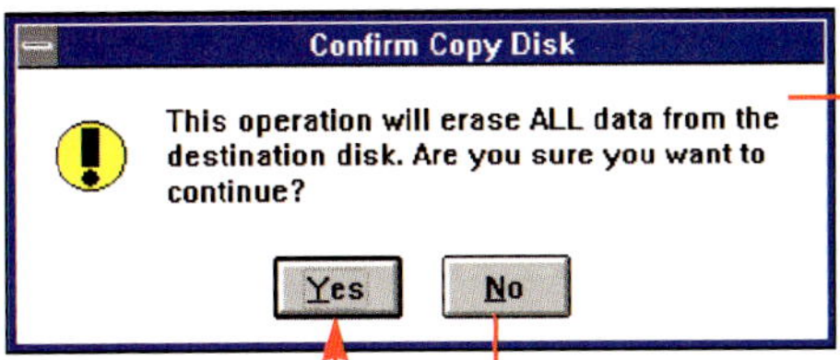

4 Choose Yes.

If you change your mind or aren't sure, choose No

5 Place the disk to copy (source disk) in the disk drive.

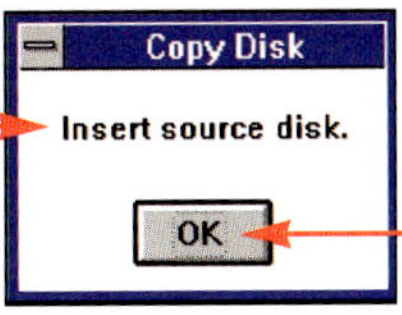

6 Choose OK.

7 Place the disk to copy to (destination disk) in the disk drive.

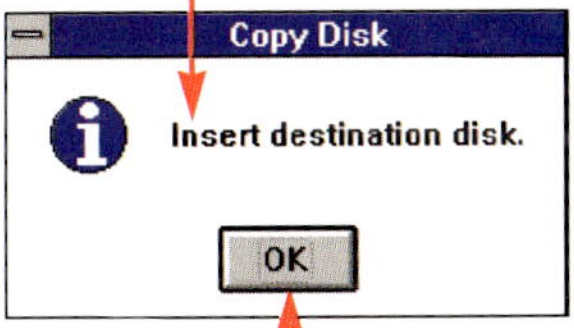

8 Choose OK.

To copy a disk with two disk drives

1 In the Main program group, double-click the File Manager icon.

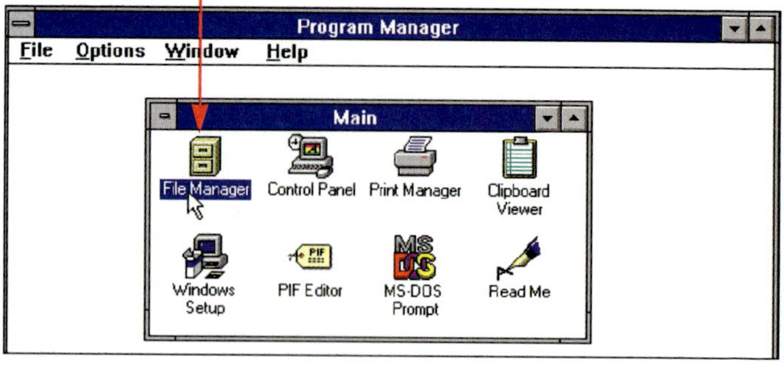

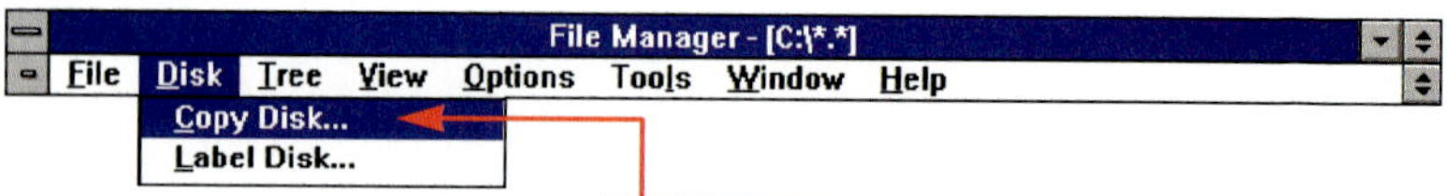

2 Choose Disk, Copy Disk.

3 Choose the drive for the source disk.

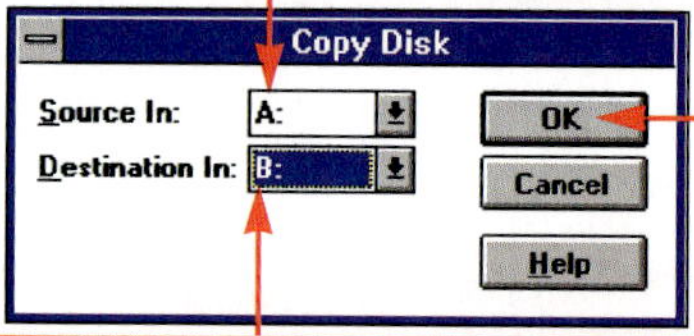

4 Choose the drive for the destination disk.

5 Choose OK.

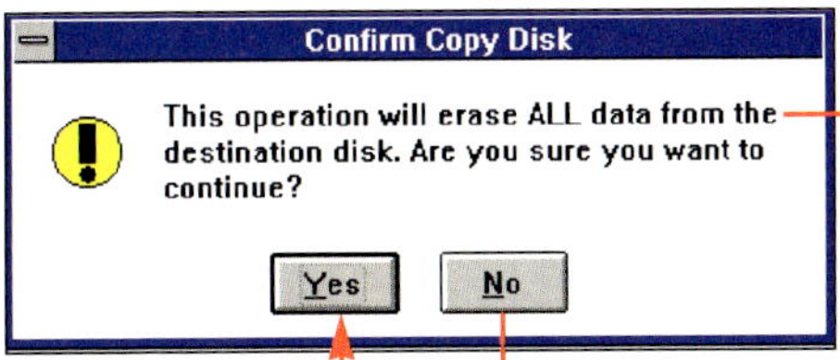

Be careful—this procedure deletes all data on the destination disk

6 **Choose Yes.**

If you change your mind or aren't sure, choose No

7 **Place the disk to copy (source disk) in the disk drive.**

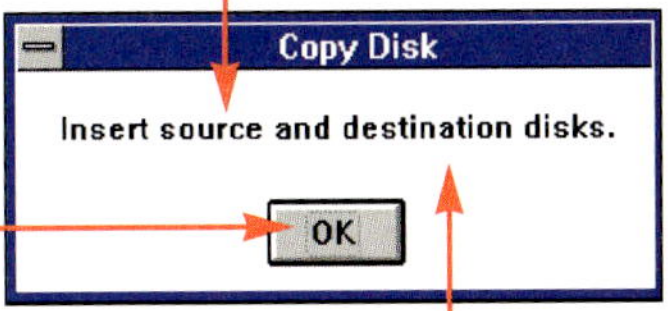

8 **Place the disk to copy to (destination disk) in the other disk drive.**

9 **Choose OK.**

Creating a Directory

File Manager's Directory feature lets you create new subdirectories on your hard disk or floppy disk. Using directories organizes program files and work files on the disk. This option is the equivalent of the DOS MD command.

To create a directory

1 **In the Main program group, double-click the File Manager icon.**

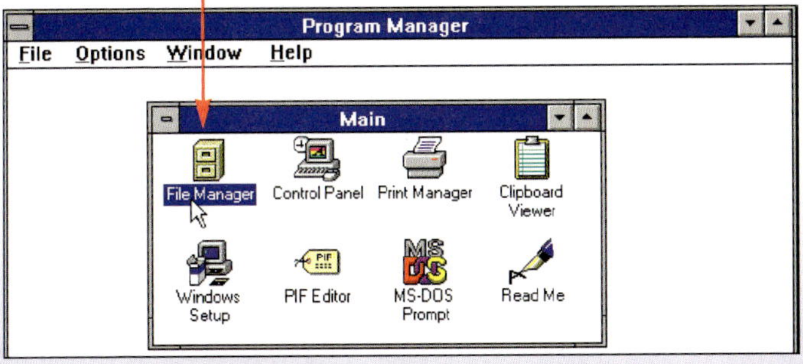

more ▶

2 Click the icon for the drive you want to contain the directory.

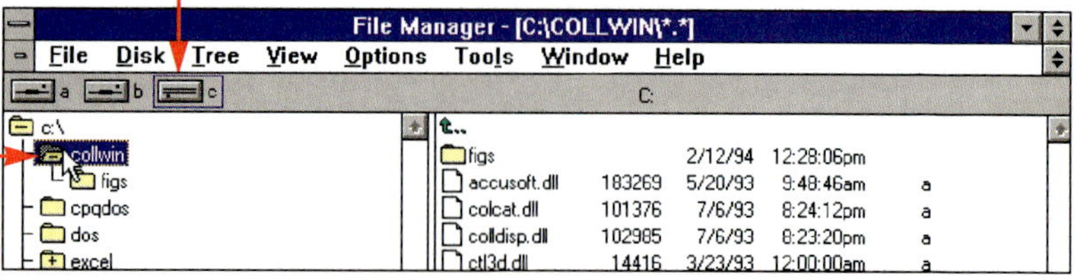

3 Click the directory in which you want to create the new subdirectory.

Double-click the directory if you want to expand it to show all subdirectories

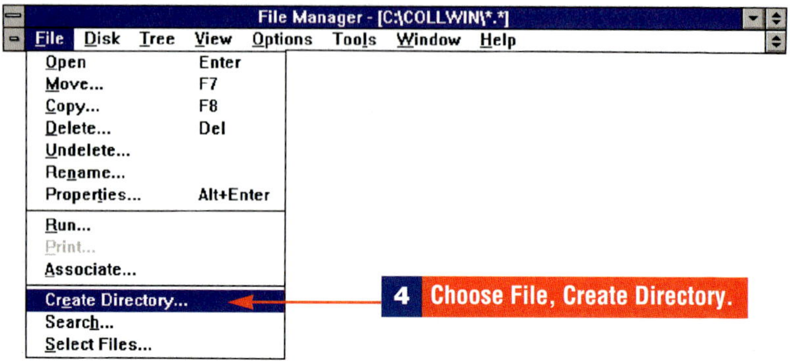

4 Choose File, Create Directory.

5 Type the new subdirectory name.

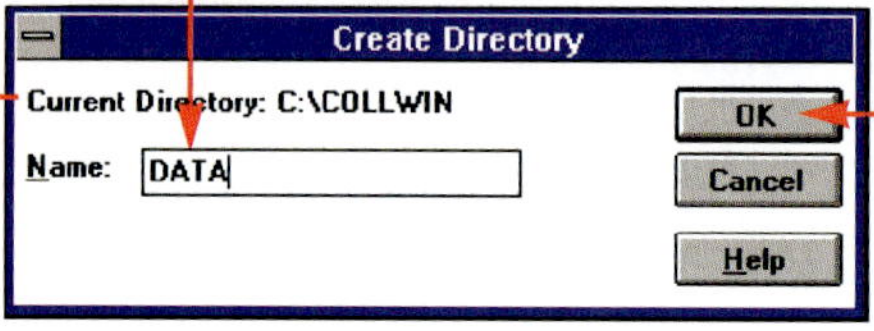

6 Choose OK.

Make sure that the path is correct

A directory name can have up to eight characters, plus an extension for DOS version 6 or later

New directory

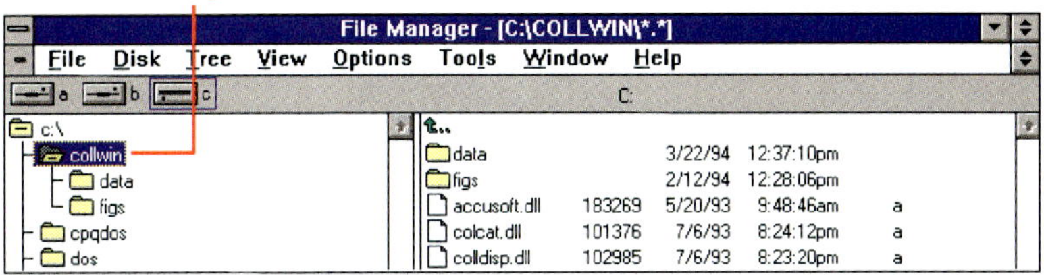

To remove a directory

1 Start File Manager.

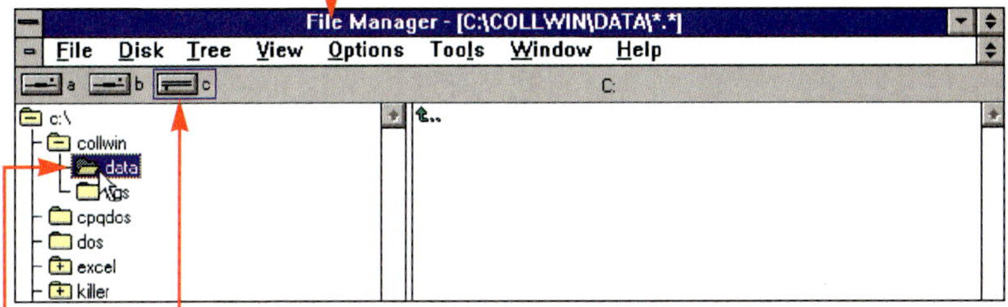

2 Click the icon for the drive containing the directory you want to remove.

3 Click the directory you want to delete.

You may have to expand a directory to see its subdirectories

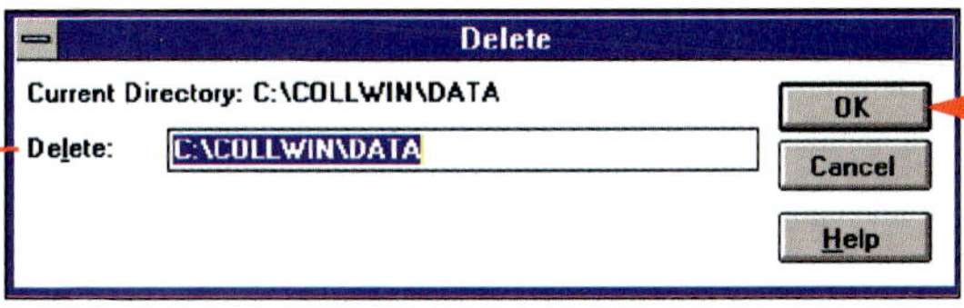

4 Press Delete on the keyboard.

Directory to be deleted

5 Choose OK to remove the directory.

more ▶

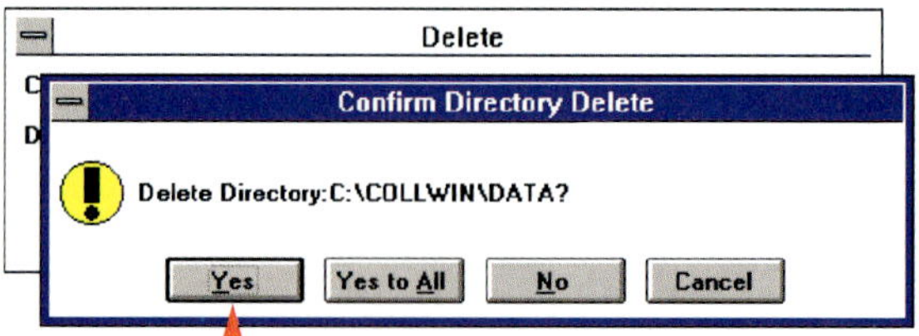

6 Choose Yes to remove the directory.

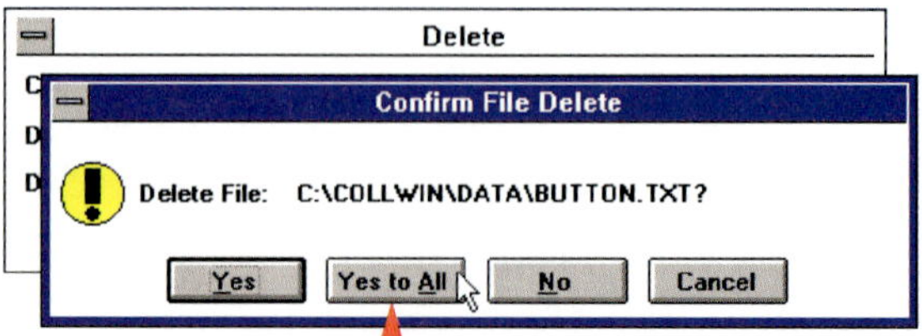

7 Choose Yes to All to remove all files in the directory.

If the directory is empty, this dialog box doesn't appear

Formatting a Floppy Disk

Formatting a floppy disk prepares the disk for use with the computer. A formatted disk is like a new, empty file folder in which you can store your work.

To format a disk

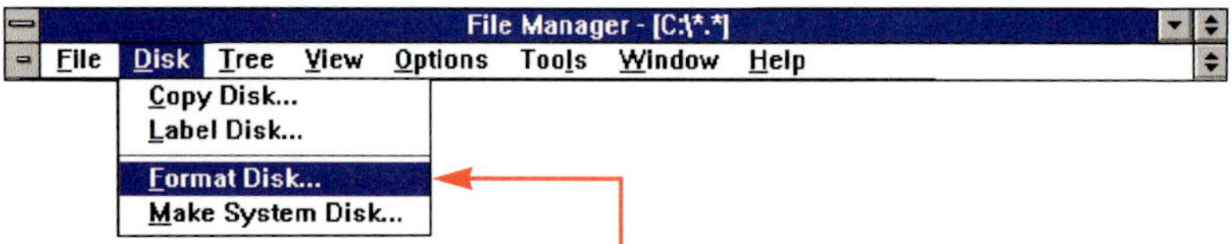

1 From the File Manager menu, choose Disk, Format Disk.

2 Place the disk you want to format in the floppy disk drive.

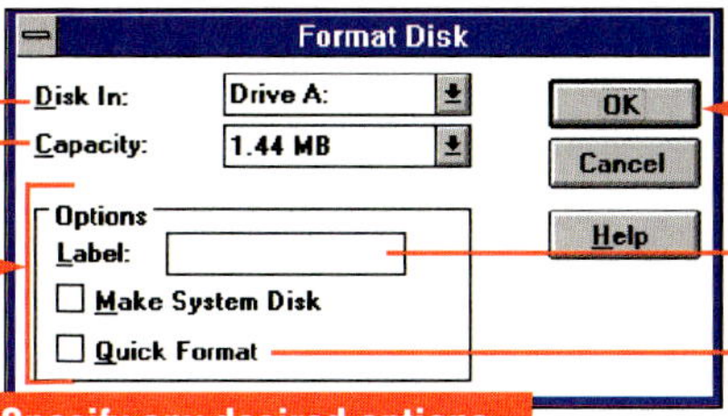

3 Specify any desired options.

Formats a previously formatted disk

Type the label you want to use (optional)

Specify the capacity of the disk, if necessary

Choose the drive you want to use, if necessary

4 Choose OK.

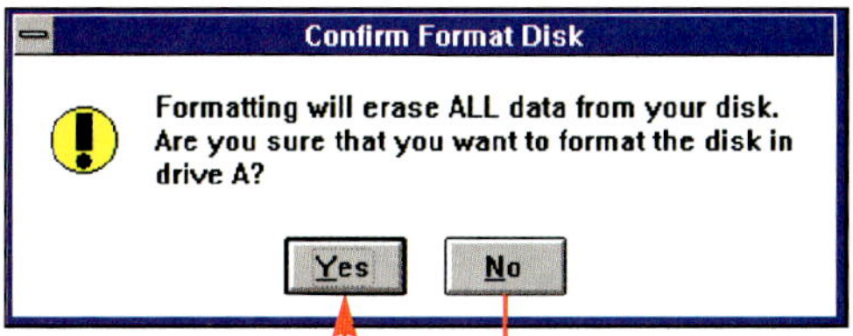

5 Choose Yes.

To cancel the disk format, choose No

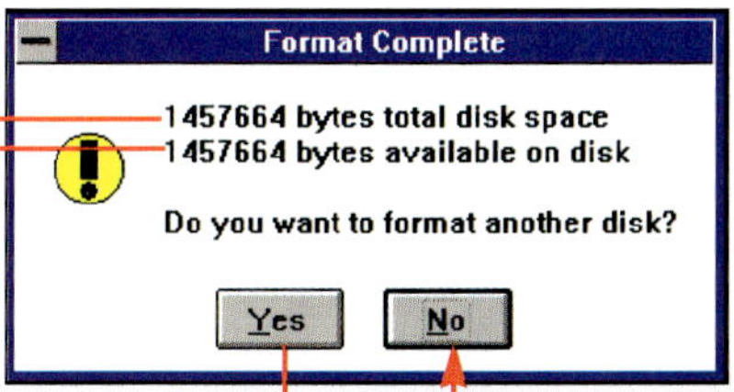

Available space on disk

Total disk space

6 Choose No.

To format another disk, choose Yes

Running DOS Commands

When you use Windows, you don't need to give up running DOS commands. You can run internal or external DOS commands such as DIR and FORMAT from within Windows.

1 From Program Manager, open the Main group window.

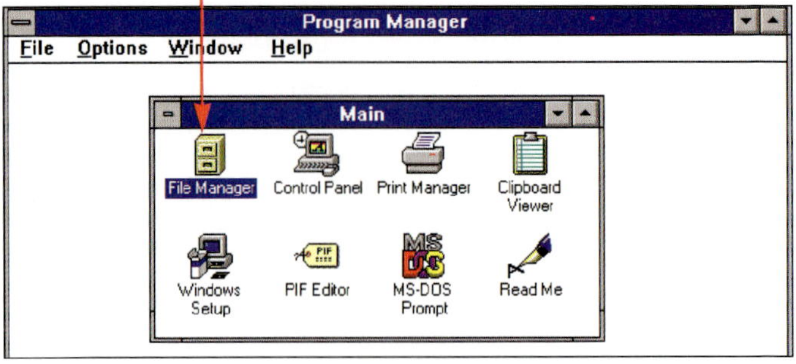

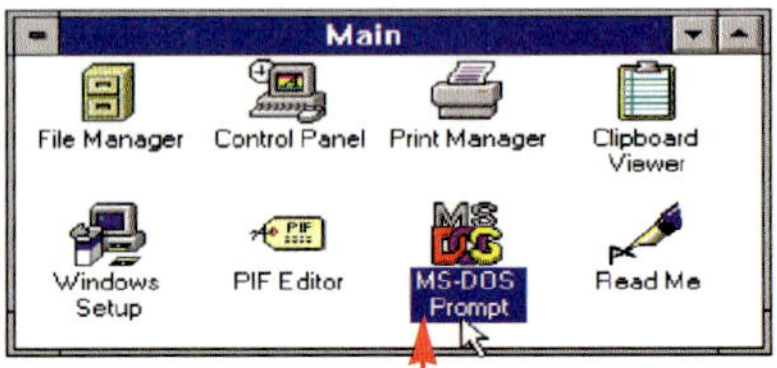

2 Double-click the MS-DOS Prompt icon.

3 Press Alt+Enter to reduce the DOS screen to a window.

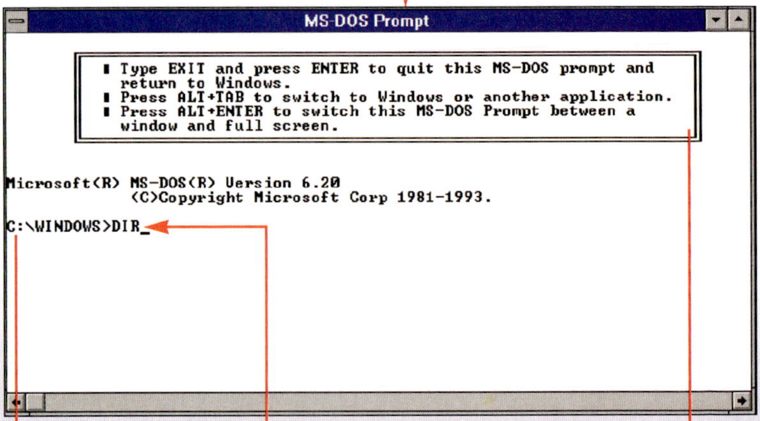

4 Type the DOS command you want to run and press Enter.

DOS prompt

Instructions for using DOS from Windows

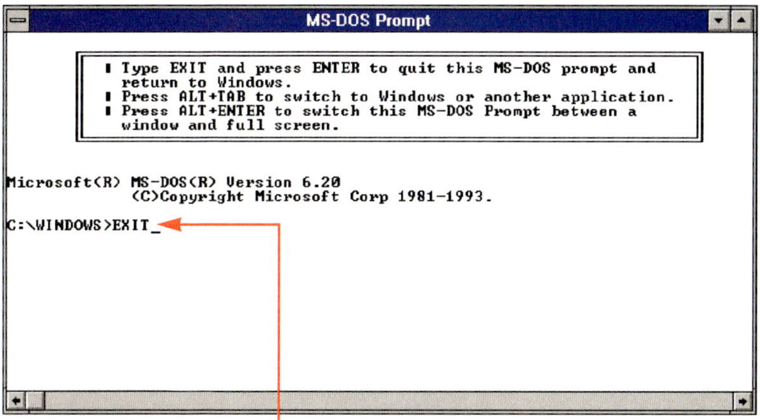

5 At the DOS prompt, type exit and press Enter.

Running a DOS Application

Windows enables you to run multiple DOS and Windows applications simultaneously (in 386 Enhanced mode). You can install a program icon that starts the DOS application; you can even add a special group for non-Windows applications.

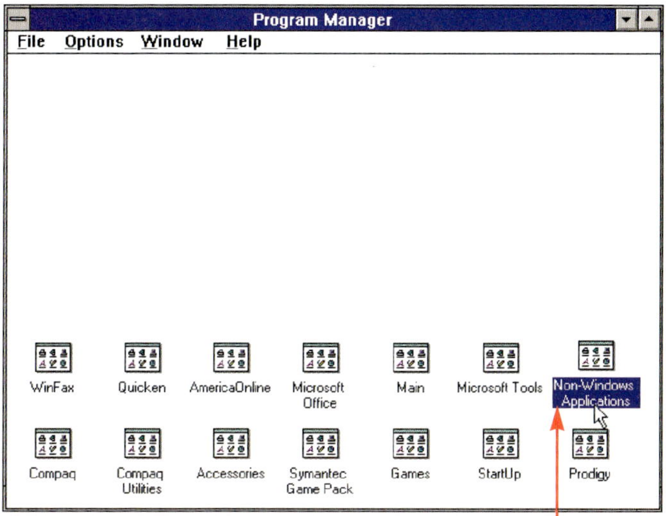

1 From Program Manager, open the non-Windows applications group.

2 Double-click the icon for the DOS application you want to run.

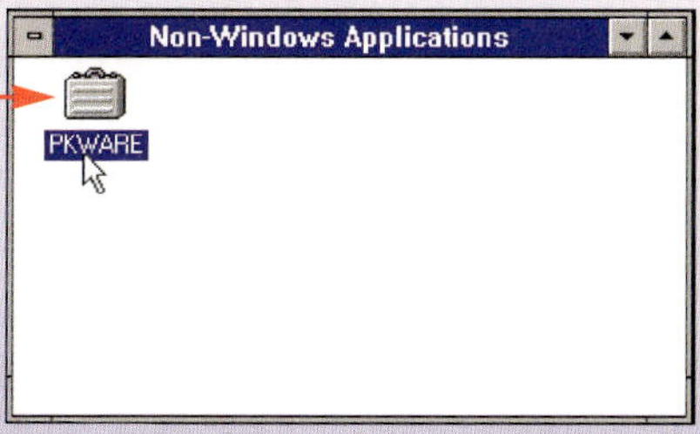

Using the PIF Editor

A set of operating characteristics must be defined for each program before Windows can run it properly. These settings are contained in a program information file called a PIF. You can customize a PIF for optimal performance.

1 From Program Manager, open the Main group window.

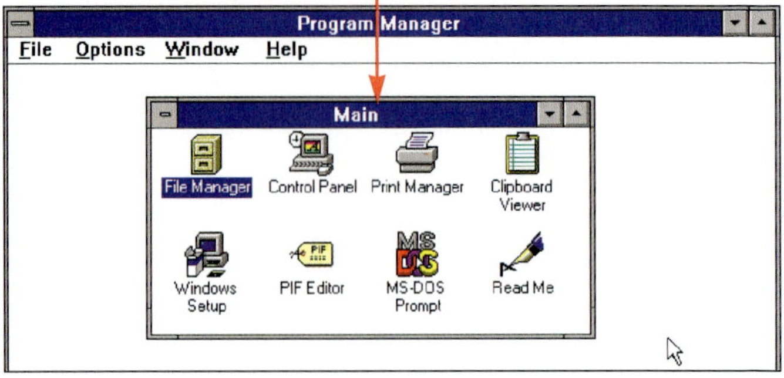

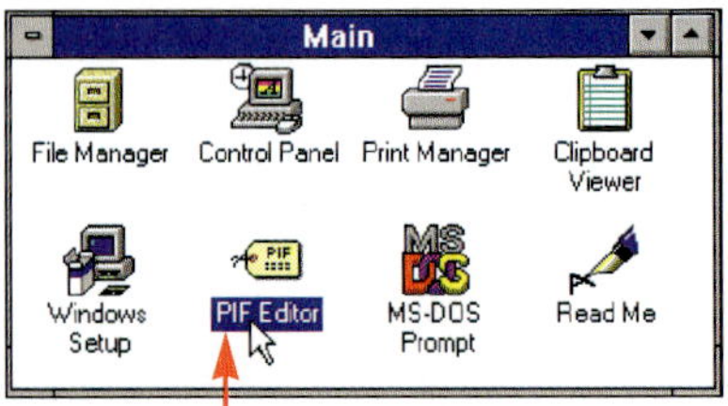

2 Double-click the PIF Editor icon.

3 Choose File, Open.

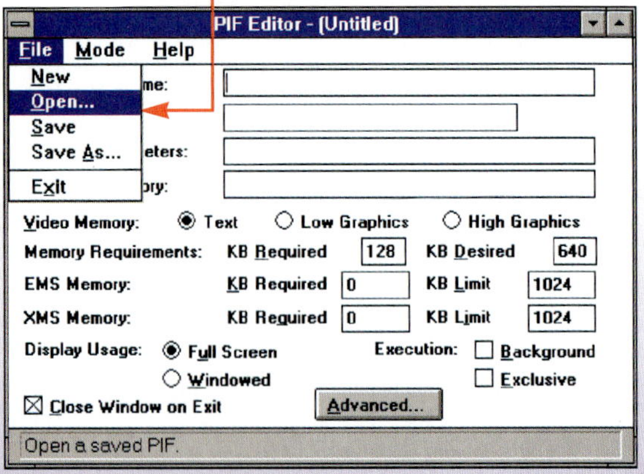

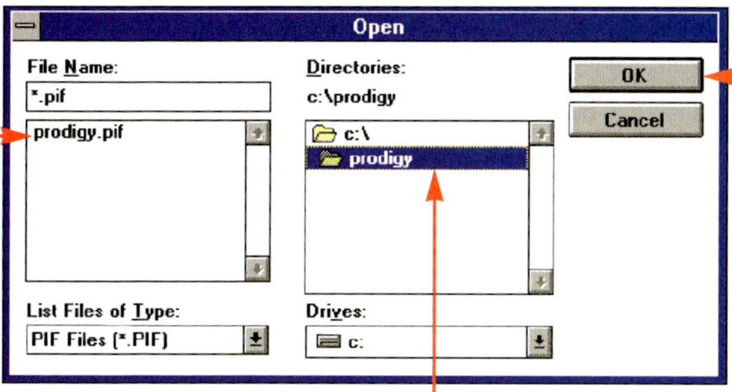

4 Change to the directory that contains the PIF you want to edit.

5 Select the PIF you want to edit.

6 Choose OK.

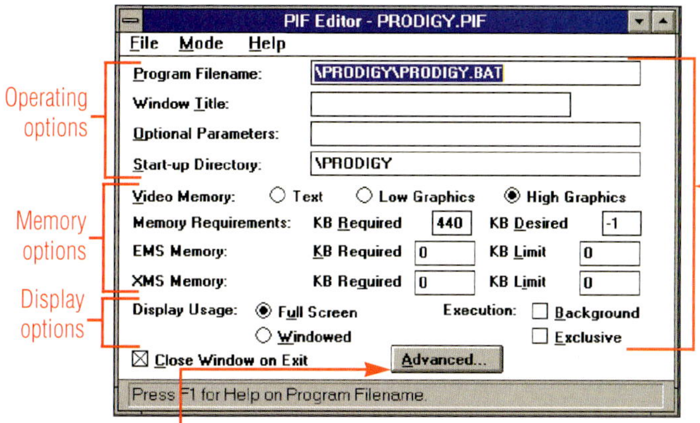

7 Make changes to the text boxes or selections.

8 If you need to change advanced PIF options, choose Advanced.

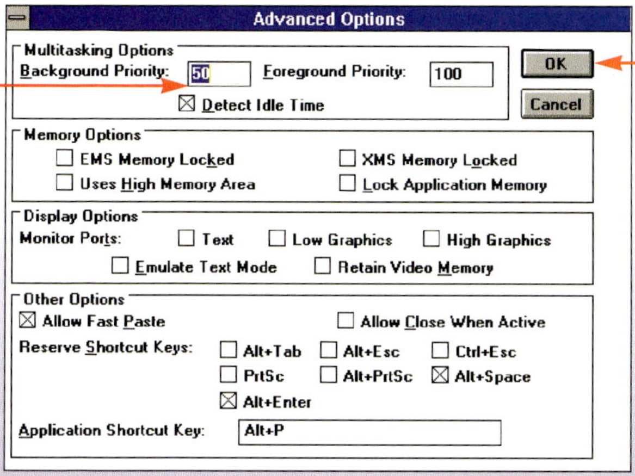

9 Specify the desired options in the Advanced Options dialog box.

10 Choose OK.

more ▶

11 Choose File, Save As.

12 Type the new file name. Windows adds the PIF extension automatically.

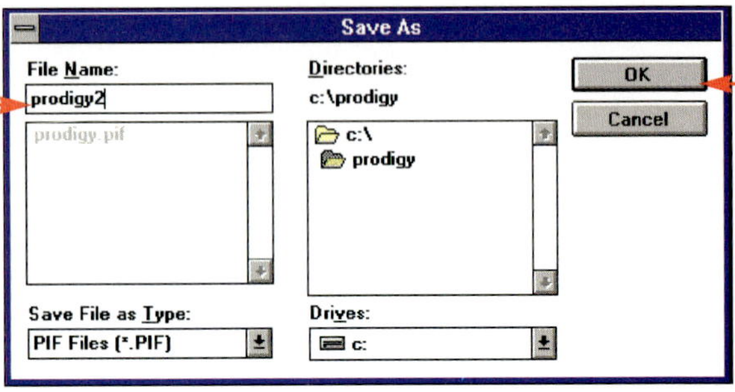

13 Choose OK.

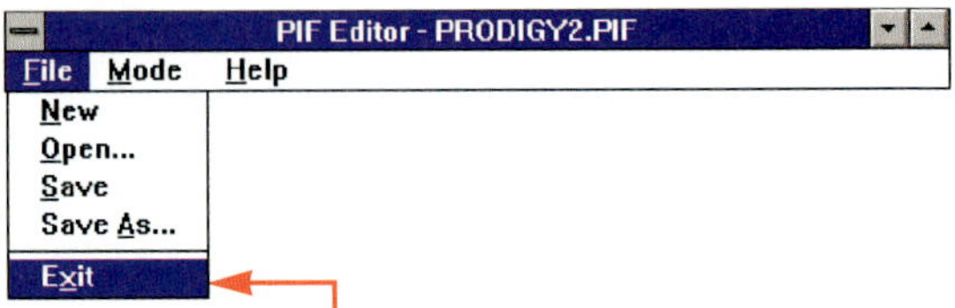

14 Choose File, Exit.

Because File Manager can be customized extensively, the steps in this section may not fit your setup exactly.

To apply settings changes in the current File Manager session to future sessions, Save Settings on Exit must be selected on the Options menu.

Expanding and Collapsing Directories

You can modify File Manager's Directory Tree window so that you can see all subdirectories or only certain levels of subdirectories. Expanding directory levels lets you find files within subdirectories at lower levels.

To see which directories are expandable, choose Tree, Indicate Expandable Branches.

To expand one level of a directory

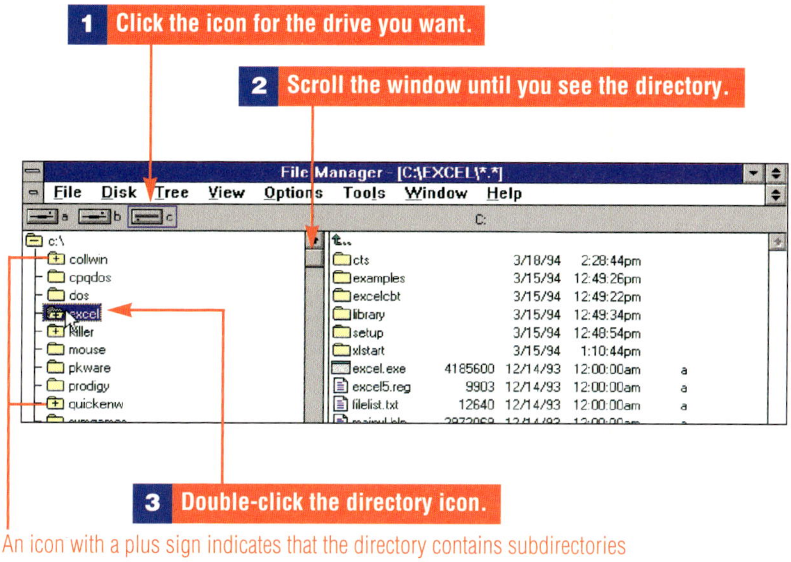

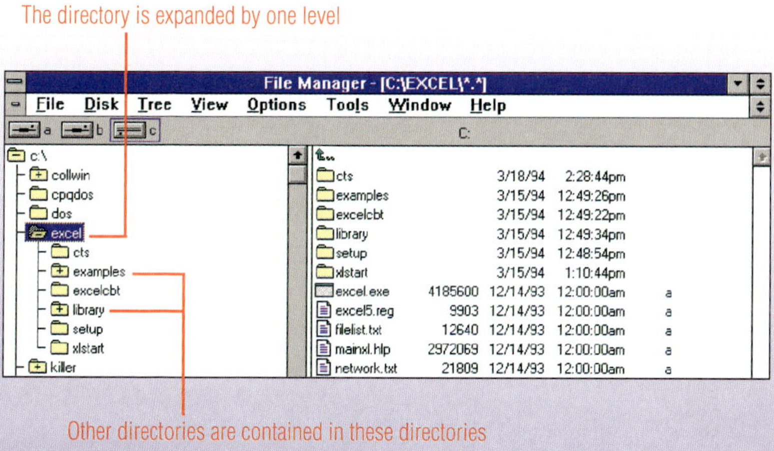

To expand an entire directory branch

1 Click the directory containing the branch you want to expand.

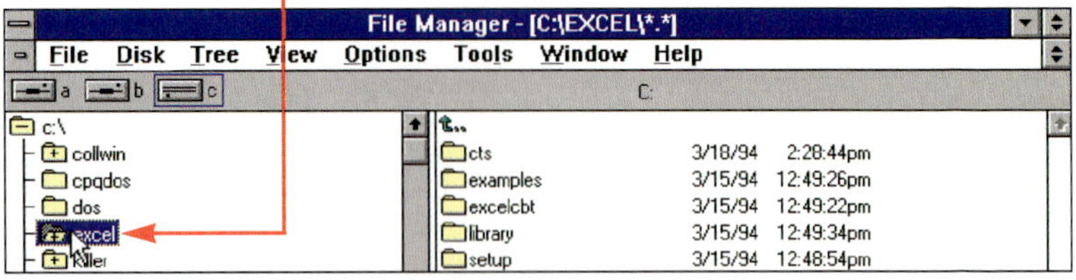

2 Press * (asterisk) to expand the branch.

The expanded branch

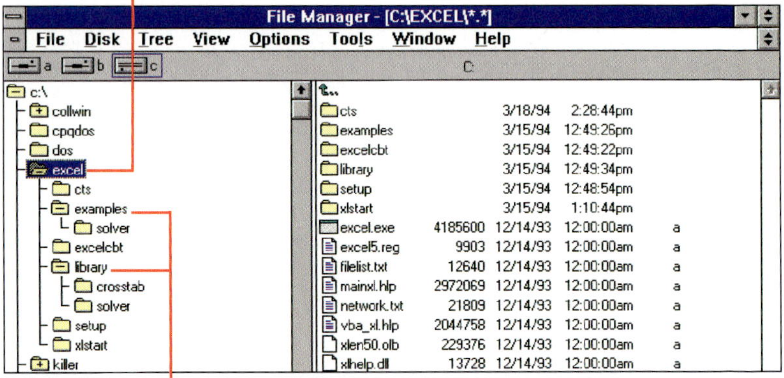

The icon displays a minus sign when all its subdirectories are expanded

To expand all directory branches

1 Click any directory.

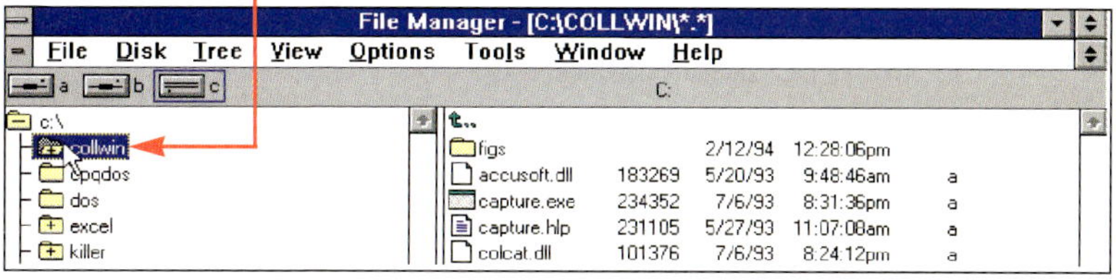

2 Press Ctrl+* (asterisk) to expand all branches.

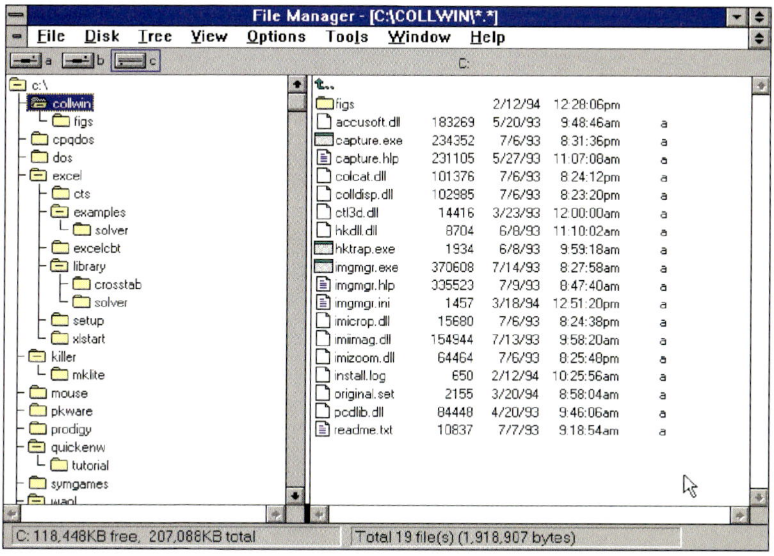

All branches are expanded (notice the minus signs)

To collapse an expanded directory

1 Double-click the directory you want to collapse.

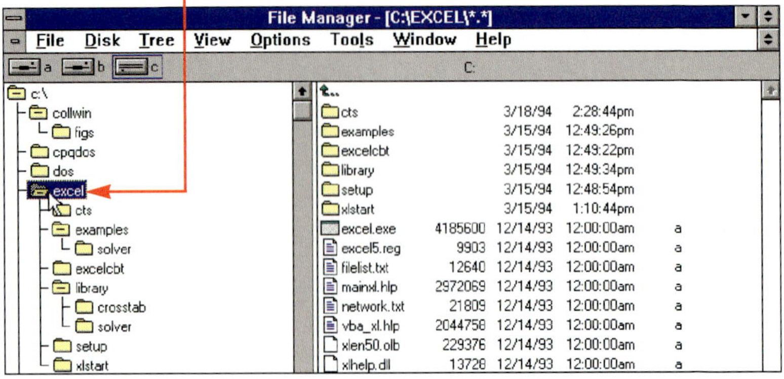

The collapsed directory (notice the plus sign)

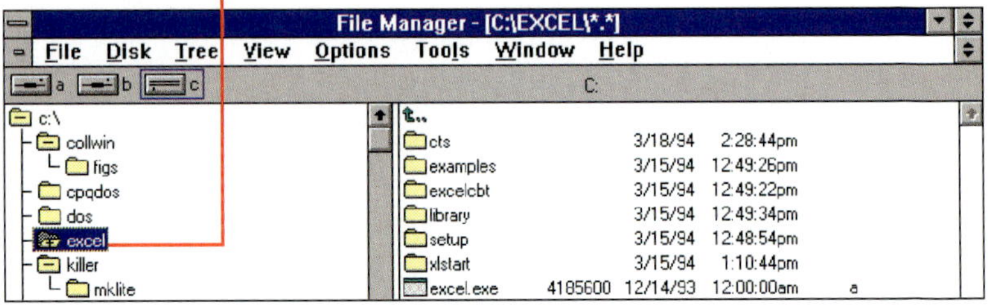

To collapse all subdirectories

1 Double-click the root directory.

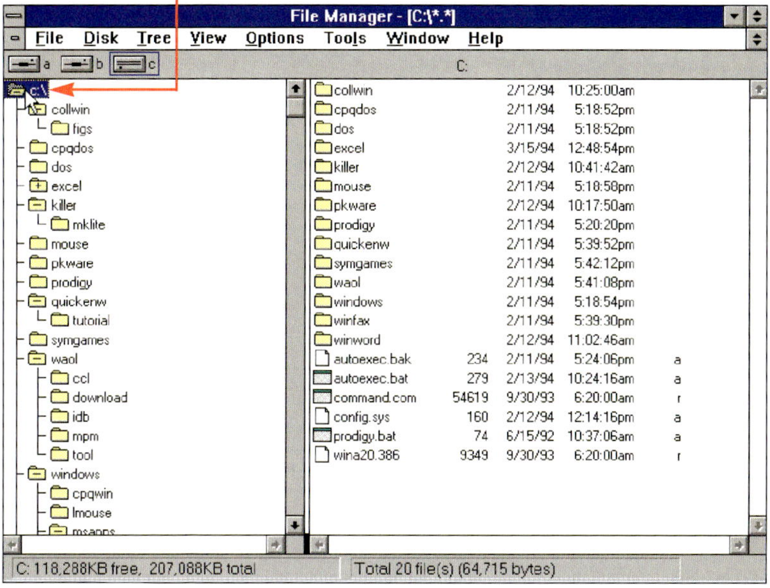

All subdirectory levels are collapsed

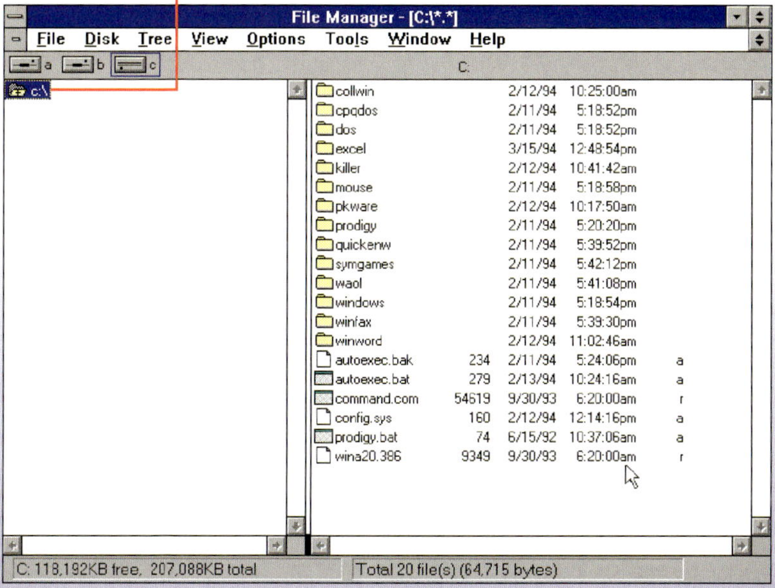

Changing the File Manager View

File Manager's View menu lets you display files with as much or as little detail as you like—file names only, file names and details, and so on. You can also sort the files in a particular order.

To display file names only

1 Choose View, Name.

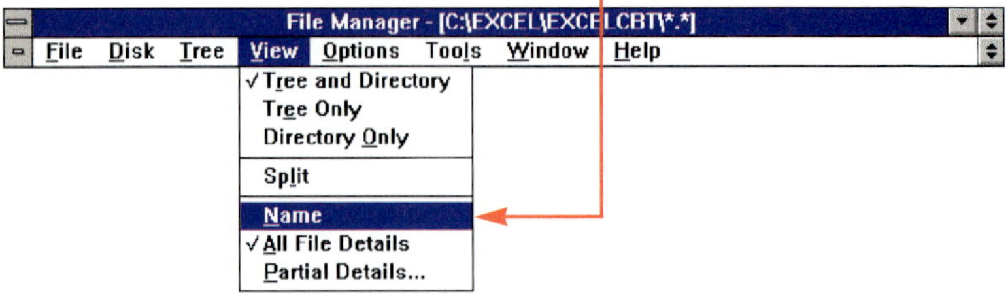

The list now displays only file names

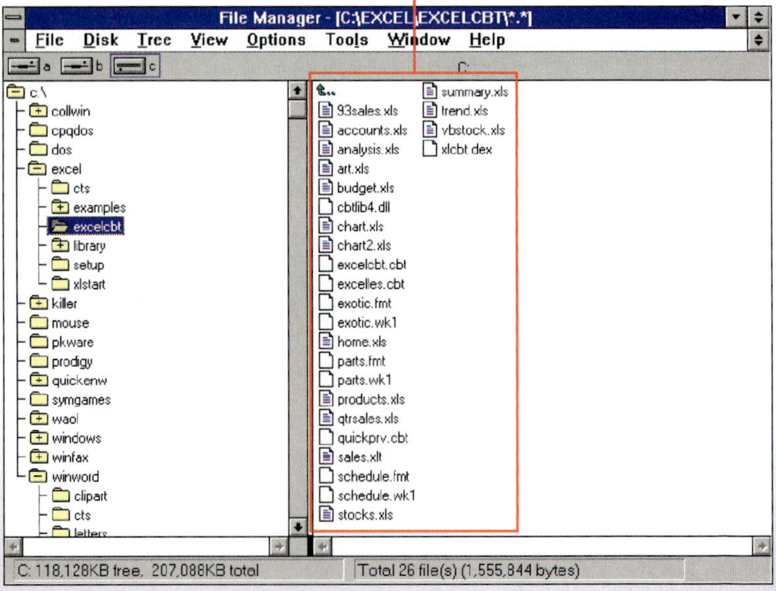

To display all details

1 Choose View, All File Details.

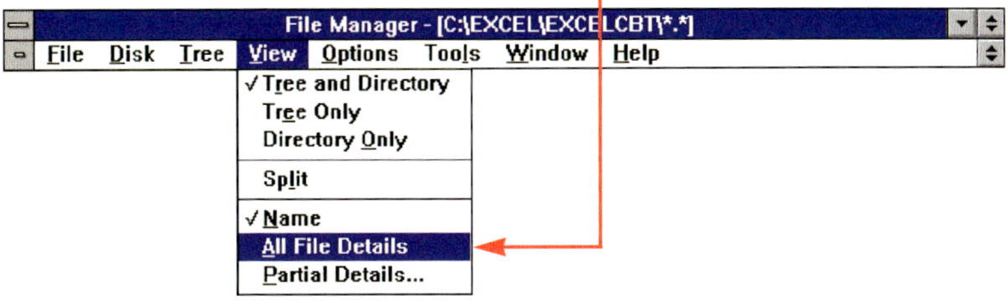

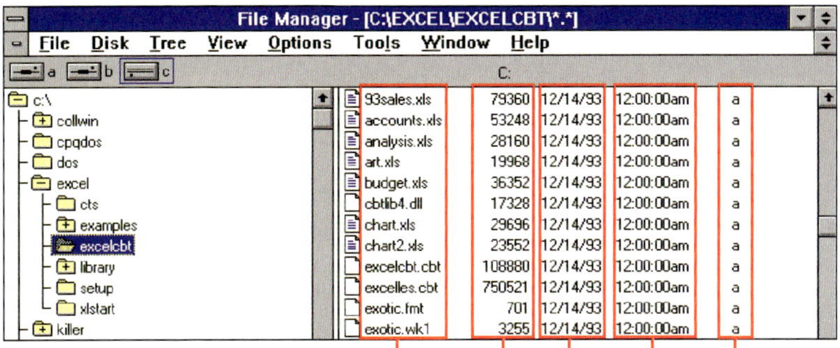

All file details are displayed

File name

File date

File attribute(s)

File size

File time

To display partial details

1 Choose View, Partial Details.

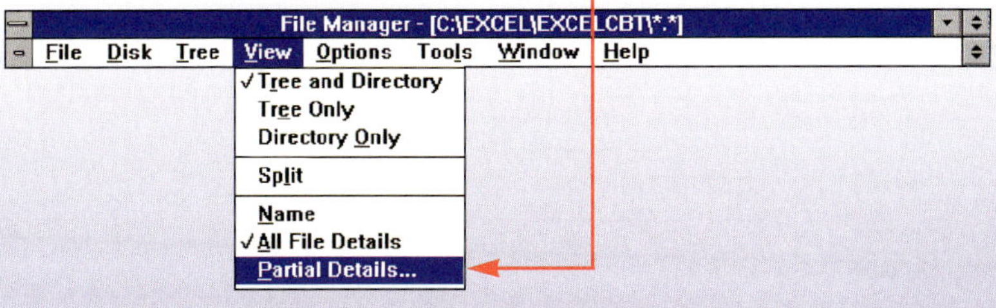

more ▶

2 Select the details you want to display.

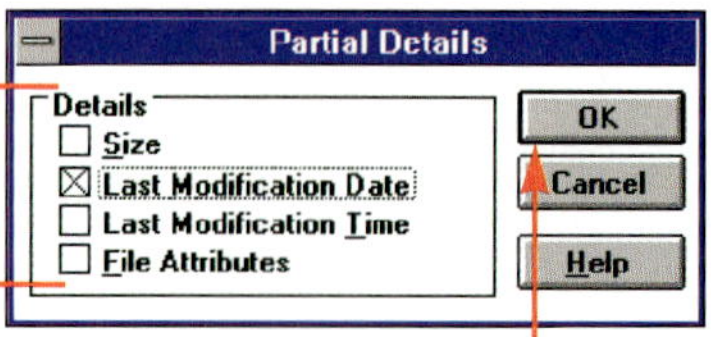

3 Choose OK.

To display a sorted file list

1 Choose View.

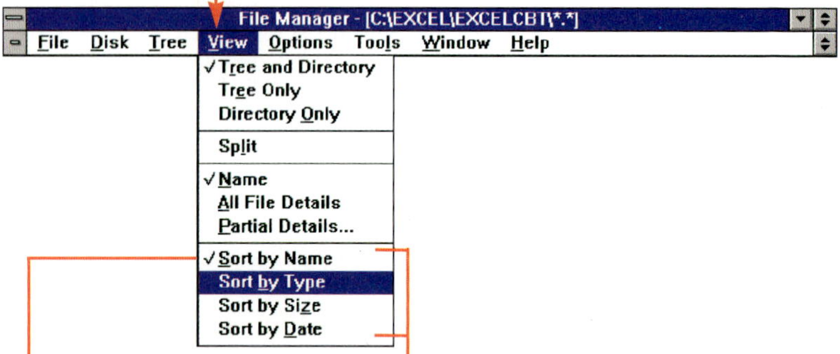

2 Select the sorting option you want: by name, type, size, or date.

A check mark indicates the current sort order

To display certain file types

1 Choose View, By File Type.

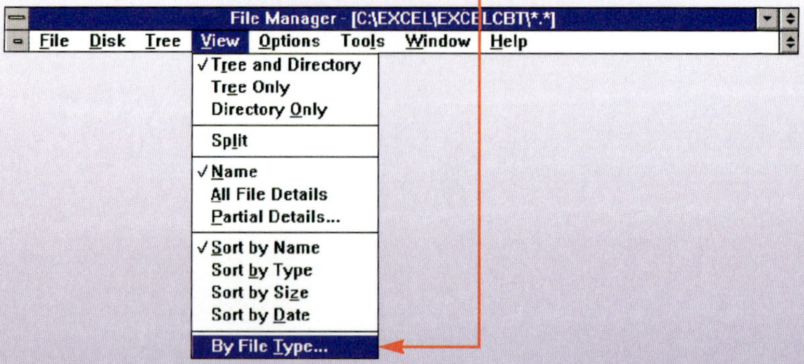

2 Select the file types you want to display.

Enter characters if you want only files with a certain extension or root name

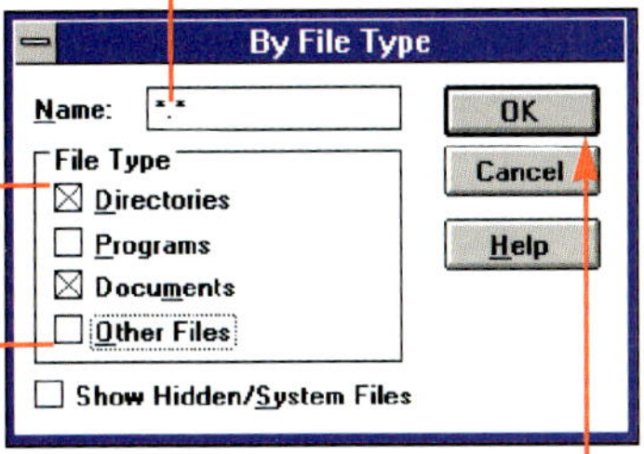

3 Choose OK.

Program, hidden, and system files display special icons

Program files

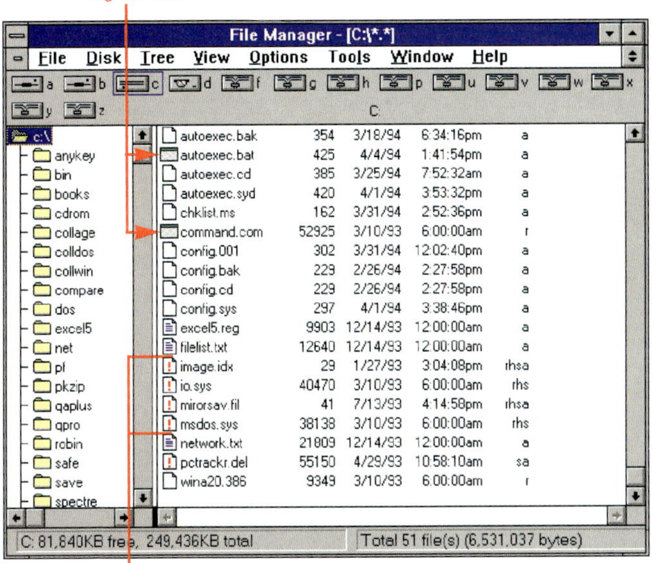

Hidden/system files

Associating Files

Associating a certain type of file with its originating program allows you to run the program just by double-clicking the file icon. This feature provides a very quick method of viewing files or of starting a program with the file in place for editing.

To associate an extension with a program

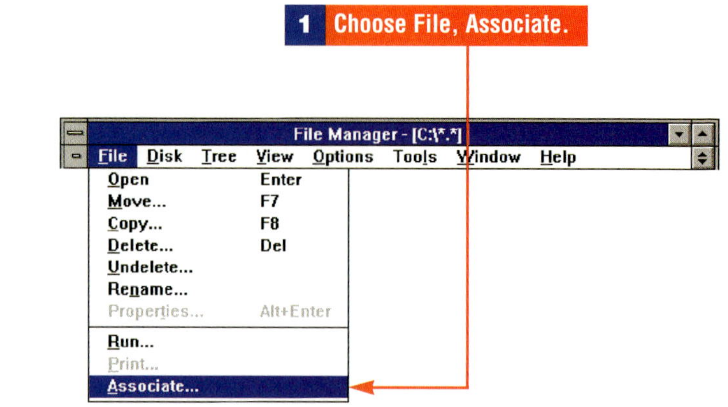

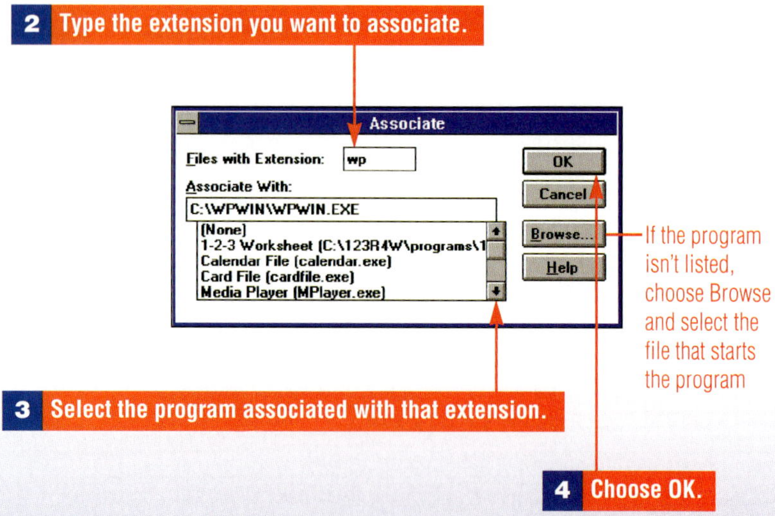

Selecting Files

For most File Manager functions, you must select the file(s) you want to use. After you select files, you can copy them, move them, delete them, and so on.

To select and deselect files

1 Click the icon of the first file you want.

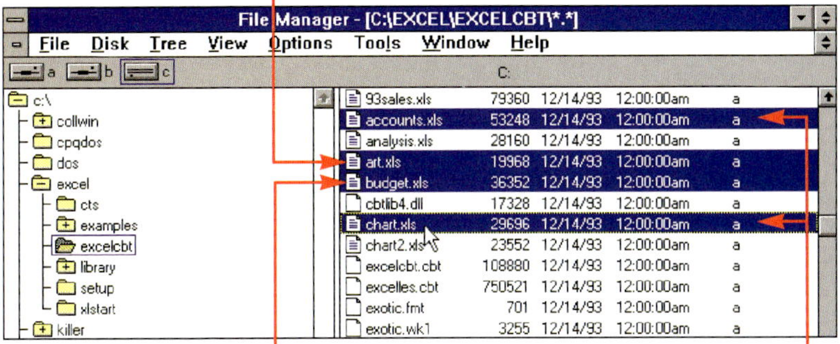

2 Hold down Shift and click the last file you want.

If the files aren't next to each other, hold down Ctrl and click each file separately

3 To deselect a selected file, hold down Ctrl and click the file again.

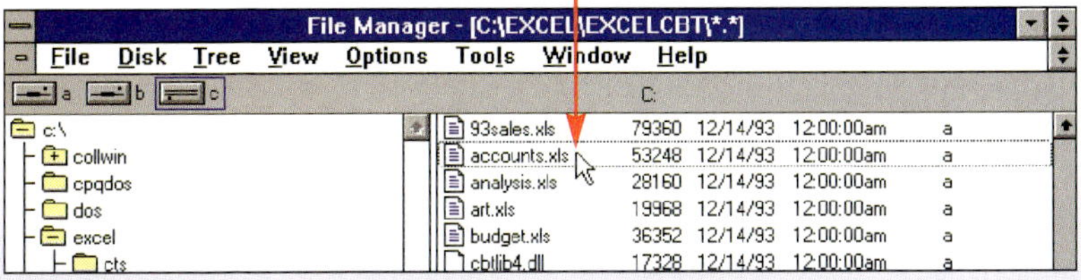

Copying Files

You can duplicate files by copying them to a different drive or directory. This feature is useful for making backup copies or for putting files on floppy disks for distribution or for use in other computers.

1 In the Main program group, double-click the File Manager icon.

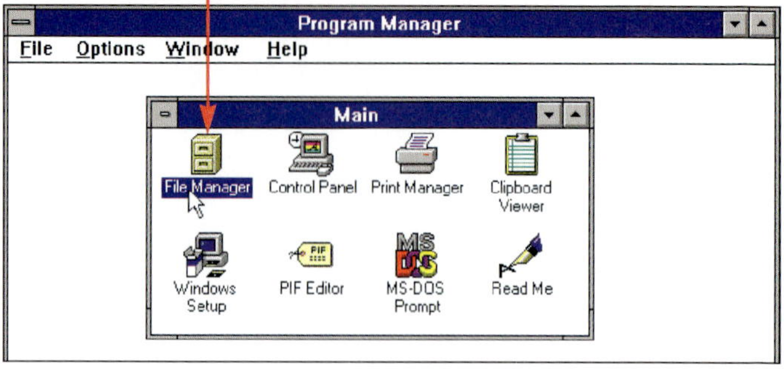

2 Insert the disk in the drive, if necessary.

3 Click the directory containing the file(s) you want to copy.

4 Select the file(s) you want to copy.

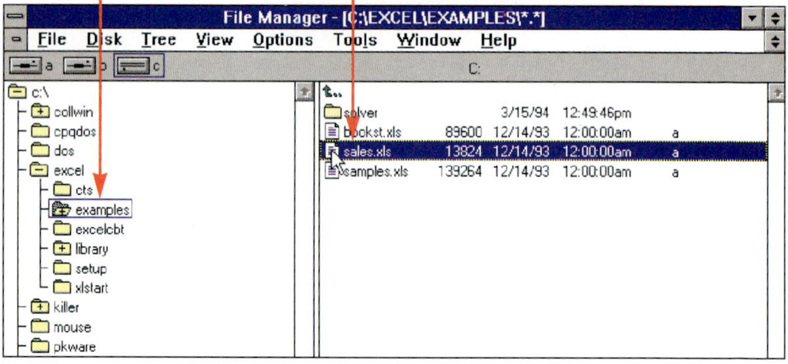

5 Hold down Ctrl and drag the file icon(s) to the destination drive or directory.

6 Choose Yes to copy the file(s).

This dialog box doesn't appear if confirmation is turned off

7 Choose Yes to replace the contents of the original file.

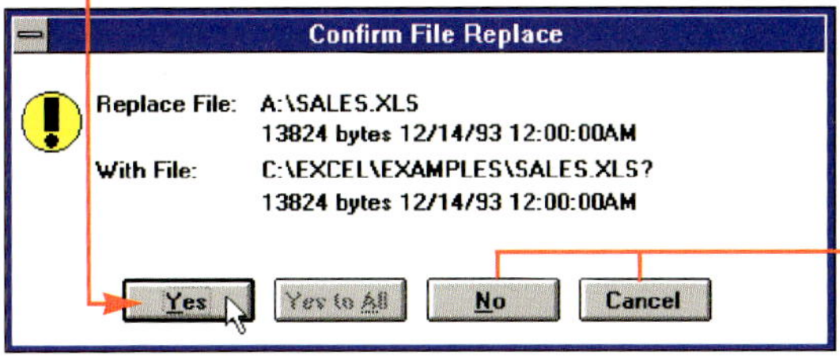

Choose No or Cancel to avoid overwriting the file

This dialog box appears only if the file already exists at the destination location

Deleting Files

You can delete files from a disk or directory when you want to eliminate duplicates or when the files are no longer needed.

1 Click the directory containing the file(s) you want to delete.

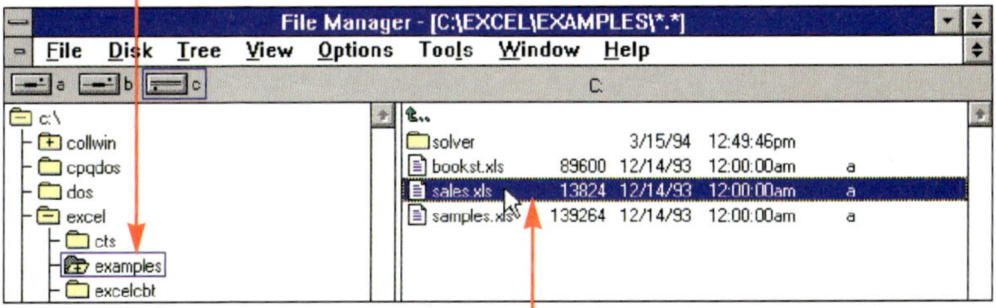

2 Click the file(s) you want to delete.

3 Press Delete.

Path

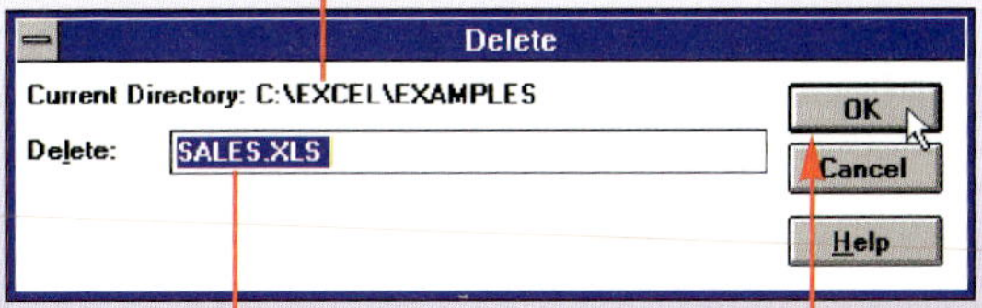

File name

4 Choose OK.

more ▶

5 Choose Yes to confirm the deletion.

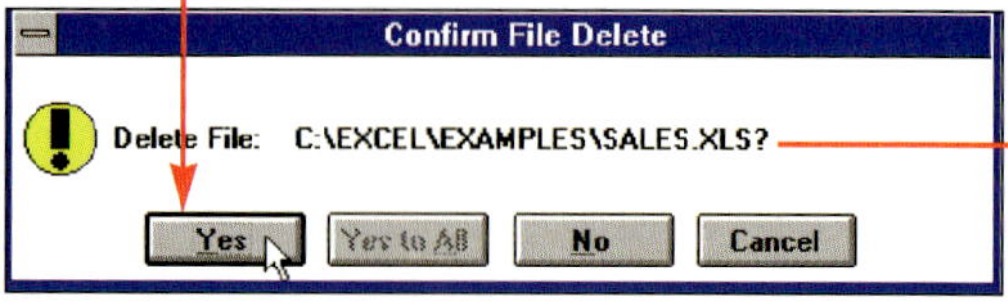

Path

This dialog box doesn't appear if confirmation is turned off

Finding Files

File Manager's Search feature helps you find a file (or set of files) when you don't remember in what directory the file is located, or you're not sure of the file name. When searching, try to use characters that are unique to the file(s) you want to find (for example, a specific extension like XLS).

1 Click the root directory to begin searching at the top of the tree.

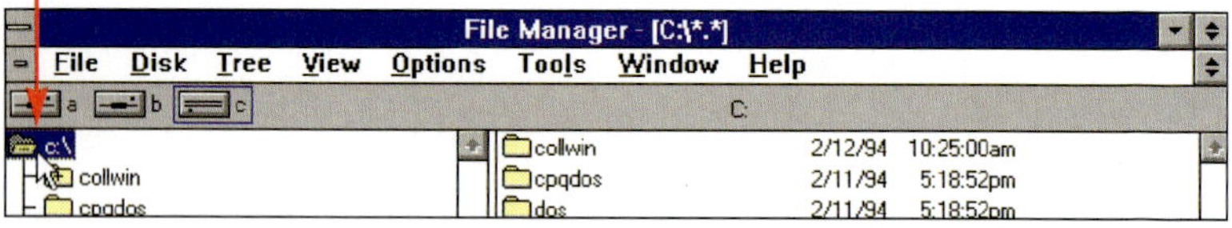

2 Choose File, Search.

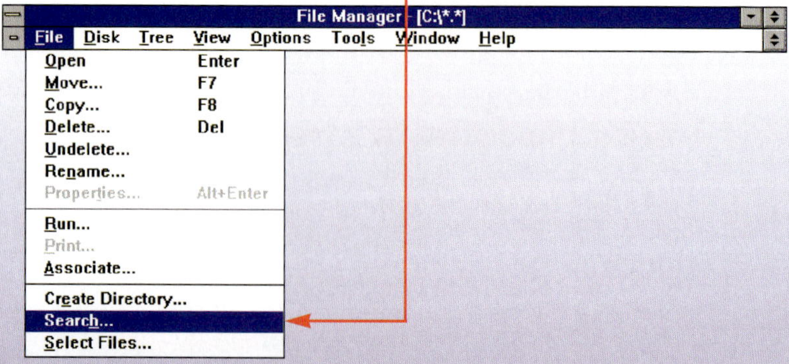

3 Type the search string (characters from the file name) you want to find.

Start from the root directory to search the whole disk

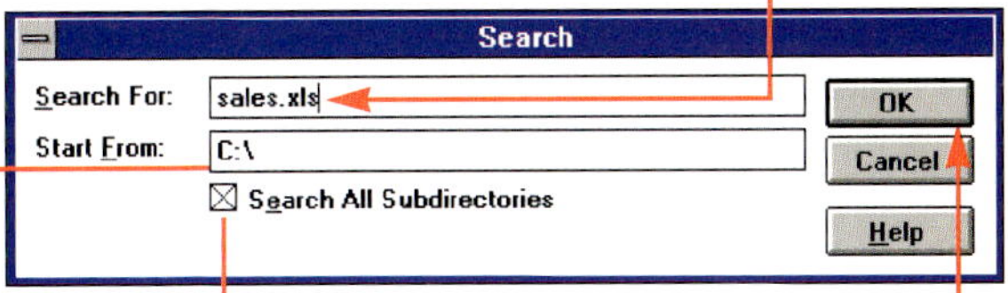

4 Choose OK.

Select Search All Subdirectories if you don't know which directory contains the file

You can use wild cards (? and *) to replace one character or multiple characters, respectively

5 Double-click the Control menu box to close the Search Results window.

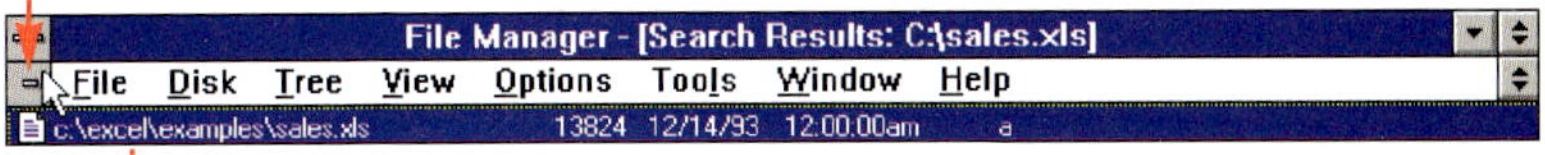

Location or path to the file

You can copy, move, delete, or rename the file(s) from the Search window

Moving Files

File Manager enables you to move a file from one drive and directory to another drive or directory. Moving files is helpful, for example, when you create a new directory and want to group certain existing files together in that new directory.

1 Insert the disk in the drive, if necessary.

2 Click the directory containing the file(s) you want to move.

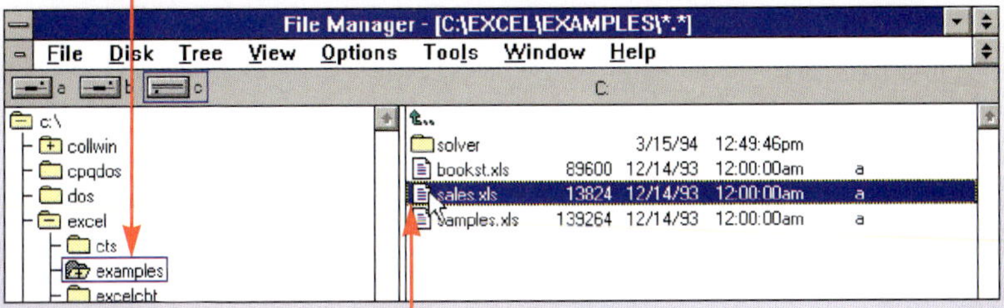

3 Select the file(s) you want to move.

4 Hold down the Shift key and drag the file icon(s) to the destination.

more ▶

5 Choose Yes to move the file(s).

This dialog box doesn't appear if confirmation is turned off

Renaming Files

Renaming a file is useful if you accidentally gave the file the wrong name, or if you want to name a set of files with names that are similar. When you rename a file, you cannot assign a name that already exists in that directory.

1 Click the directory containing the file you want to rename.

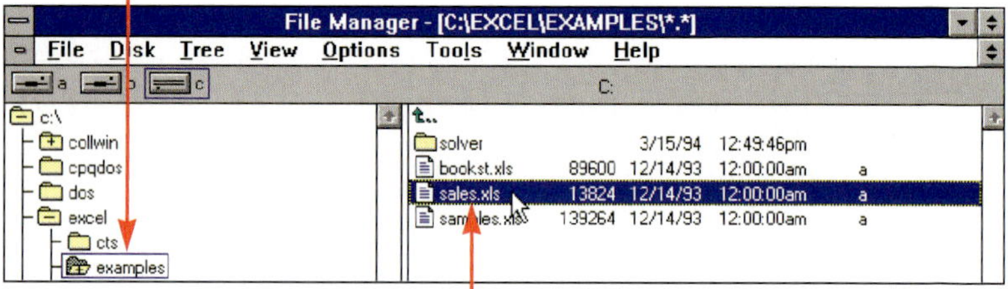

2 Click the file you want to rename.

Files must be renamed one at a time

3 Choose File, Rename.

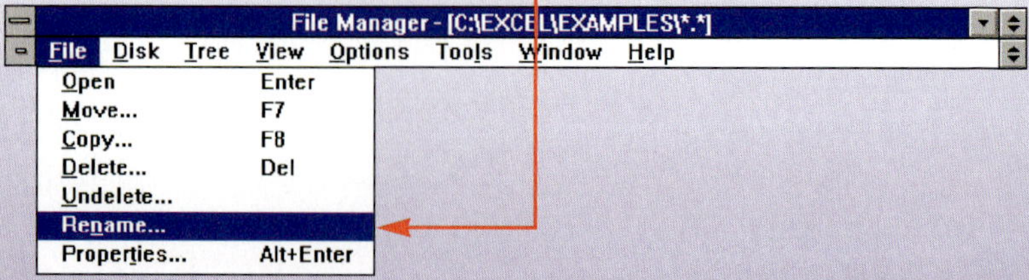

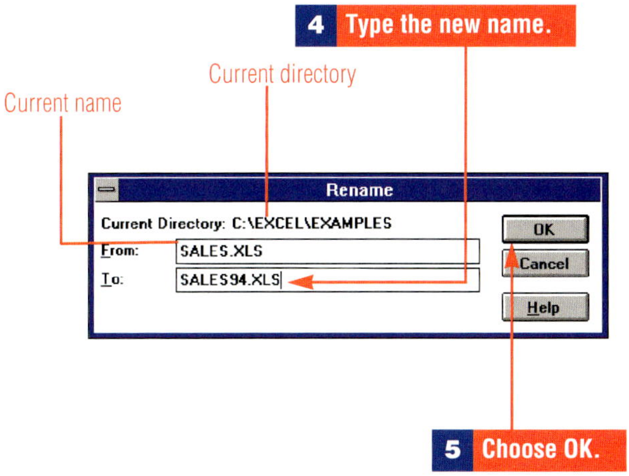
4 Type the new name.
Current directory
Current name
Rename
Current Directory: C:\EXCEL\EXAMPLES
From:
SALES.XLS
To:
SALES94.XLS
OK
Cancel
Help
5 Choose OK.

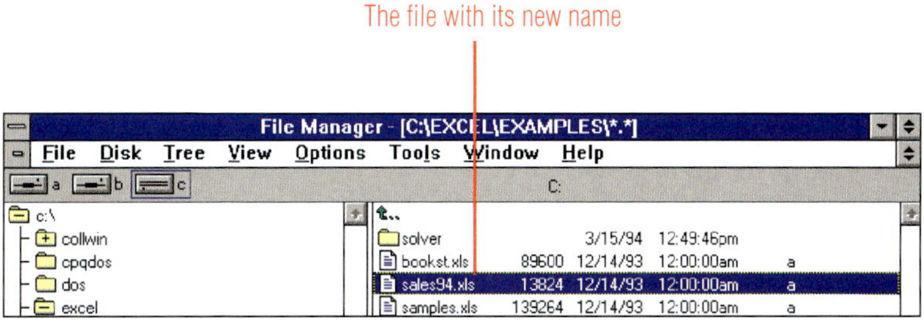
The file with its new name
File Manager - [C:\EXCEL\EXAMPLES*.*]
File Disk Tree View Options Tools Window Help
c:\
collwin
cpqdos
dos
excel
solver 3/15/94 12:49:46pm
bookst.xls 89600 12/14/93 12:00:00am a
sales94.xls 13824 12/14/93 12:00:00am a
samples.xls 139264 12/14/93 12:00:00am a

Getting Help with Common Tasks

Windows offers many ways to get help. If you cannot remember how to perform a task, use the Windows Help system to get information. The Help feature has its own menu system.

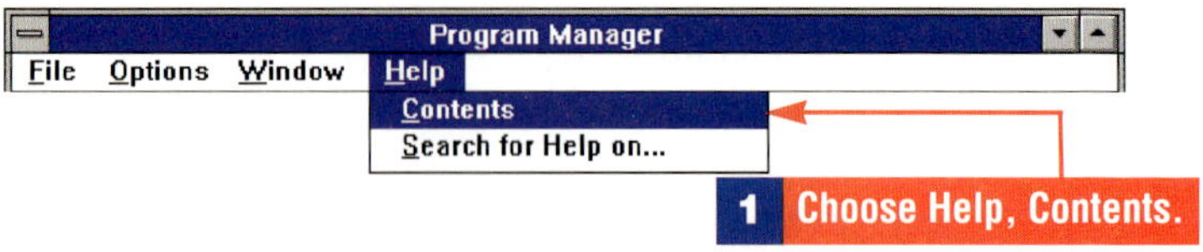

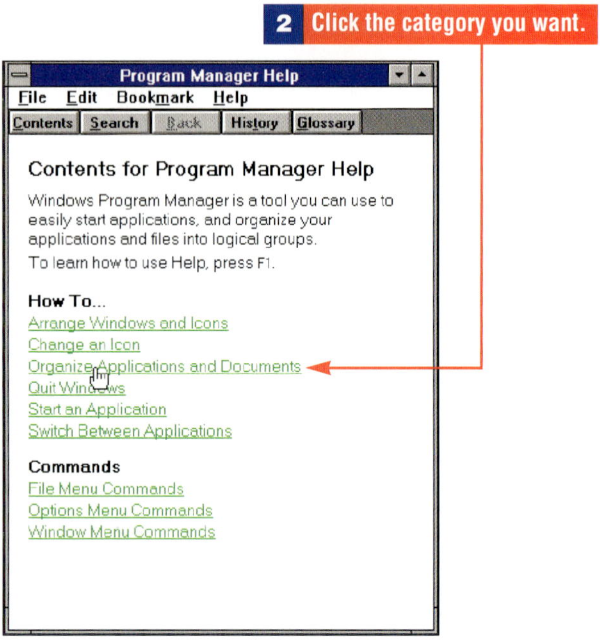

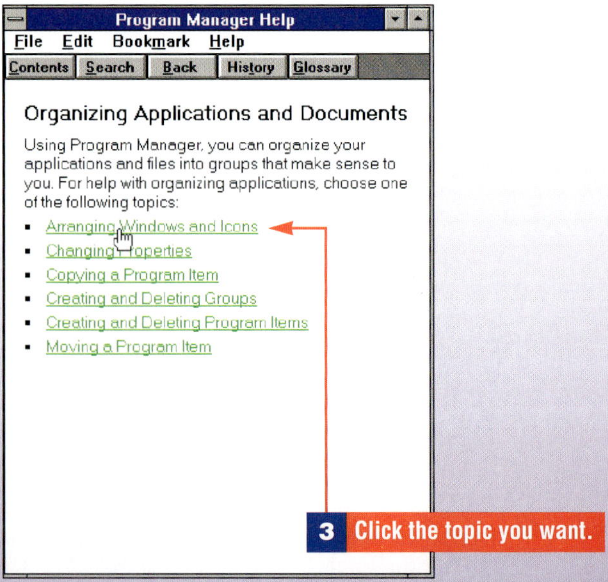

4 Scroll as necessary to read the Help description.

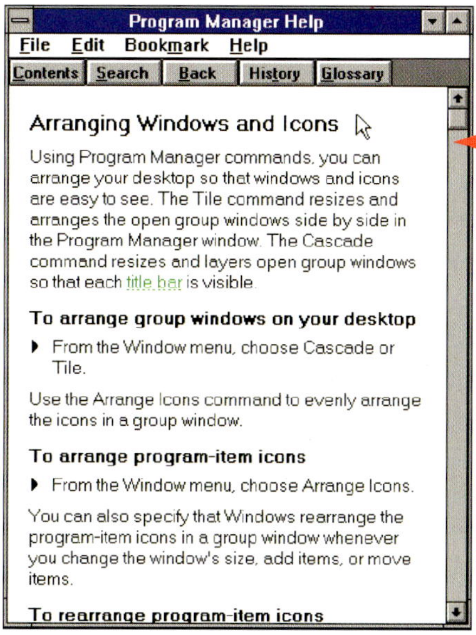

5 Choose File, Exit to exit Help.

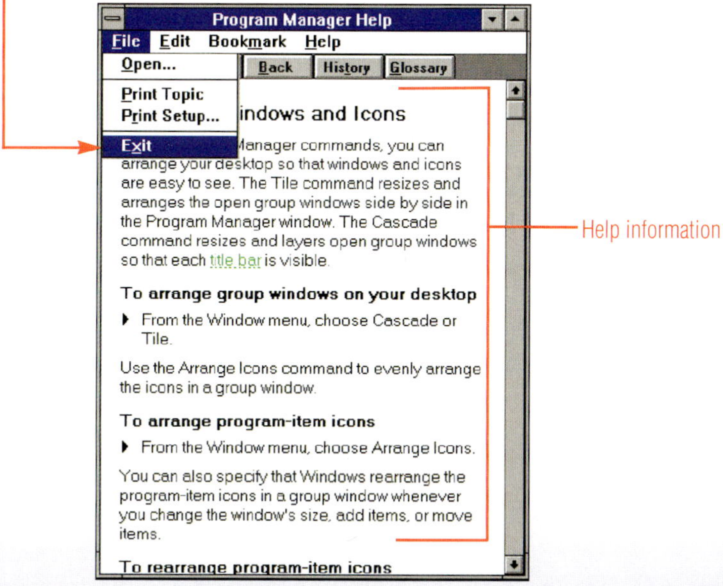

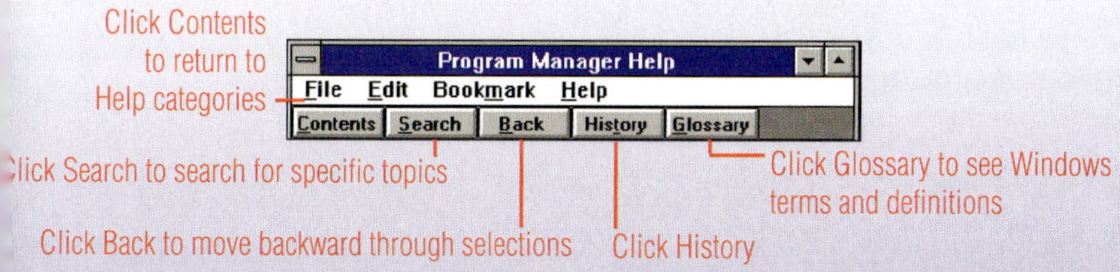

Looking Up a Topic

The Search for Help On command lets you search for help on a particular topic.

1 Choose Help, Search for Help on.

2 Type the name of the feature for which you want help.

3 Click a subject and then click Show Topics.

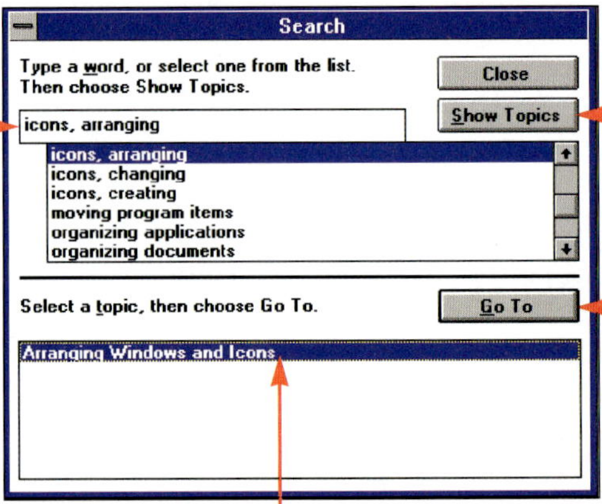

4 The topics for the subject appear in the bottom box. Click the one you want.

5 Click the Go To button.

6 Double-click the Help window's Control menu box to exit Help.

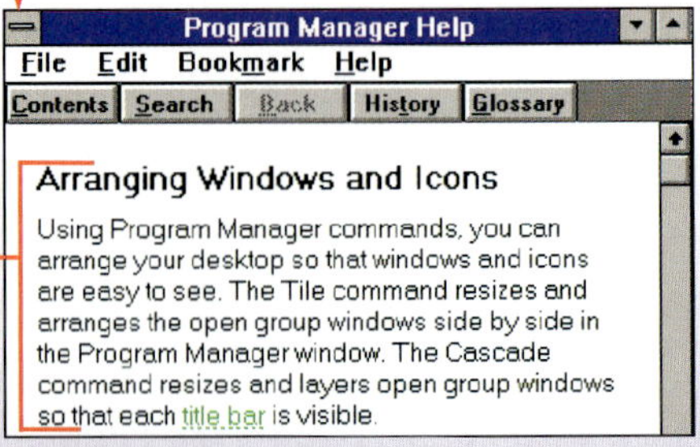

Help information

Getting Help in a Dialog Box

You can get help on the options in a dialog box when the dialog box is on-screen.

1 Choose a menu command that displays a dialog box.

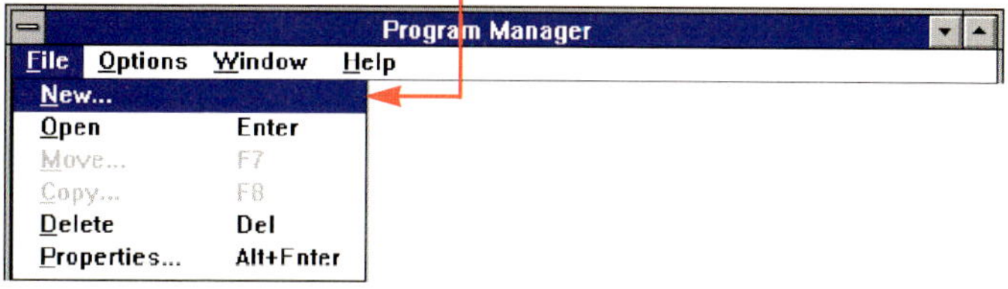

2 Click the Help button.

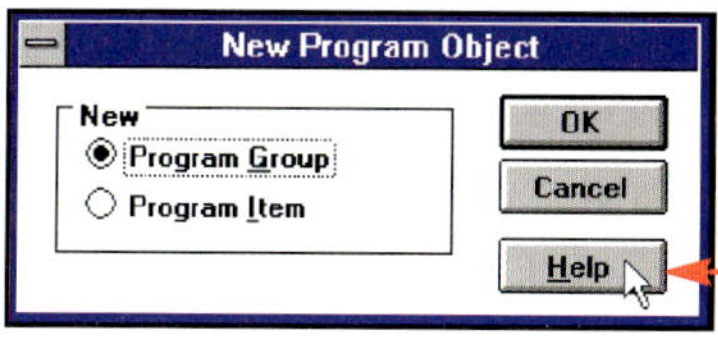

3 Double-click the Help window's Control menu box to exit Help.

Help information

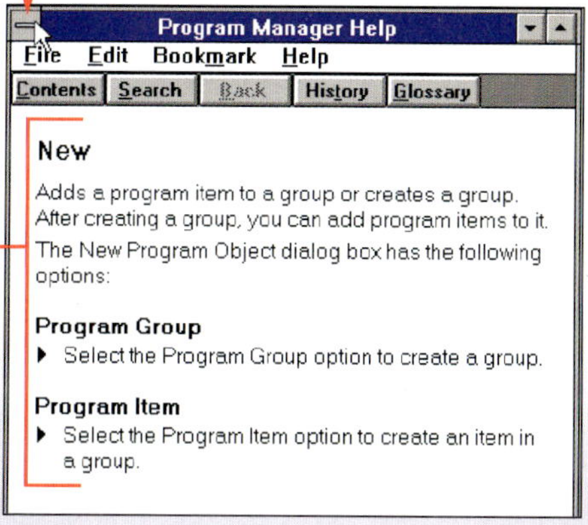

Using the Windows Tutorial

The Windows Tutorial shows you how to perform certain tasks in Windows by stepping through a series of short interactive lessons.

1 Choose Help, Windows Tutorial.

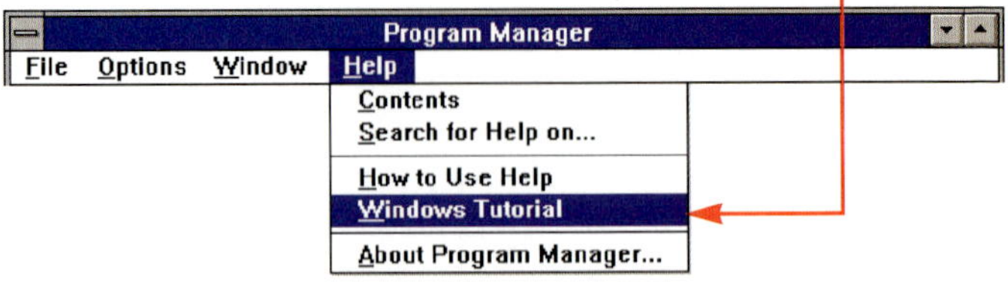

2 Choose the type of lesson you want.

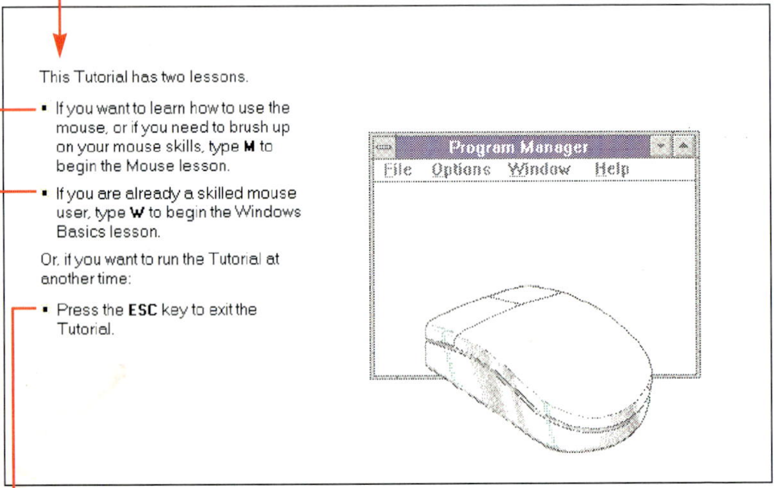

Press Esc to exit the Windows Tutorial

Press W to go through the Windows Basics lesson

Press M to go through the Mouse lesson

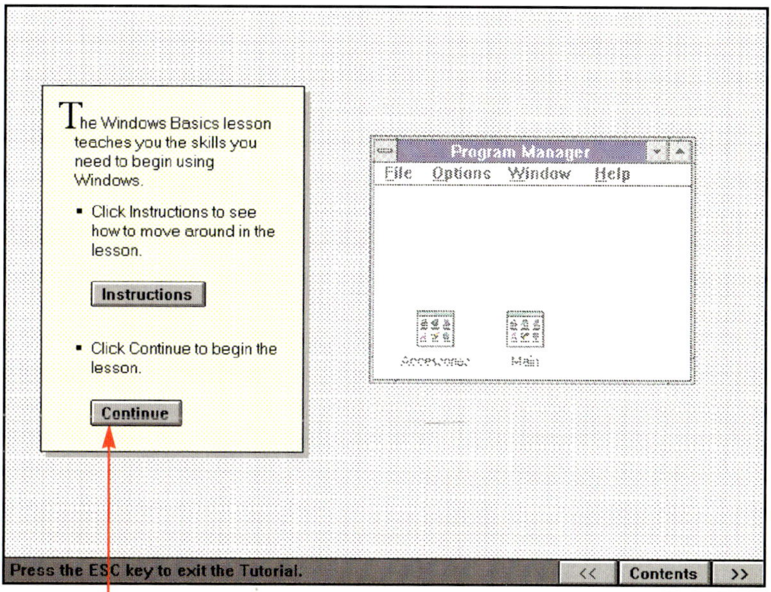

3 Click the Continue button to begin the lesson.

4 Follow the steps in the lesson.

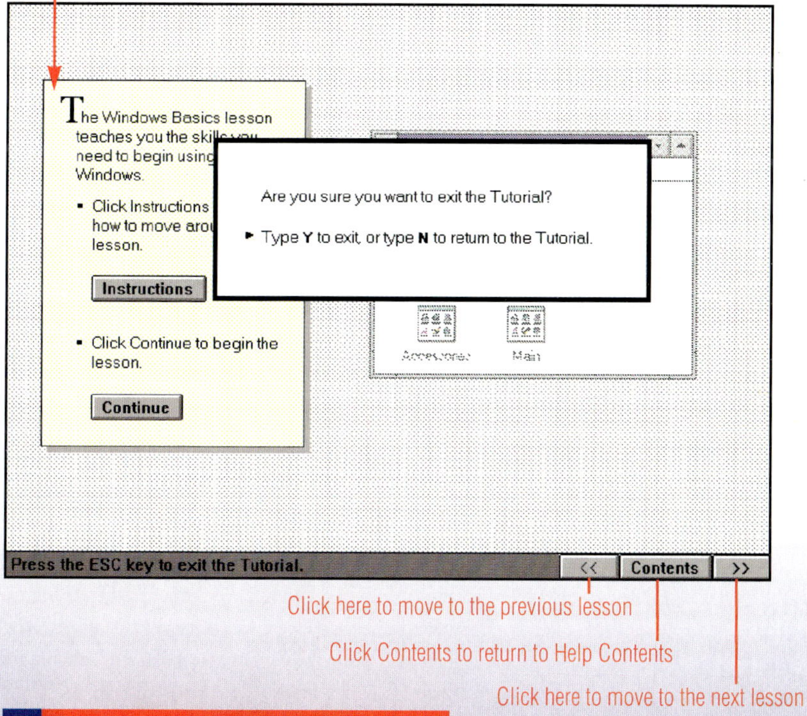

5 Press Esc to exit the Windows Tutorial.

6 Type Y to exit or N to continue.

Switching Programs

Windows allows you to move different applications into the foreground, to switch from one application program to another.

To switch applications with the keyboard

1 Press Alt+Esc or Alt+Tab to move from one application to another.

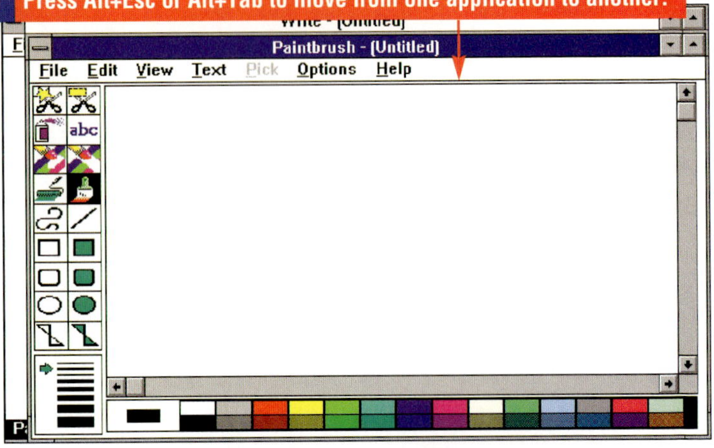

To switch applications with the Task List

1 Press Ctrl+Esc or double-click the desktop to open the Task List.

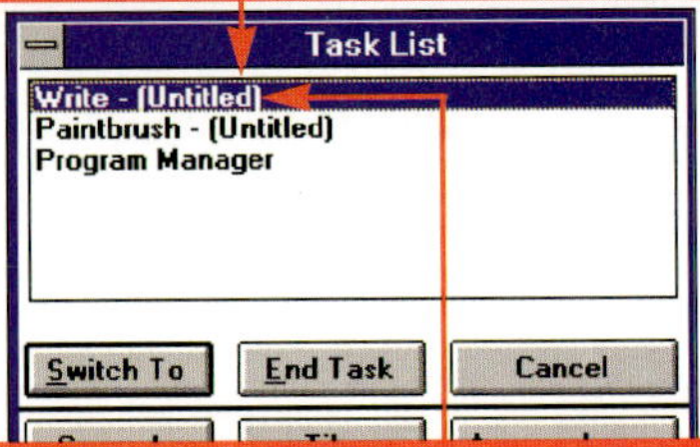

2 Double-click the application you want to make active.

To switch applications with the mouse

1 Point to the application's window and click, or double-click the application's icon.

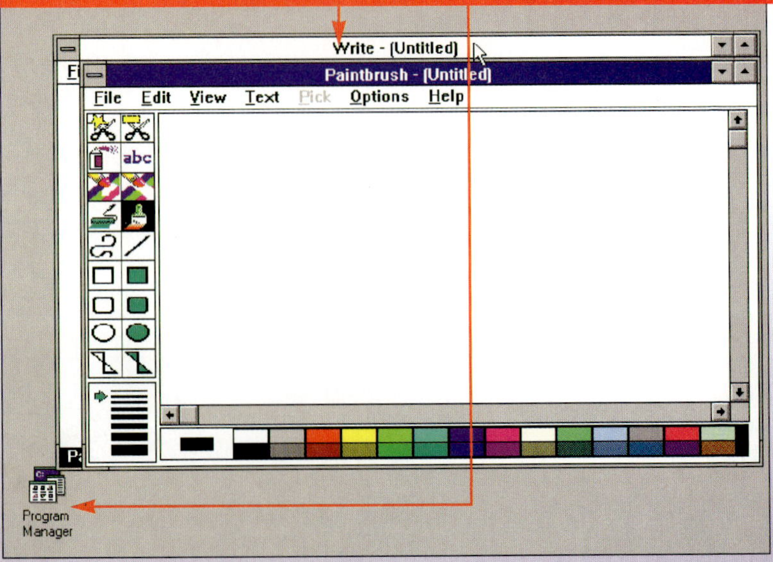

Using the Clipboard

The Clipboard stores text or graphics temporarily, while you transfer them between two applications or within an application.

To store and retrieve information in the Clipboard

1 Select the text or graphics to place in the Clipboard.

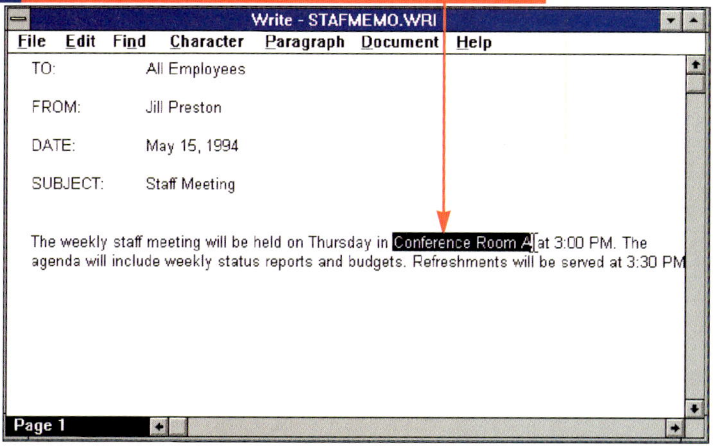

2 Choose Edit, Copy to copy text or graphics.

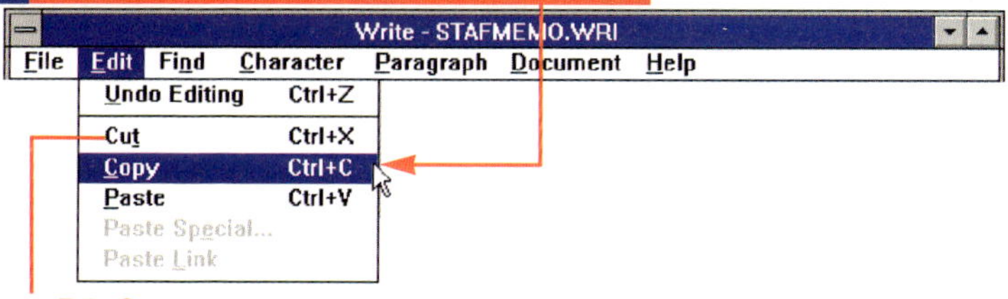

Choose Edit, Cut to remove text or graphics

3 Switch to the application where you want to place the text or graphics.

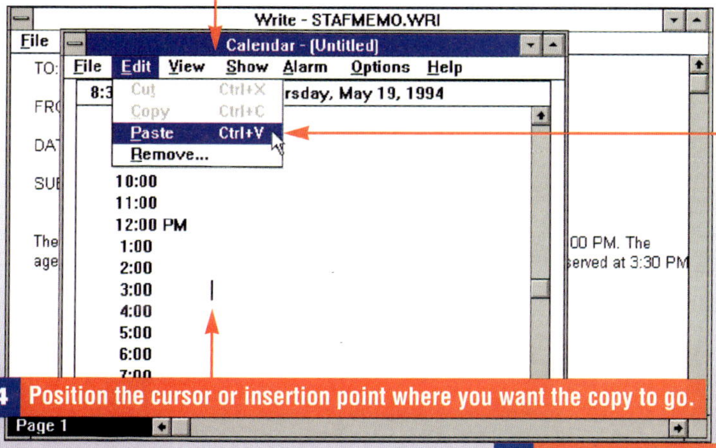

4 Position the cursor or insertion point where you want the copy to go.

5 Choose Edit, Paste.

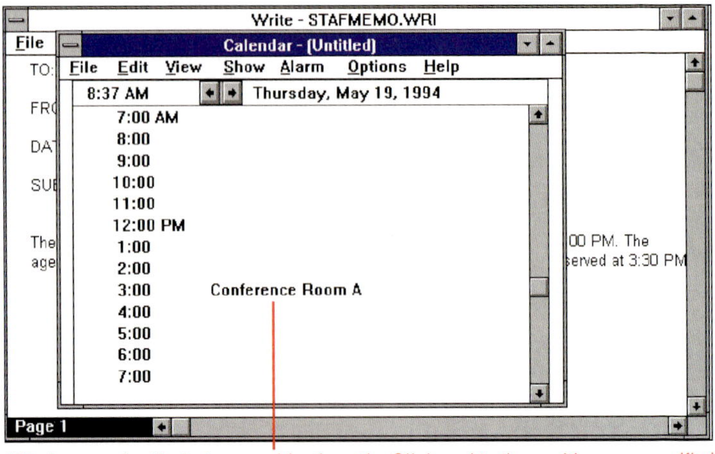

Windows copies the text or graphics from the Clipboard to the position you specified

To view the information in the Clipboard

1 From Program Manager, open the Main program group.

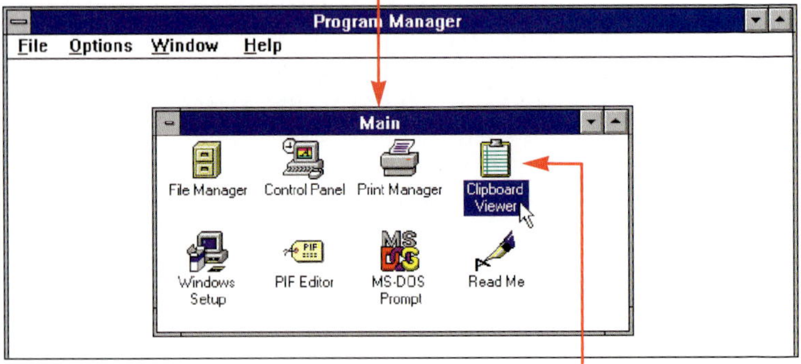

2 Double-click the Clipboard Viewer icon.

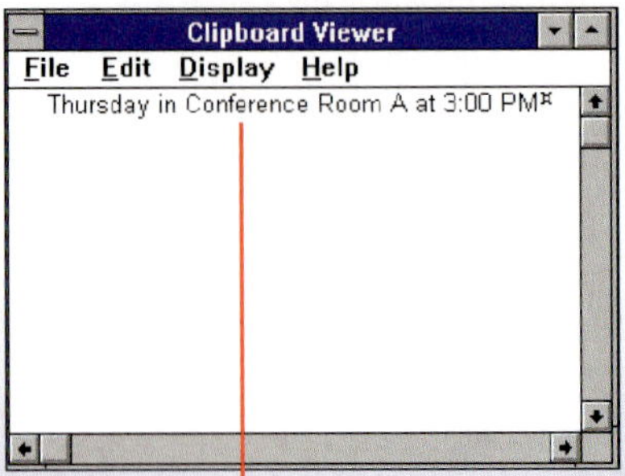

The Clipboard contains the information that you last copied or cut

To save the information in the Clipboard for later use

1 From the Main program group, double-click the Clipboard Viewer icon.

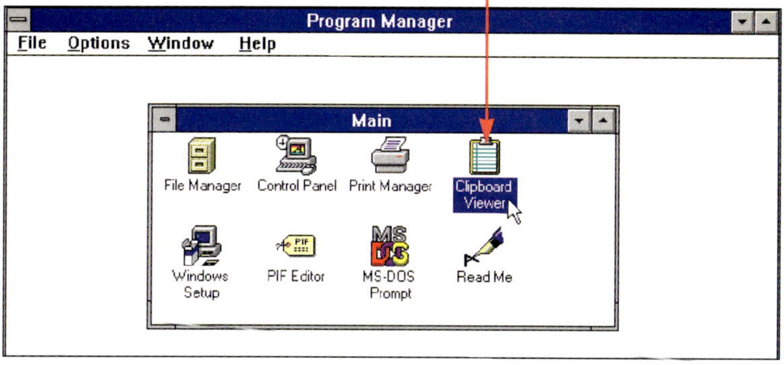

2 From the Clipboard Viewer menu, choose File, Save As.

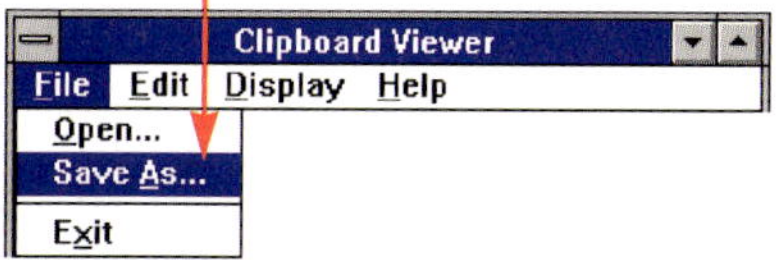

3 Choose the directory in which you want to save the file.

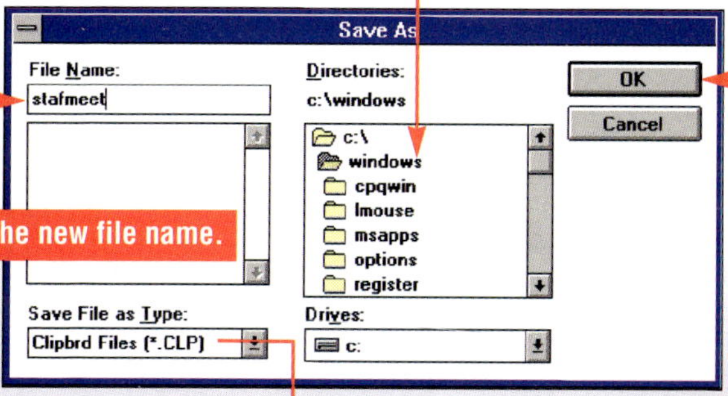

4 Type the new file name.

5 Choose OK.

Windows automatically adds the CLP file extension

To open a Clipboard file

1 From the Main program group, double-click the Clipboard Viewer icon.

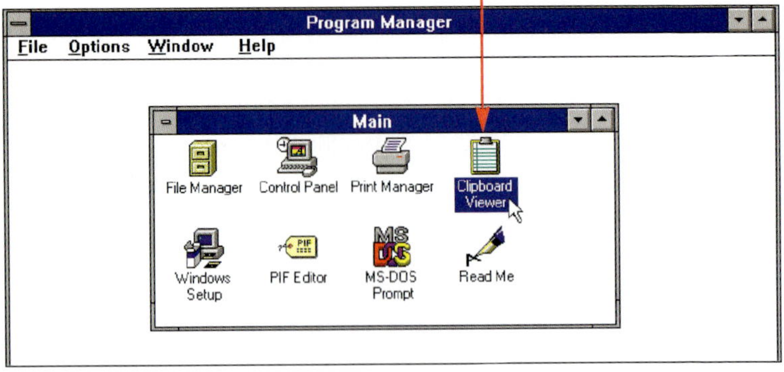

2 From the Clipboard Viewer menu, choose File, Open.

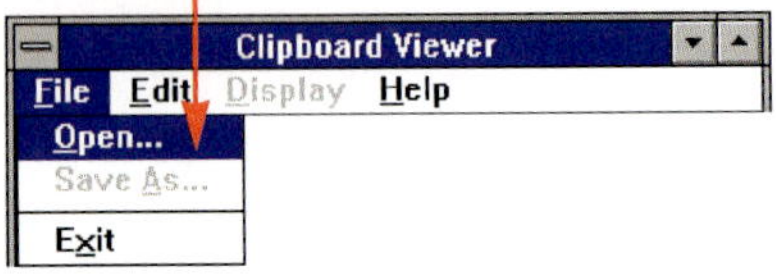

3 Choose the directory containing the file.

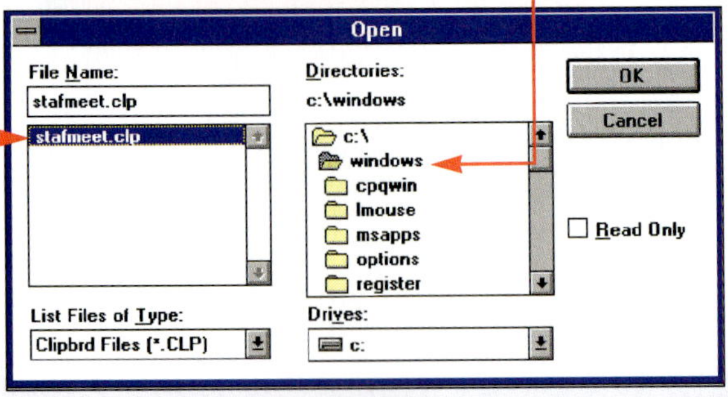

4 Double-click the Clipboard file name.

5 If you have something in the Clipboard, choose Yes to clear it.

Linking and Embedding

Linking and embedding insert data from one application into another. The server is the sending application and the client is the receiving application.

To link an object

1 Start or select the server program.

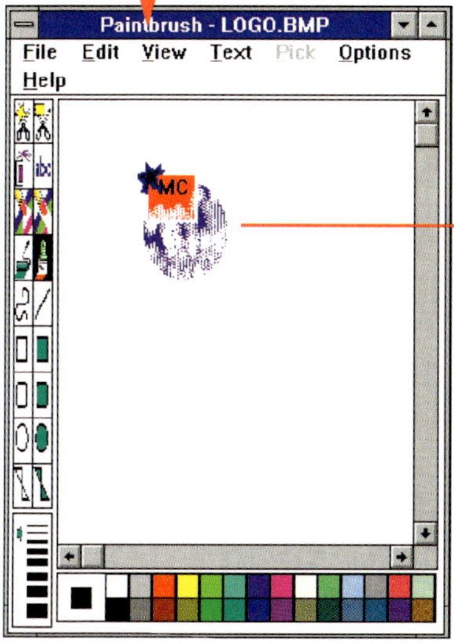

Create and save the object if it has not been created

2 Select the object you want to link.

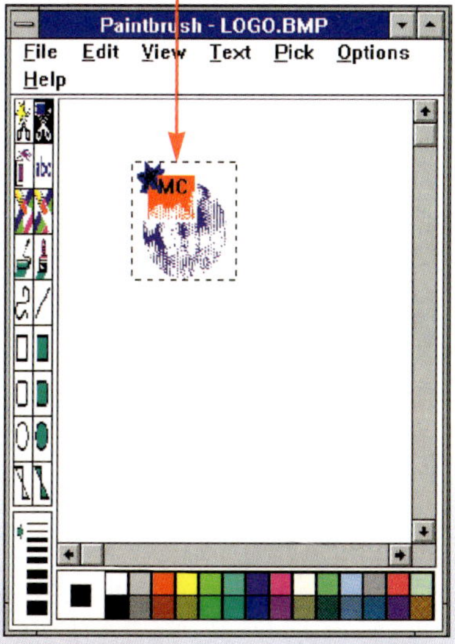

3 Choose Edit, Copy.

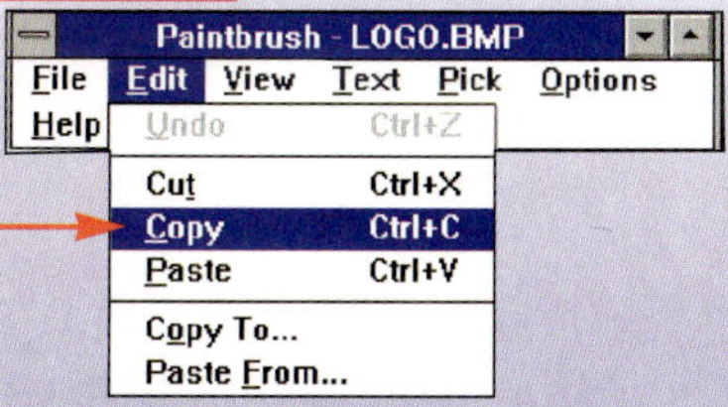

more ▶

4 Start or select the client program.

5 Open the file where you want to place the linked item.

6 Position the cursor or insertion point where the object should be linked.

7 Choose Edit, Paste Link.

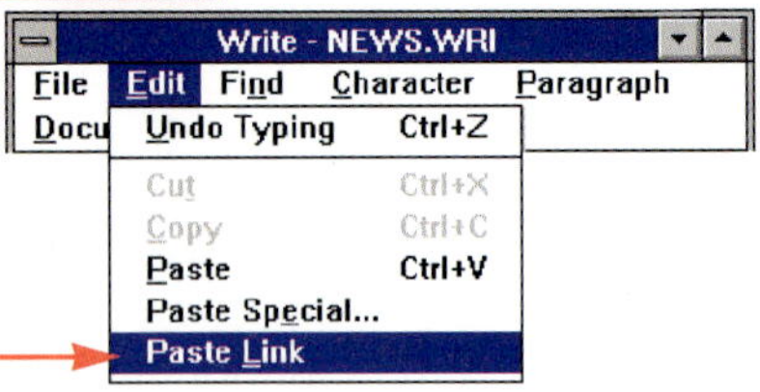

The linked object in the client application

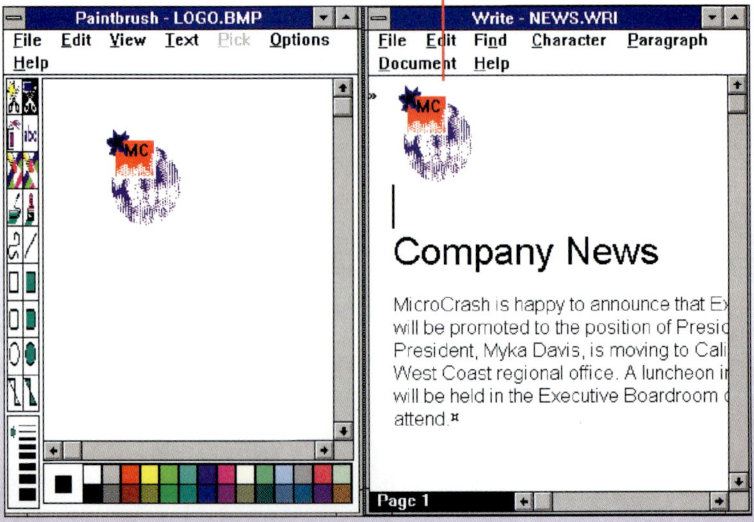

When you change the linked item in the server application, the same changes occur in the client application

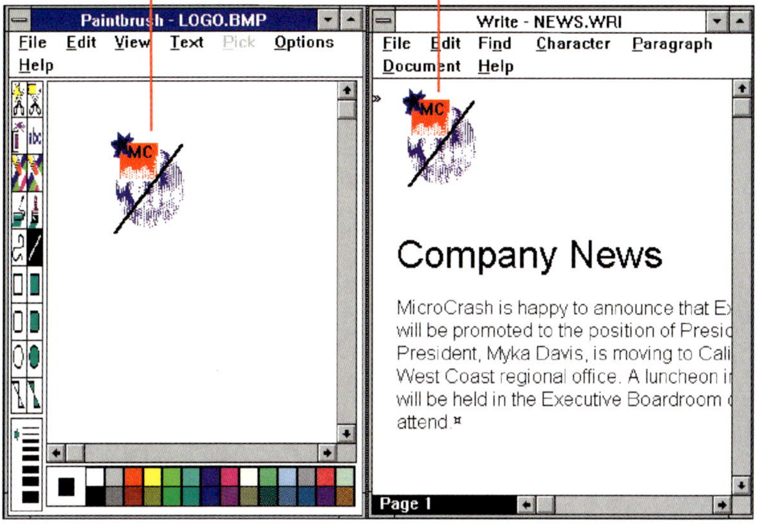

To embed an object

1 Start or select the server program.

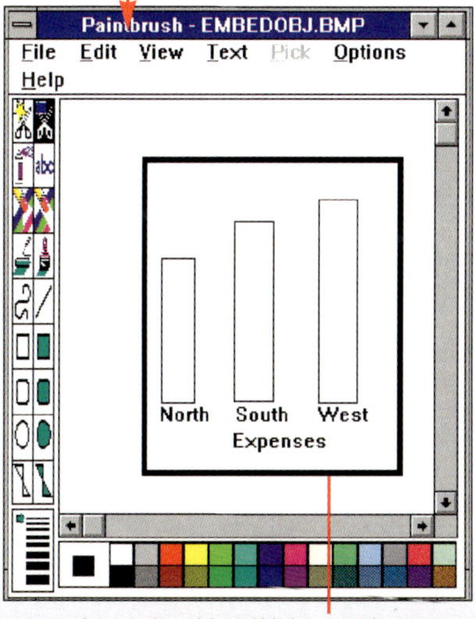

Create and save the object if it has not been created

more ▶

2 In the server program, select the object you want to embed.

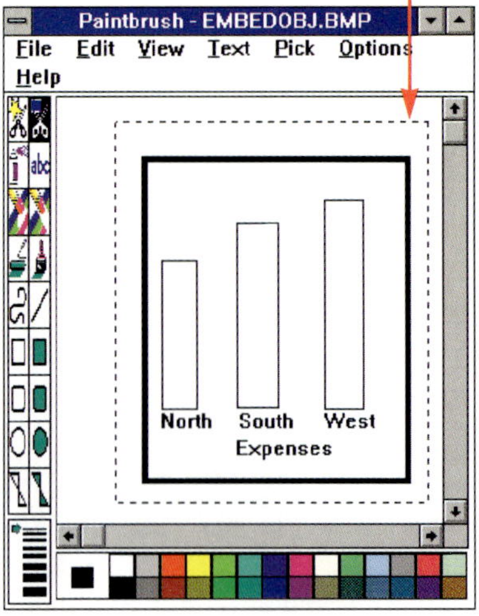

3 Choose Edit, Copy.

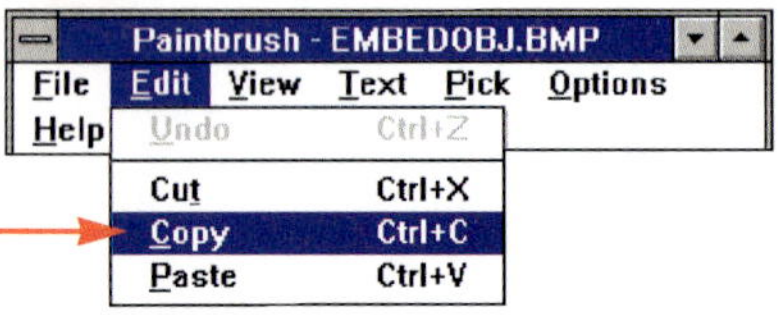

4 Start or select the client program.

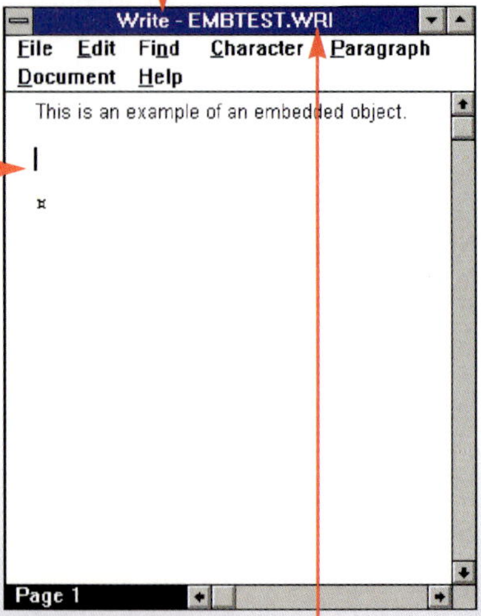

5 Open the file you want to use.

6 Position the cursor where you want to place the embedded object.

7 Choose Edit, Paste

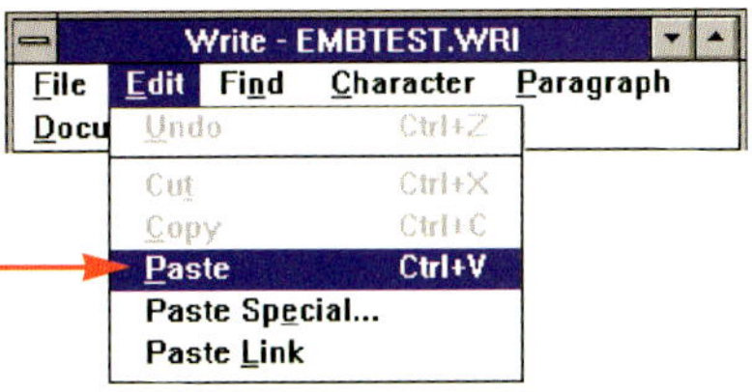

The embedded object in the client application

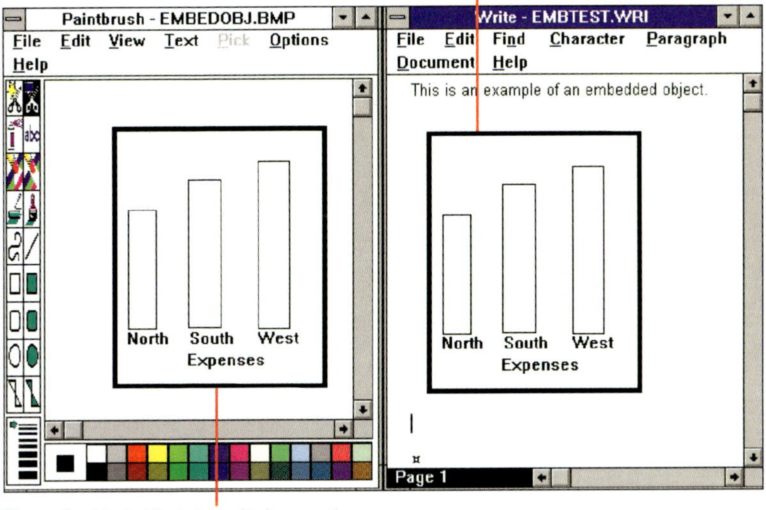

The embedded object doesn't change when you change the original in the server application

Packaging Objects

Object Packager is a program that enables you to store any linked or embedded object as an icon for inclusion in a program.

To use Object Packager

1 Open the file containing the data you want to package.

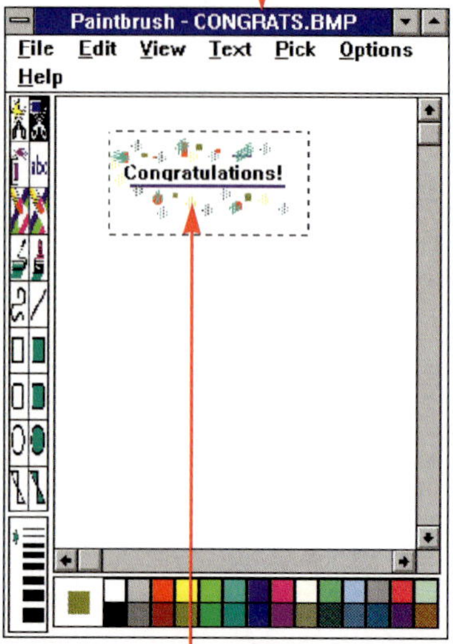

2 Select the text or graphic you want to package.

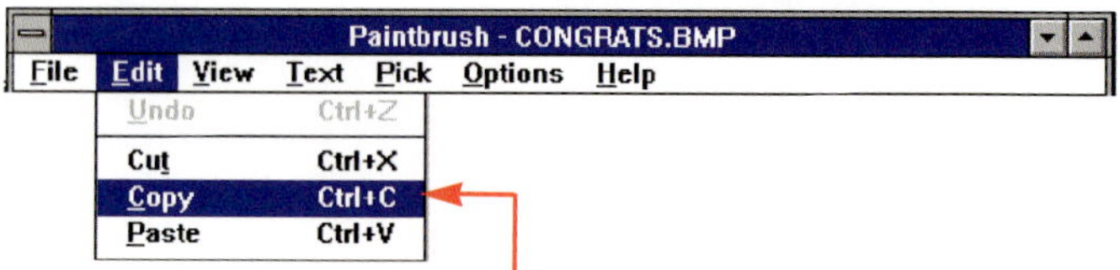

3 Choose Edit, Copy.

4 From the Accessories program group, double-click the Object Packager icon.

5 Choose Edit, Paste to create an embedded package.

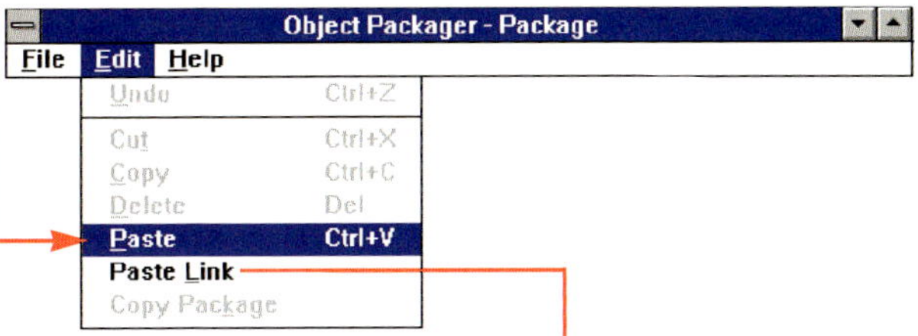

Choose Edit, Paste Link to create a linked package

6 Choose Edit, Copy Package to copy the package to the Clipboard.

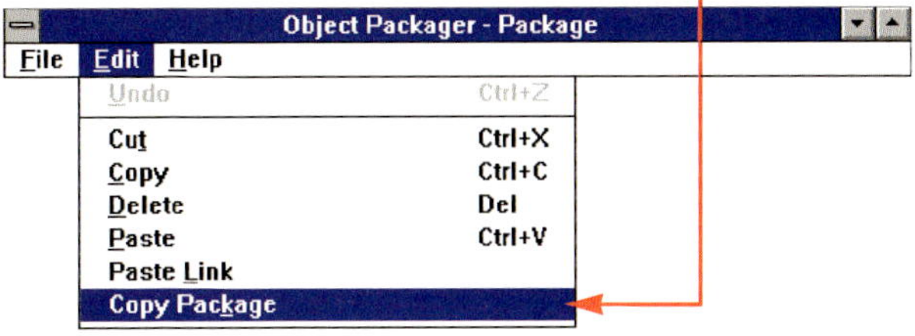

7 Activate the client application and open the client file.

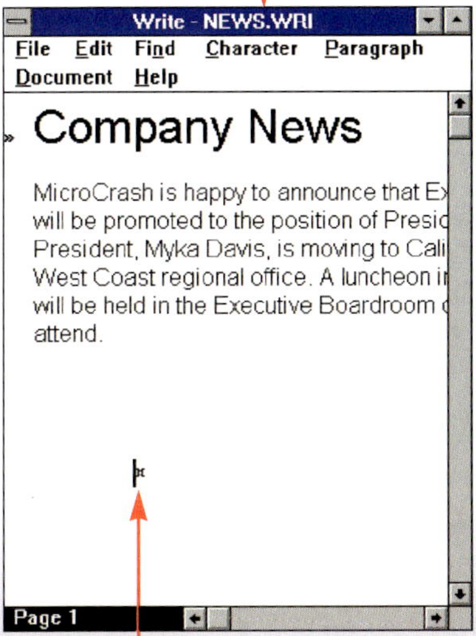

8 Move the insertion point to where you want the package.

more ▶

9 Choose Edit, Paste Special.

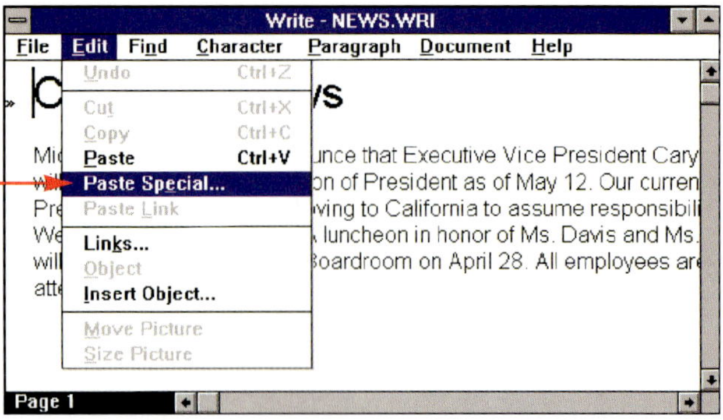

10 Select the type of file you want to paste.

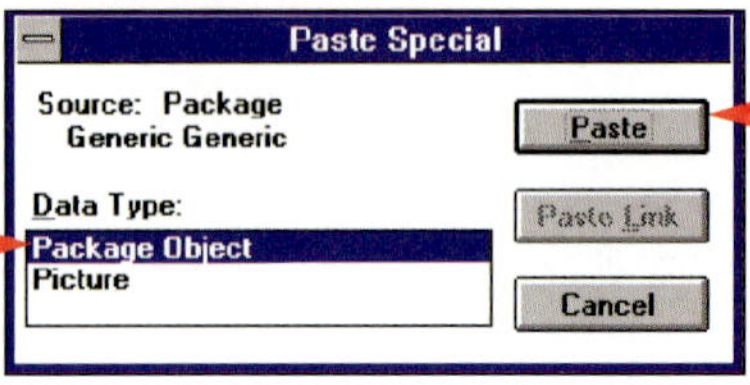

11 Choose Paste.

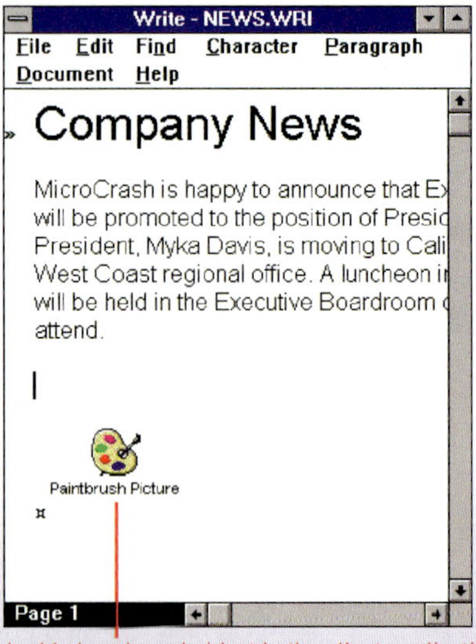

The embedded packaged object in the client application

Double-click the package icon to view the packaged object in the server application

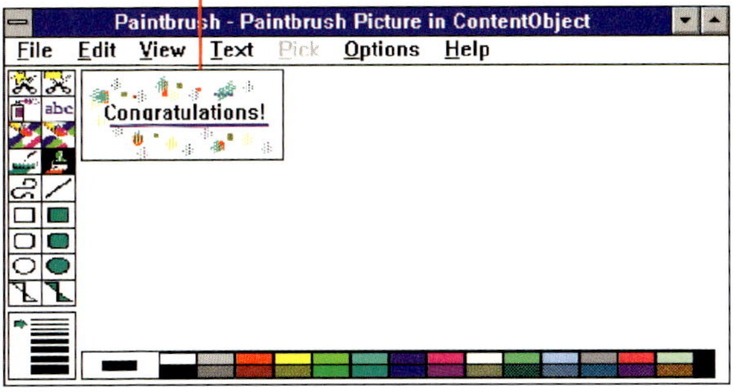

To change the icon for your package

1 In the Object Packager window, click Appearance.

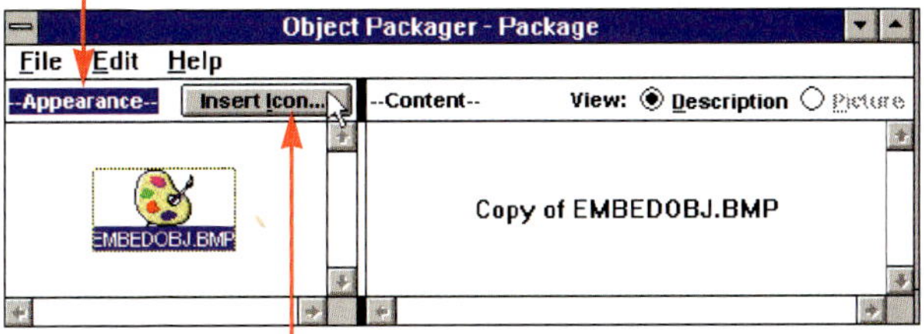

2 Click Insert Icon.

3 Click Browse.

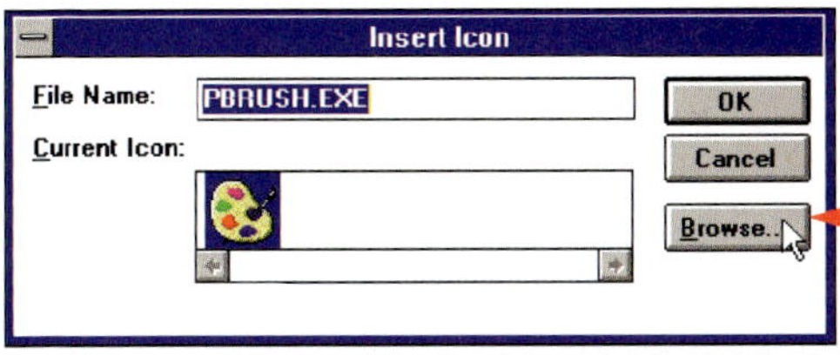

more ▶

4 Double-click program.exe or moricons.dll.

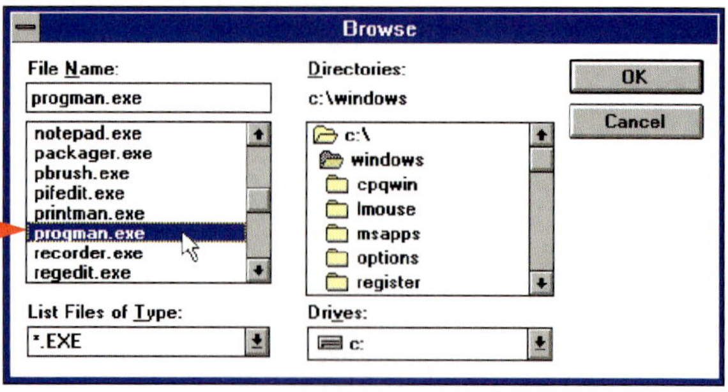

5 Scroll the Current Icon list and click the icon you want.

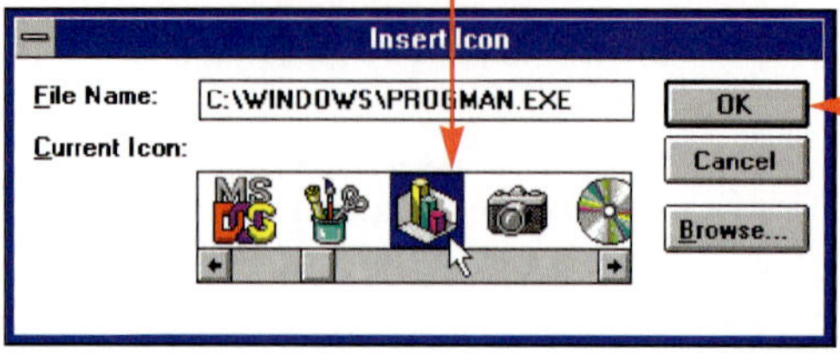

6 Choose OK.

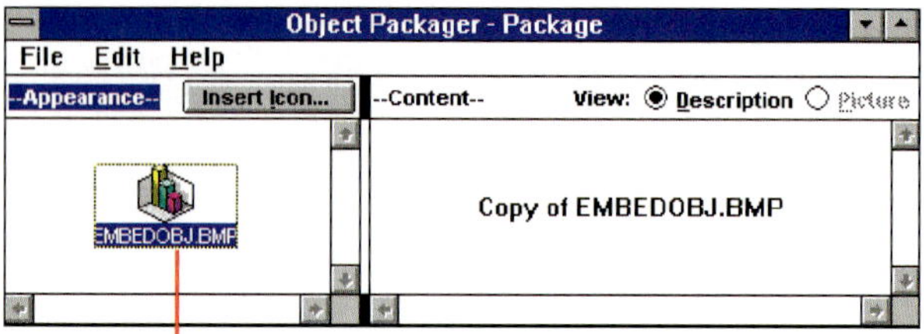

The new object icon

Setting Colors

Windows enables you to customize screen colors, making it easy to identify each Window element on-screen.

To select a new color scheme

1 From Program Manager, open the Main group window.

2 Double-click the Control Panel icon.

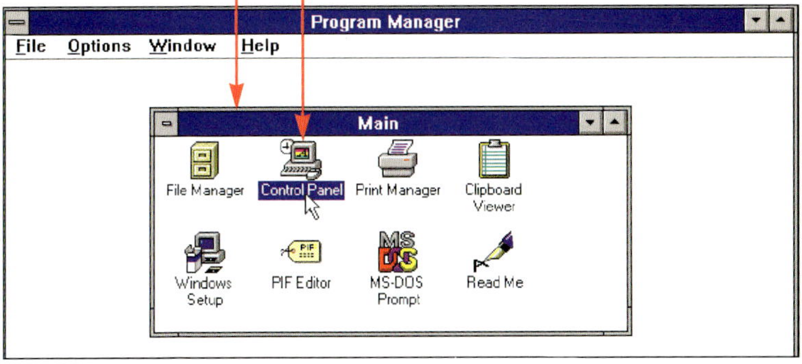

3 Double-click the Color icon.

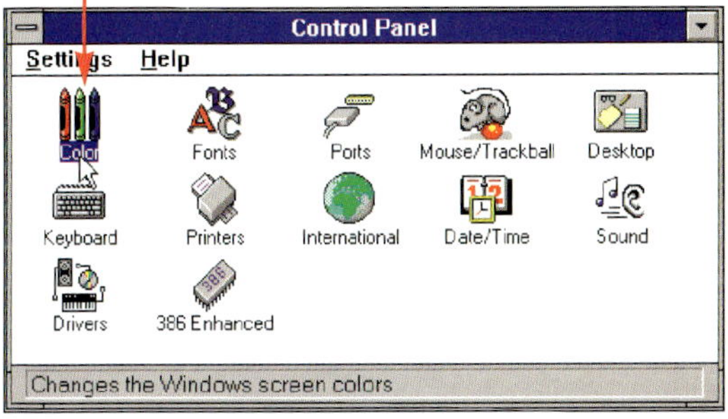

4 Click the Color Schemes arrow button.

5 Click the color scheme you want.

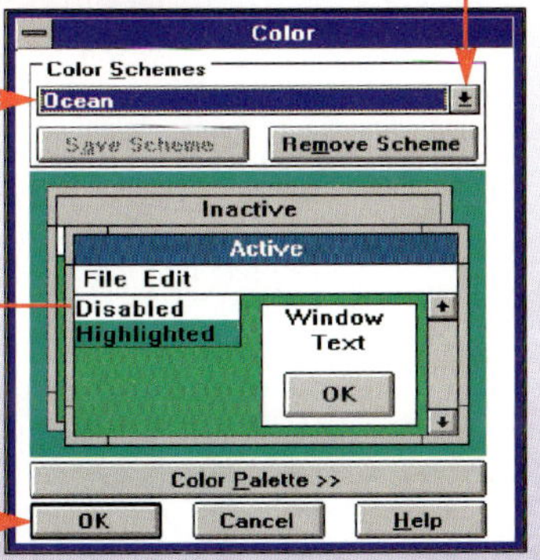

Sample screen

6 Choose OK.

To change the color of a screen element

1 From the Color dialog box, click the Color Palette button.

Sample screen

2 Click the Screen Element arrow button.

3 Click the screen element for which you want to change color.

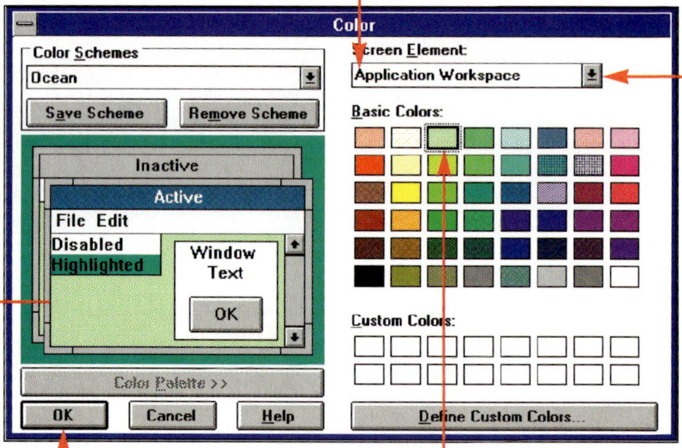

4 Click the color you want to use.

5 Choose OK.

Setting Fonts

Windows lets you add and remove fonts for the operating environment. Programs written to take advantage of the Windows environment can access these fonts.

To add fonts to Windows

1 From Program Manager, open the Main group window.

2 Double-click the Control Panel icon.

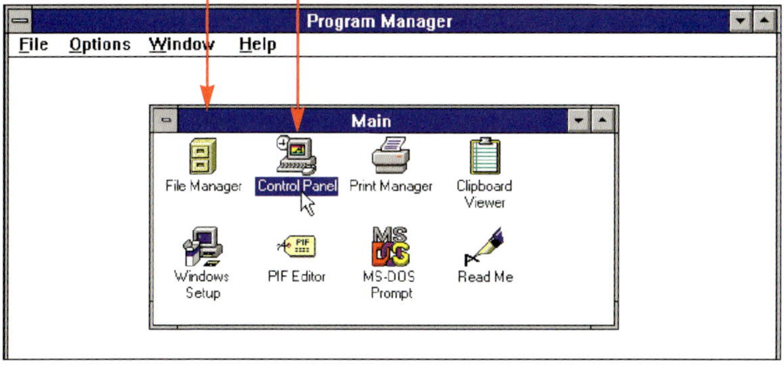

3 Double-click the Fonts icon.

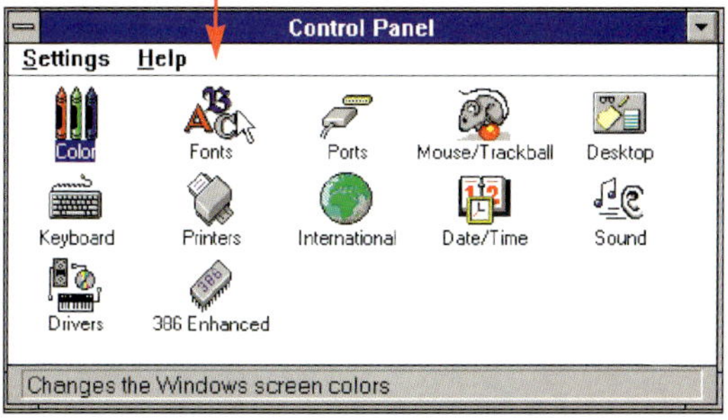

4 Click the Add button.

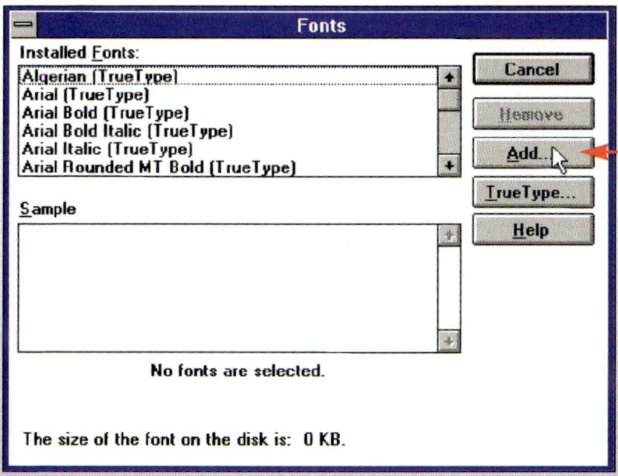

more ▶

5 Click the drive that contains the new fonts.

6 Click the directory that contains the new fonts.

7 Click the font you want to add.

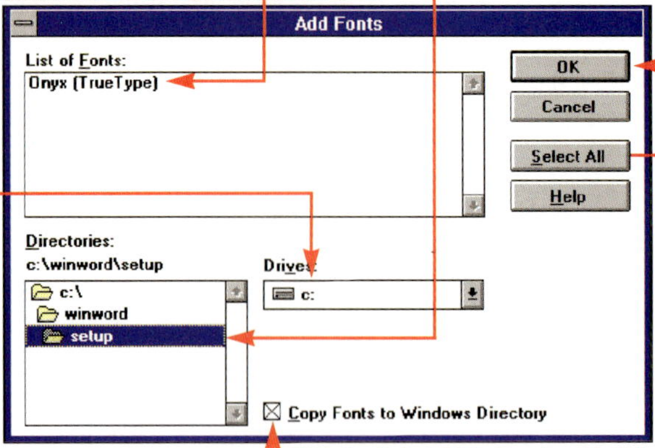

Click the Select All button to add all fonts in the list

8 Select the Copy Fonts to Windows Directory option.

9 Choose OK.

To remove fonts from Windows

1 In the Fonts dialog box, click the font you want to remove.

2 Click the Remove button.

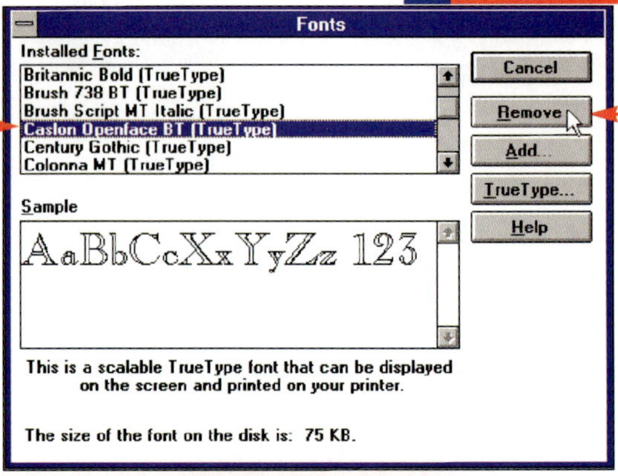

3 Select the Delete Font File From Disk option.

4 Click Yes to remove the font.

To cancel the procedure, click No

Setting the Pattern

The default Windows desktop background is a solid color, but you can replace the solid color with a pattern. The pattern is a small design or picture that is repeated many times on your desktop to form a mosaic.

1 From Program Manager, open the Main group window.

2 Double-click the Control Panel icon.

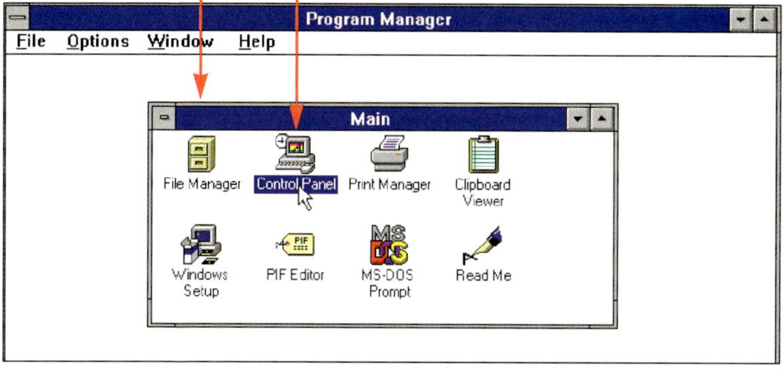

3 Double-click the Desktop icon.

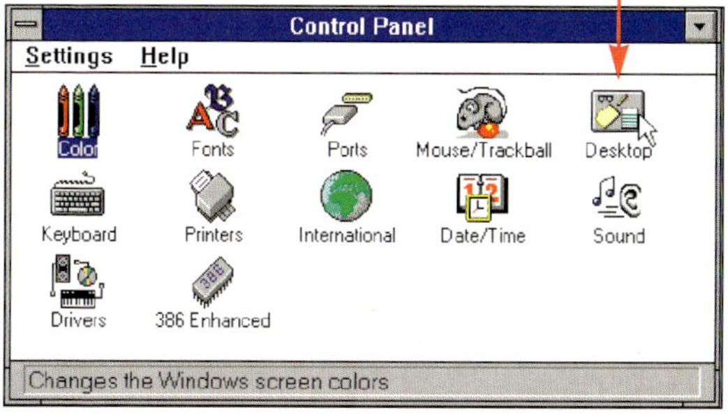

4 In the Pattern section, click the Name arrow button.

If you don't want a pattern, choose (None)

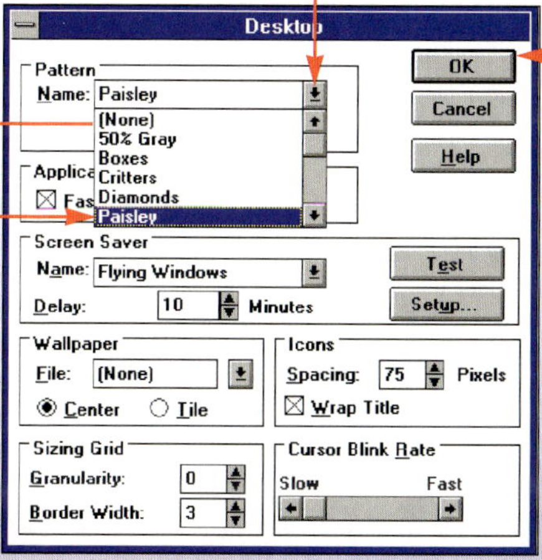

5 Click the pattern you want to use.

6 Choose OK.

Setting Screen Savers

You can set a screen saver that blanks the screen after a specified period of inactivity. A screen saver contains a moving graphic or pattern, reminding you that the computer is still turned on.

1 From Program Manager, open the Main group window.

2 Double-click the Control Panel icon.

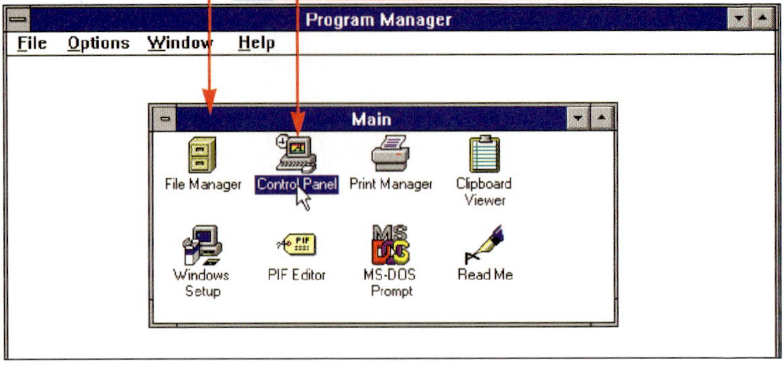

3 Double-click the Desktop icon.

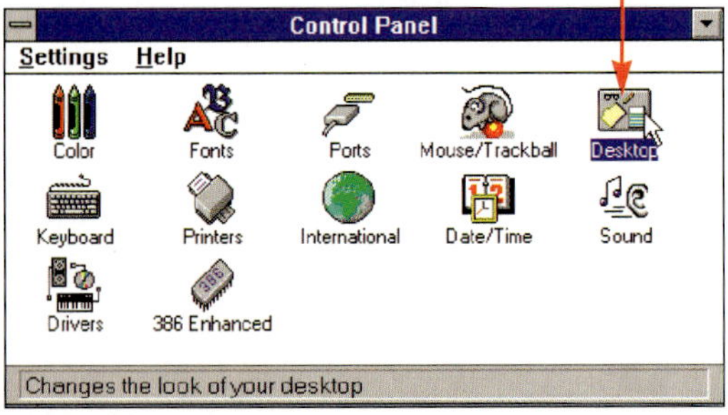

4 In the Screen Saver section, click the Name arrow button.

5 Click the screen saver you want to use.

Click the Test button to display the screen saver

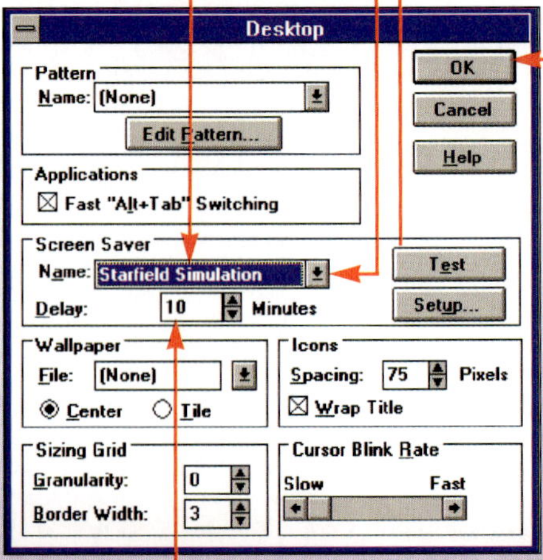

6 Select the number of minutes before the screen saver is activated.

If you don't want a screen saver, choose (None)

7 Choose OK.

Setting Wallpaper

You can attach a bit-mapped file as "wallpaper" for the desktop. Tiled wallpaper contains repeated pictures to cover the whole desktop. Centered wallpaper places one picture in the middle of the desktop; extra space around the wallpaper is filled with the desktop color.

1 From Program Manager, open the Main group window.

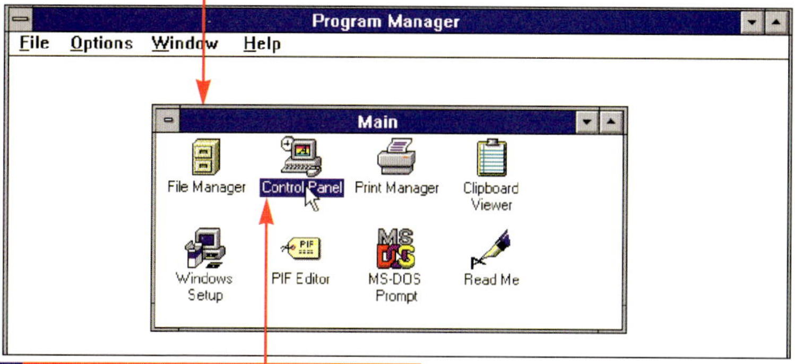

2 Double-click the Control Panel icon.

3 Double-click the Desktop icon.

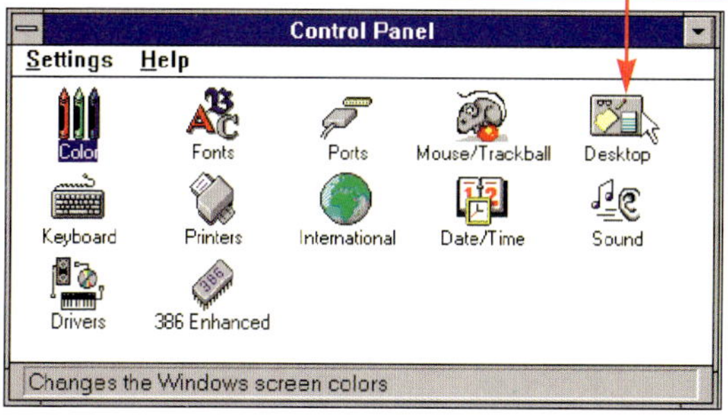

4 In the Wallpaper section, click the File arrow button.

5 Click the wallpaper you want to use.

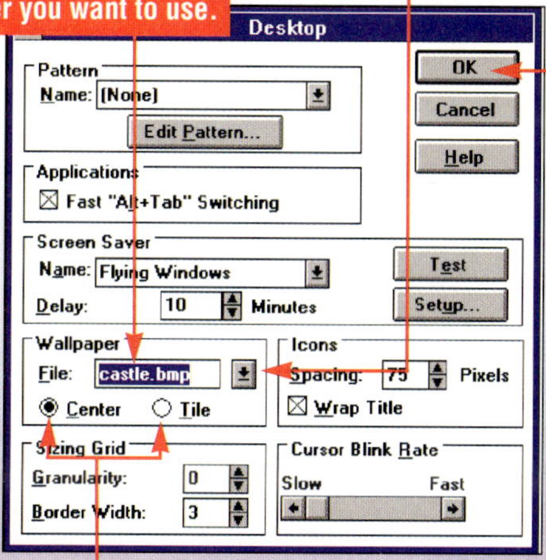

6 Specify how the wallpaper appears on-screen.

7 Choose OK.

If you don't want wallpaper, choose (None).

Recording a Macro

Macros are special instructions that control Windows programs—repeating keystrokes and mouse movements exactly as you record them.

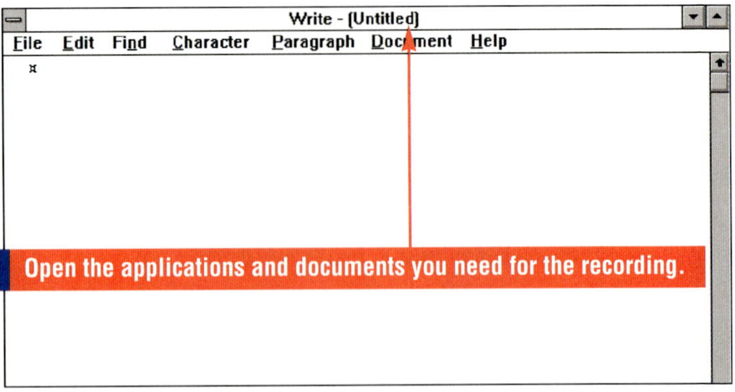

1 Open the applications and documents you need for the recording.

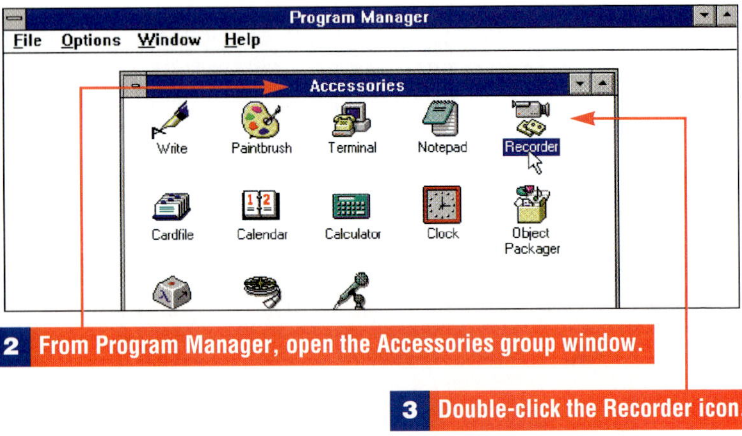

2 From Program Manager, open the Accessories group window.

3 Double-click the Recorder icon.

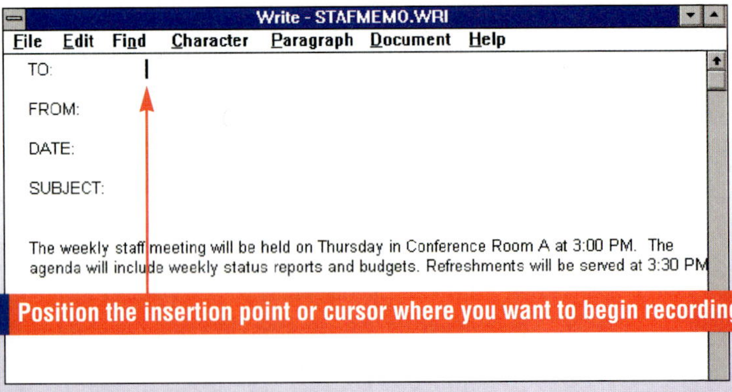

4 Position the insertion point or cursor where you want to begin recording.

Or select the text or graphics you want the macro to work on

5 Click the Recorder window to activate it.

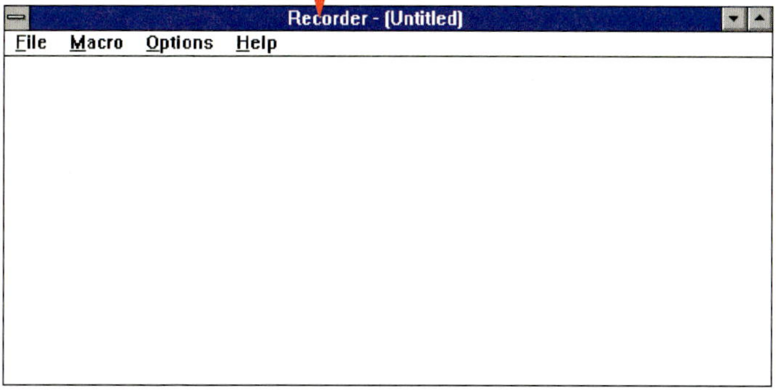

6 Choose Macro, Record.

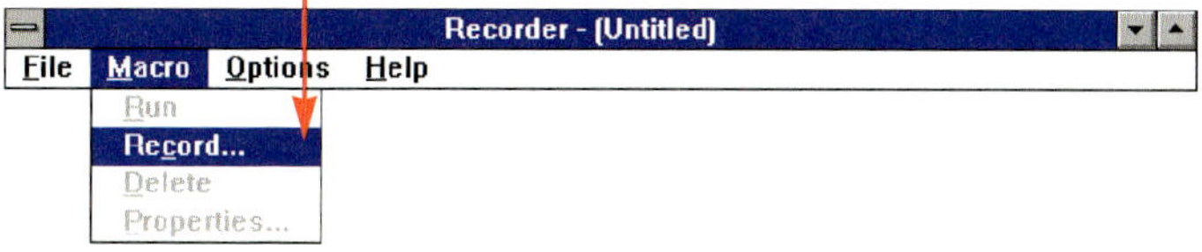

7 Type the macro name (up to 40 characters).

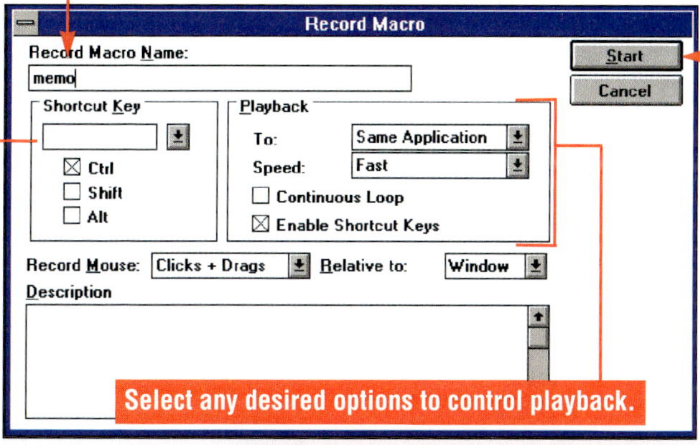

Select any desired options to control playback.

9 Choose Start to begin recording the macro.

You can specify a shortcut key to play the macro—a letter, special key, or key combination

more ▶

10 Perform the procedure you want to record (for example, type a heading).

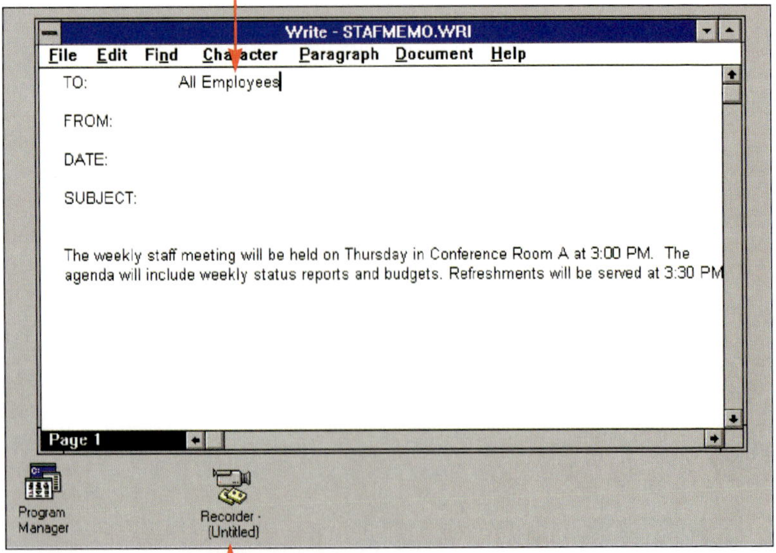

11 To stop the Recorder, click the blinking Record icon.

12 Click the Save Macro option.

To cancel any recording you have done, click Cancel Recording

13 Choose OK.

Saving a Macro

Windows places the recorded macro in the current Recorder file along with other macros. You must save the file to disk to keep your macro; otherwise you lose the macro when you exit the Recorder.

1 From the Recorder menu, choose File, Save As.

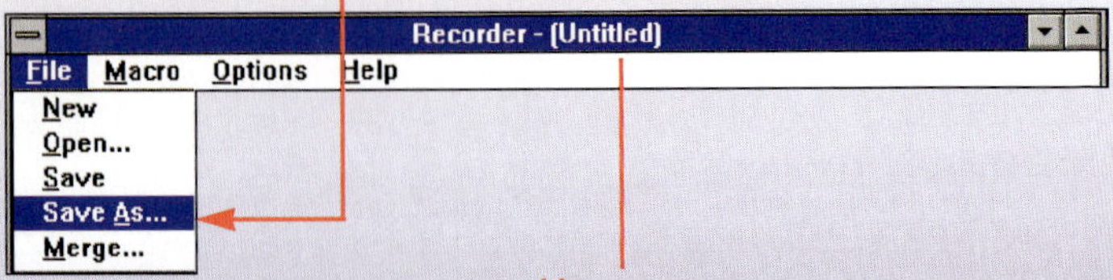

Macro name

2 Choose the drive where you want to save the macro.

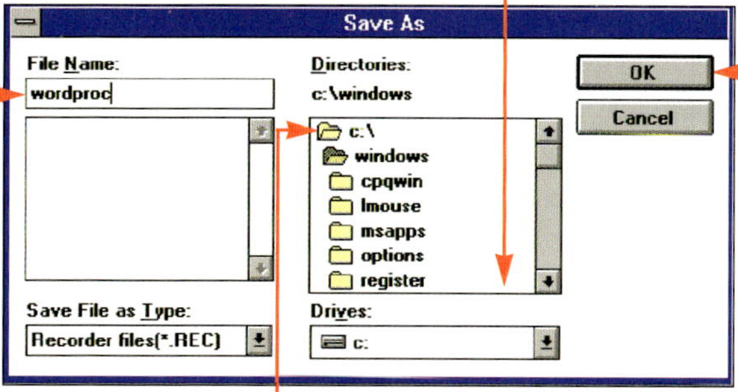

3 Choose the directory where you want to save the macro.

4 Type the file name (up to 8 letters). Windows adds the REC extension.

5 Choose OK.

Playing a Macro

After you record and save a macro, you can play it back at any time, using one of two methods to invoke the macro. Before you play a macro, however, you must open the Recorder file that contains the macros you want to use.

To open a Recorder file

1 From the Recorder menu, choose File, Open.

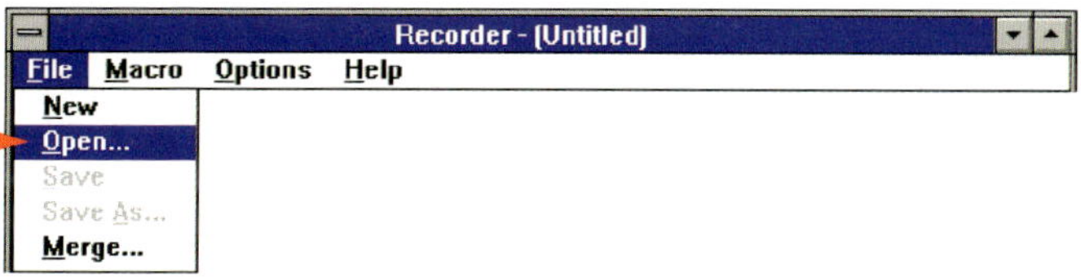

2 Choose the drive and directory where the macro is stored.

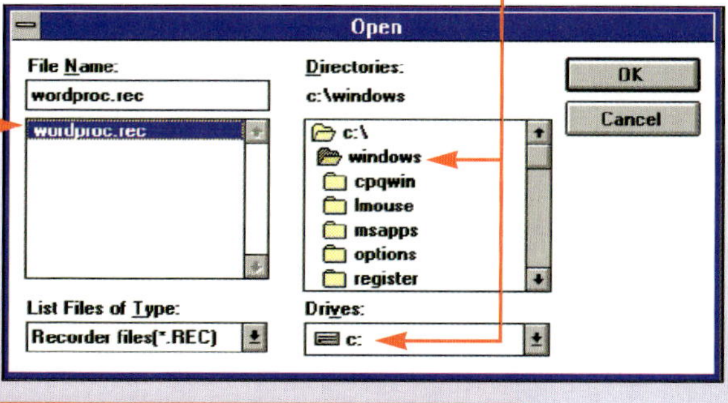

3 Double-click the Recorder file you want to use.

To play a macro

1 Activate the application in which you want to play the macro.

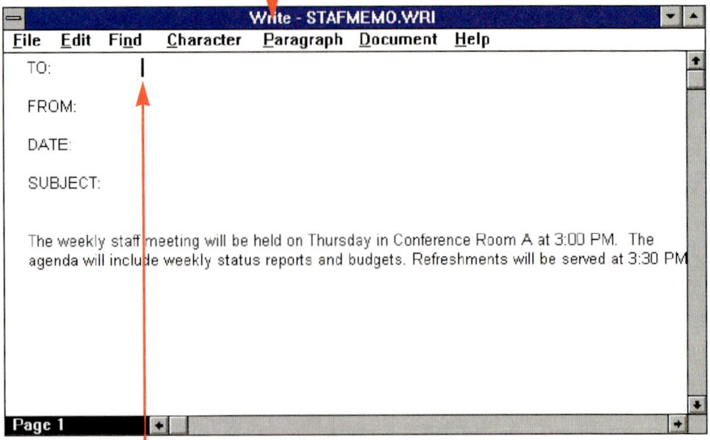

2 Position the insertion point or cursor, or select the text or graphics.

3 Activate the Recorder window.

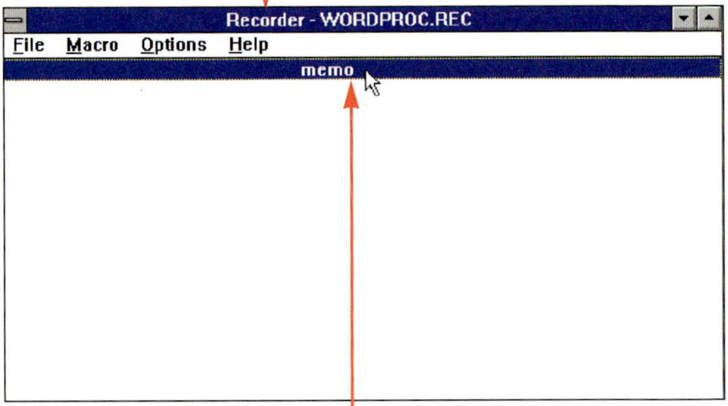

4 Double-click the name of the macro you want to play.

Or press the shortcut key assigned to the macro

Deleting a Macro

If you no longer need a macro, you can delete the macro from the Recorder file.

1 Open the Recorder file containing the macro you want to delete.

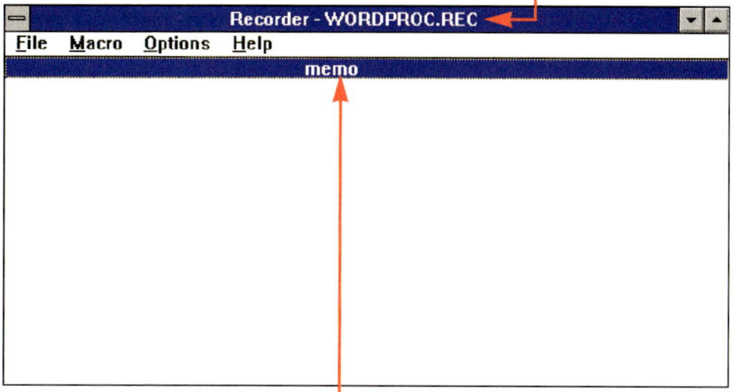

2 Click the name of the macro you want to delete.

3 Choose Macro, Delete.

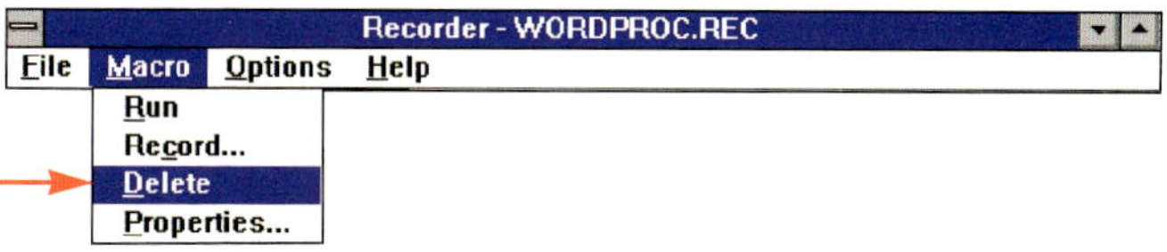

4 Choose OK.

5 Choose File, Save to save the Recorder file.

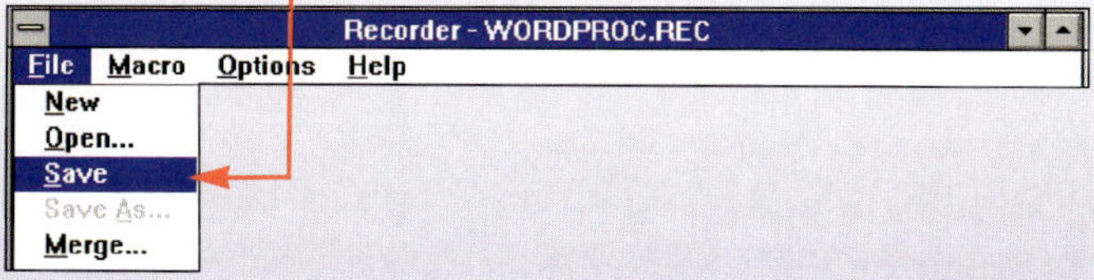

Network Setup

Windows for Workgroups 3.11 includes utilities for communicating with the other members of your workgroup. Some utilities are added to existing Windows programs (File Manager and Print Manager); others are available as separate applications.

File Manager includes features that enable the sharing of drives and directories. Print Manager allows sharing of and connection to network printers.

To share a directory

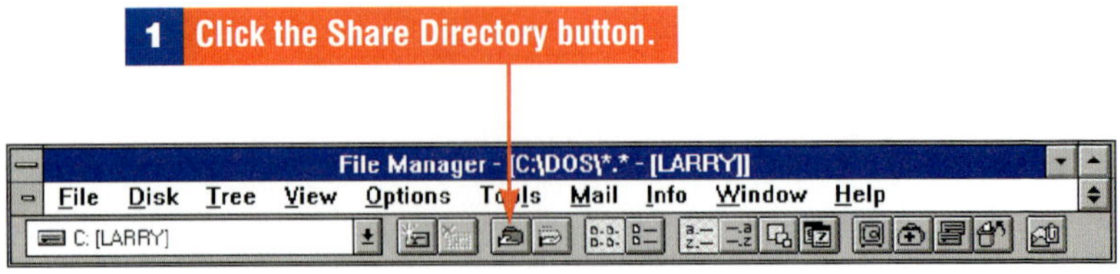

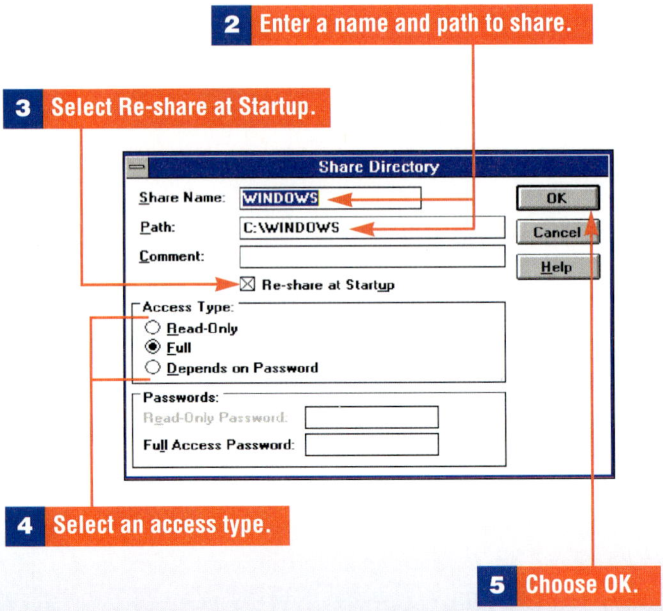

To connect to a network drive

1 Click the Connect Network Drive button.

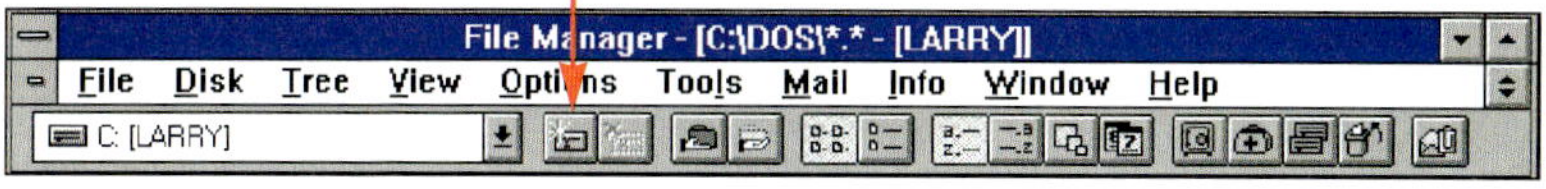

2 Choose the drive.

3 Enter a computer name and path.

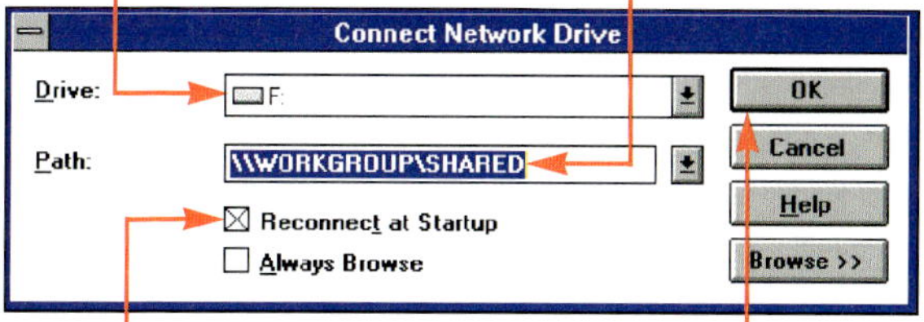

4 Select Reconnect at Startup.

5 Choose OK.

To enable printer sharing

1 Choose Printer, Share Printer As.

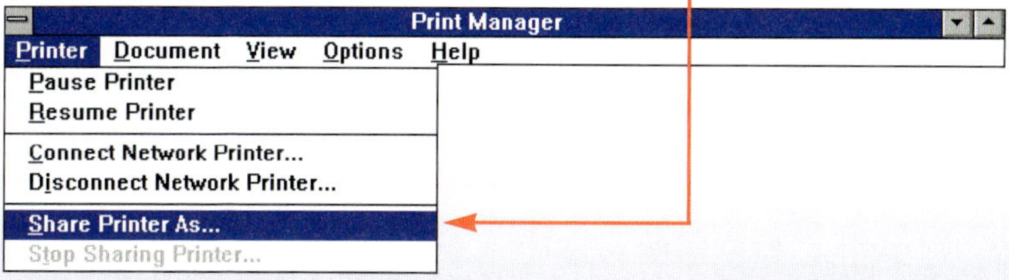

more ▶

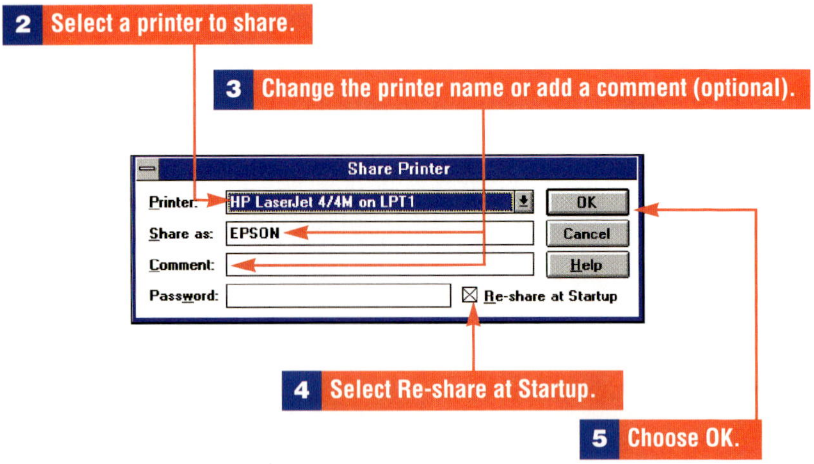

To connect to a network printer

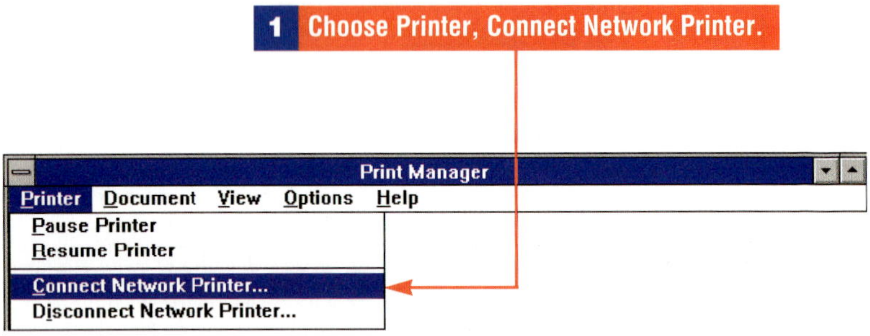

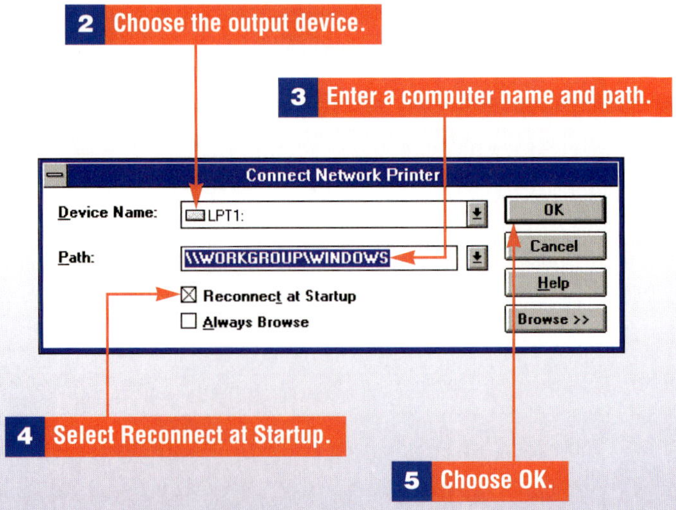

Using Mail

The Mail utility in Windows for Workgroups enables users to send, read, reply to, forward, and delete messages between two or more computers.

To send a message

1 Click the Compose button.

2 Enter the recipient's name.

3 Enter all copied recipients.

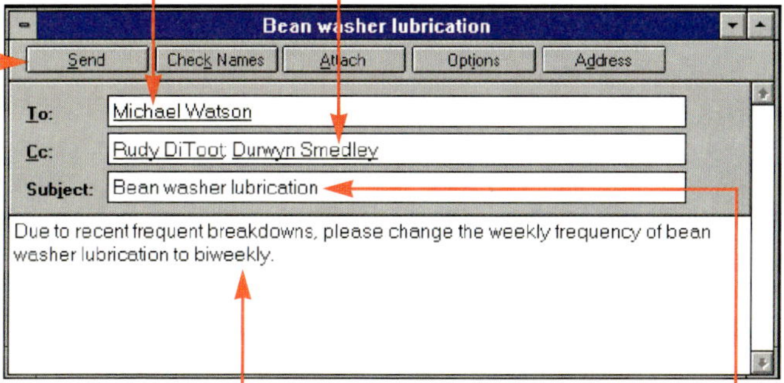

4 Enter the message title.

5 Enter the message.

6 Choose Send.

To read a message

1 Double-click the Inbox folder.

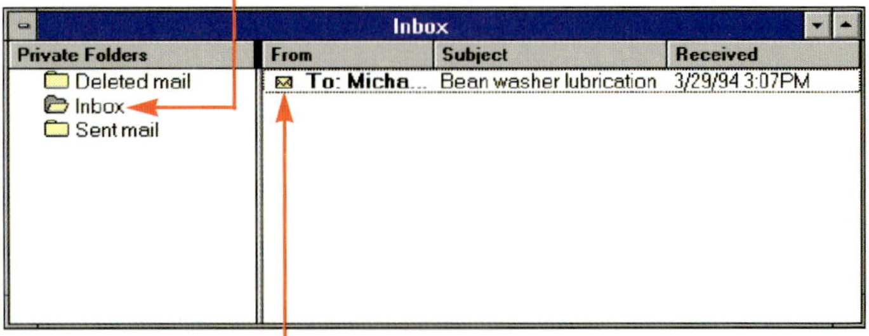

2 Double-click the message you want to read.

To reply to a message

1 Double-click the Inbox folder.

2 With the message highlighted, click the Reply button.

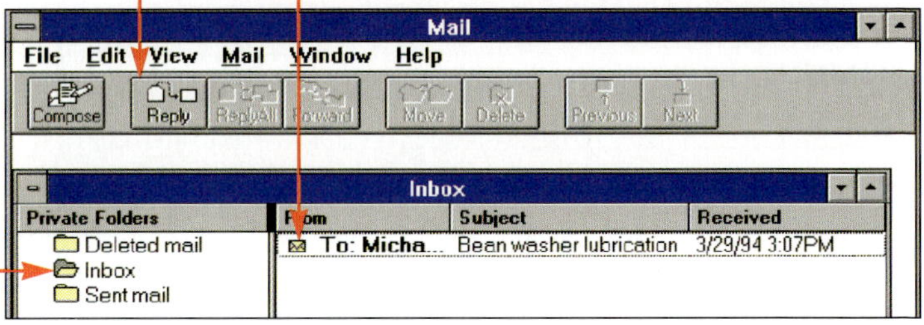

3 Enter a reply above the existing message.

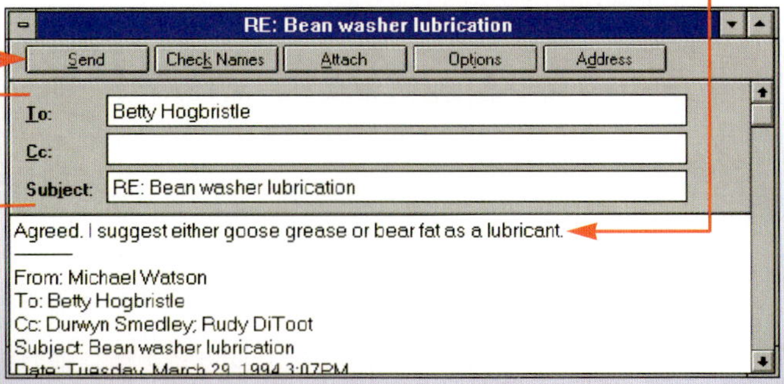

4 Optionally, change To, Cc, or Subject information.

5 Choose Send.

To forward a message

1 Double-click the Inbox folder.

2 Highlight the message and click the Forward button.

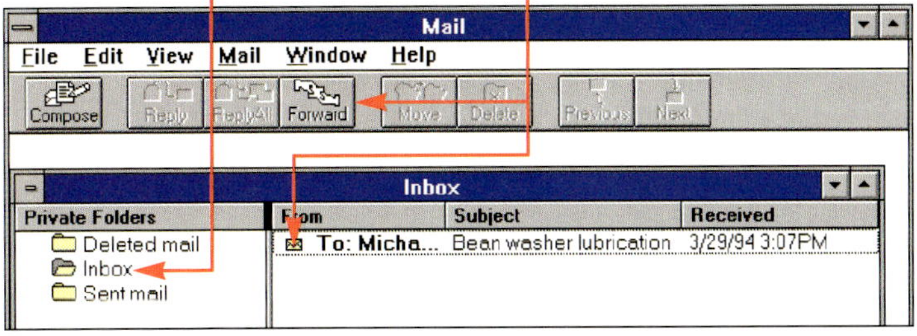

3 Enter the recipient's name.

4 Optionally, change Cc or Subject information.

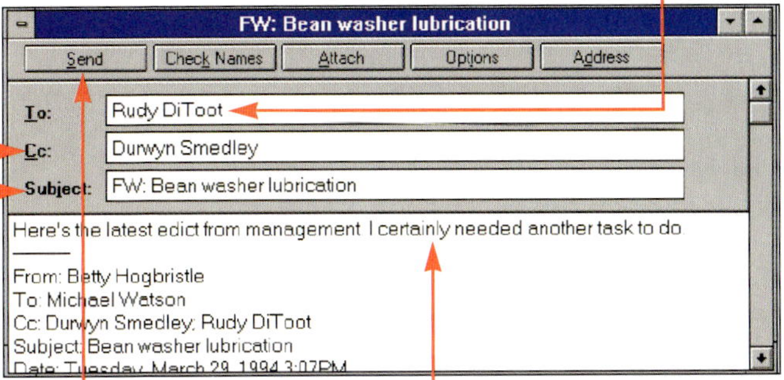

5 Optionally, add a message.

6 Choose Send.

To delete a message

1 Double-click the folder containing the message.

2 Highlight the message and click the Delete button.

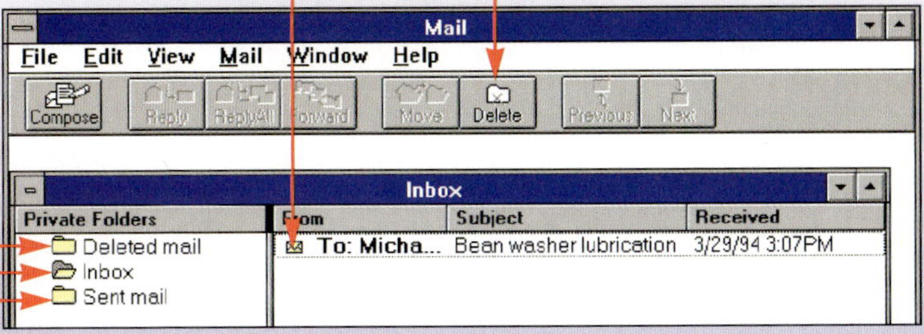

Using Schedule+

The Windows for Workgroups Schedule+ utility generates schedules and reminder messages for group appointments and meetings. This feature replaces the Calendar utility in Windows 3.1 and 3.11.

To schedule a group appointment

1 Choose Appointments, New Appointment.

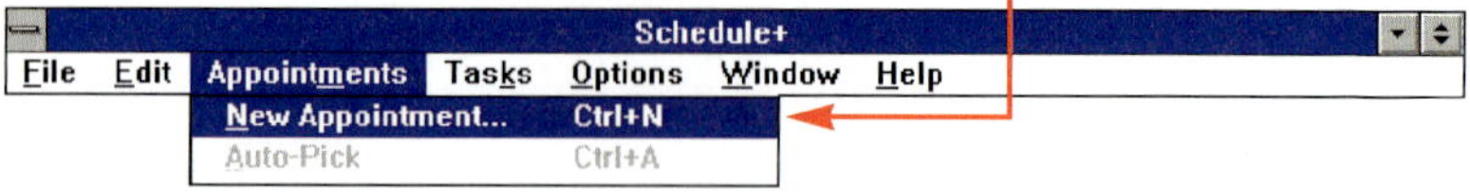

2 Enter the start and end times.

3 Enter the start and end dates.

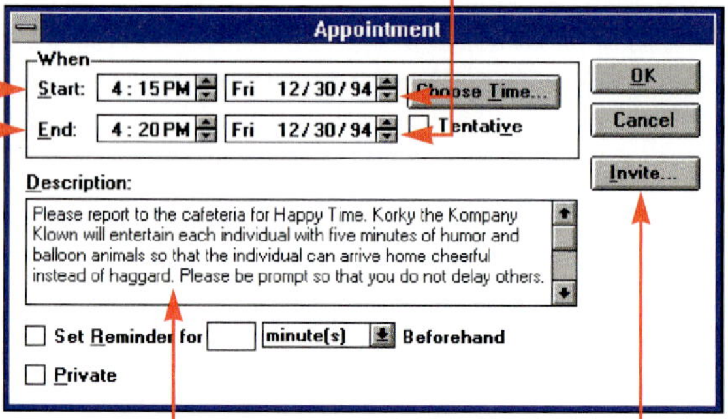

4 Enter a description of the appointment.

5 Choose Invite.

6 For each attendee, highlight the name and choose Add.

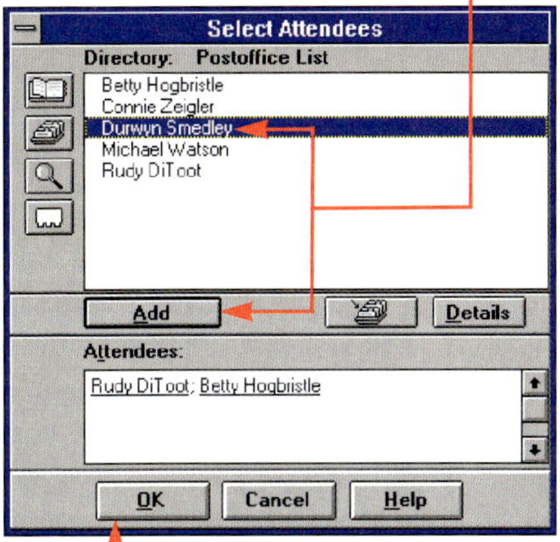

7 Choose OK.

To schedule a meeting

1 Open the Planner and choose Change.

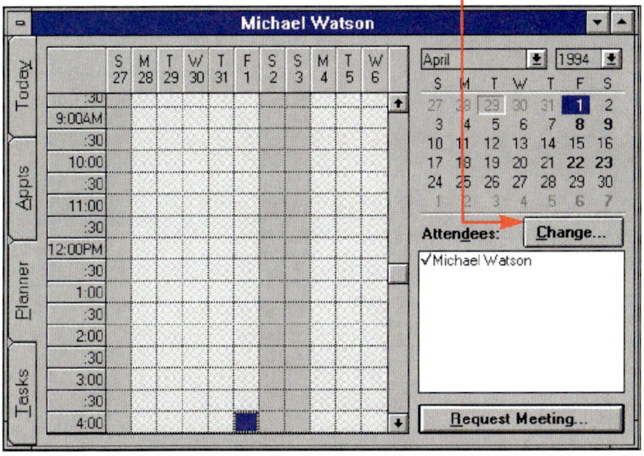

2 For each attendee, highlight the name and choose Add.

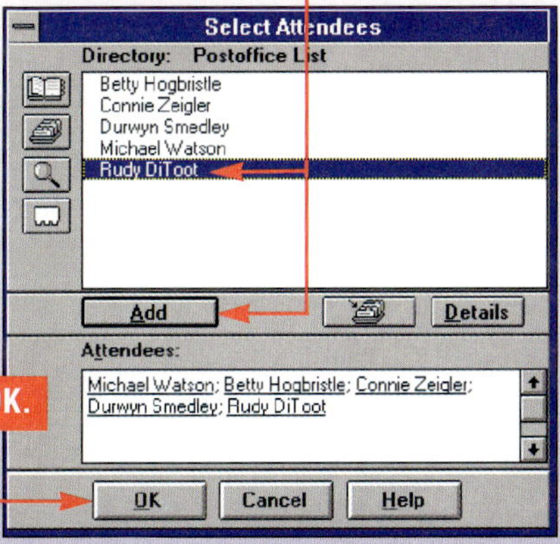

3 Choose OK.

more ▶

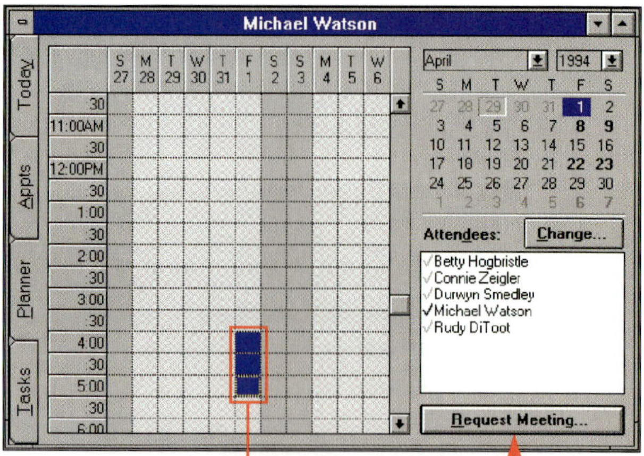

4 Select a block of time and choose Request Meeting.

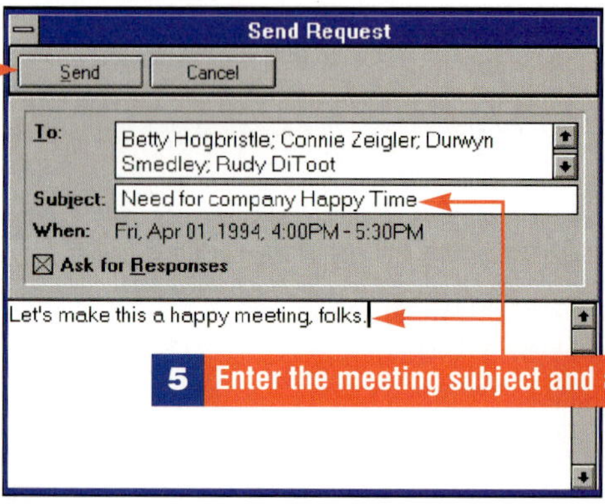

5 Enter the meeting subject and any notes.

6 Choose Send.

To reschedule a meeting

1 Open the Appointments window.

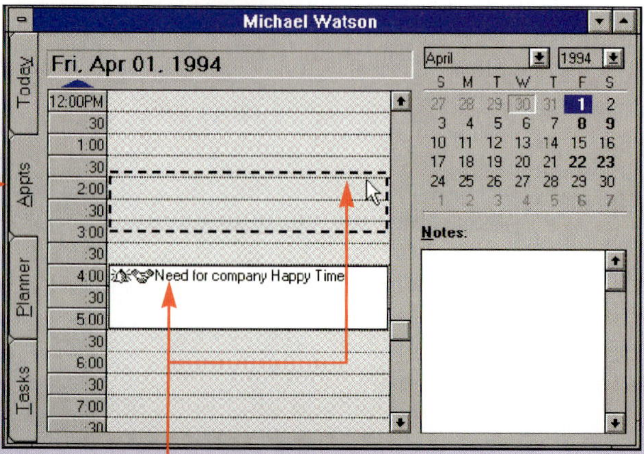

2 Drag the meeting to a new time.

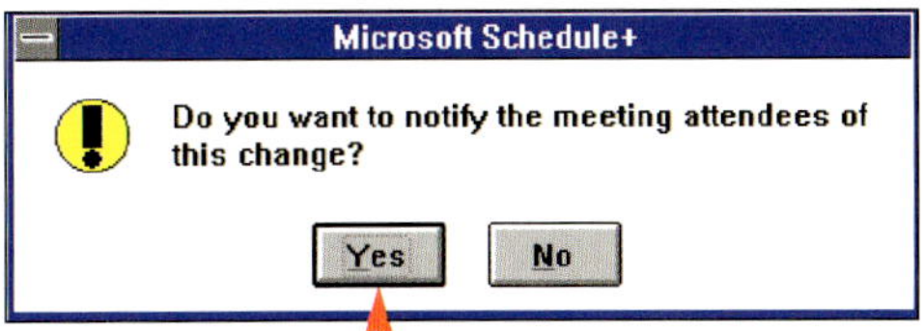

3 Choose Yes to notify other attendees.

4 Optionally, enter any notes.

5 Choose Send.

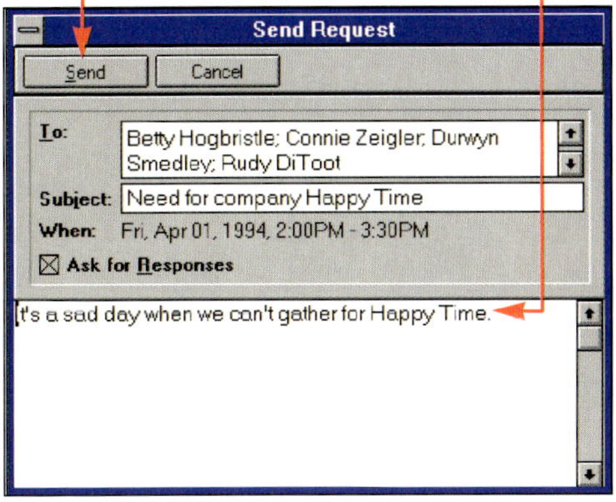

To cancel a meeting

1 Open the Appointments window.

2 Select the meeting.

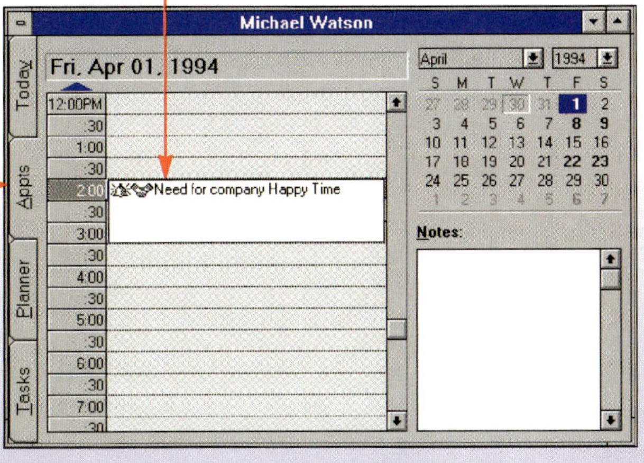

more ▶

3 Choose Edit, Delete Appt.

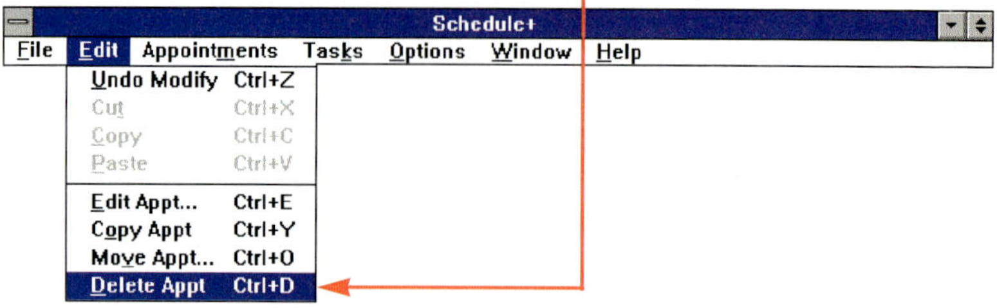

4 Choose Yes to notify other attendees.

5 Optionally, enter any notes.

6 Choose Send.

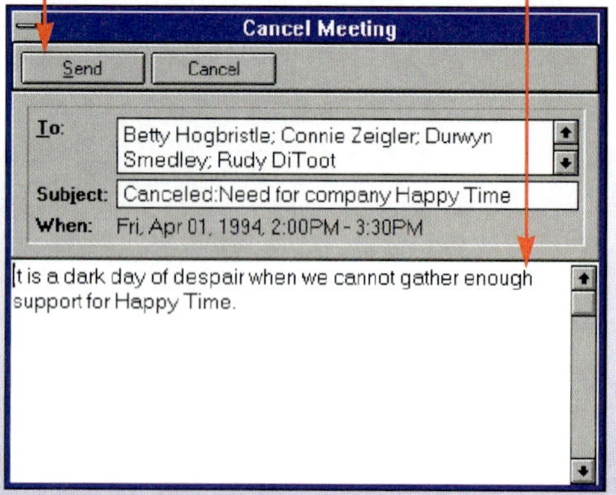

Using Chat

The Chat utility in Windows for Workgroups enables a user to have an immediate conversation with another user.

To call another user

1 Click the Dial button.

2 Enter the computer name of the user with whom you want to chat.

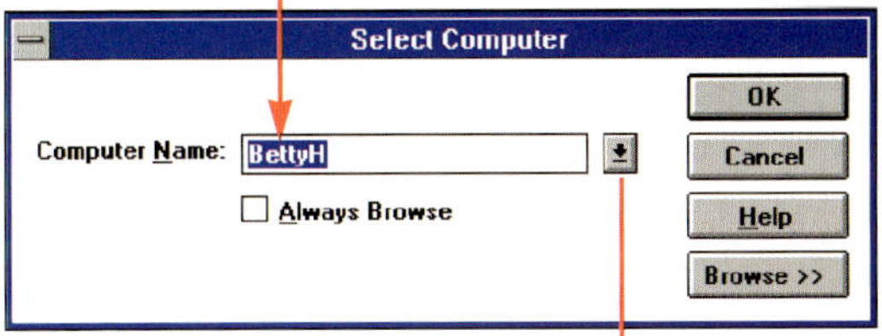

To select from a list, click the arrow button

3 Enter your message before or after the user answers.

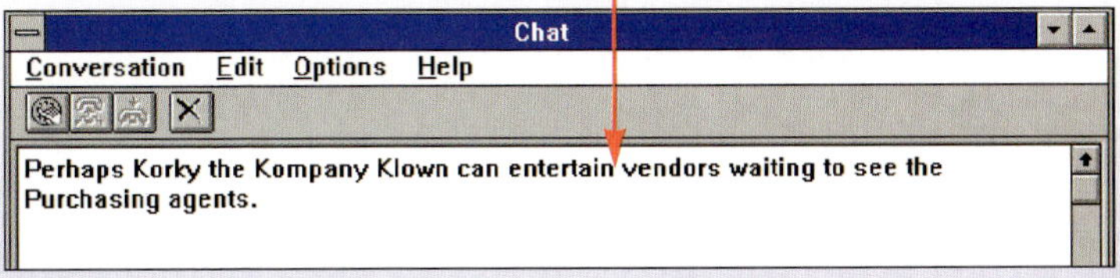

more ▶

4 The reply appears in the window.

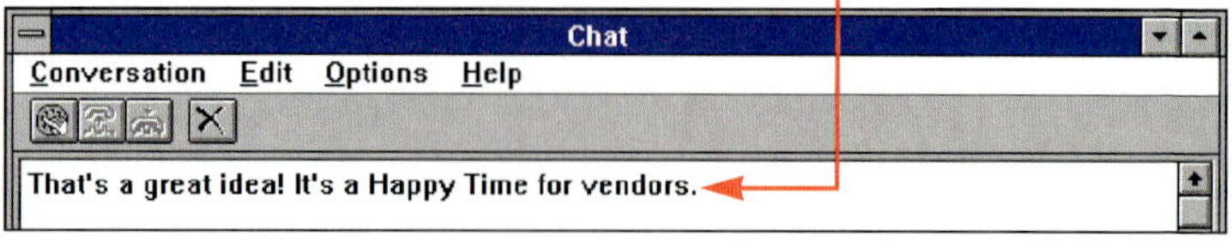

To answer a call while in another application

1 Double-click the Chat icon on the screen.

2 Click the Answer button.

The message appears in the lower half of the window

Enter your reply in the upper half of the window

Click Hangup when the conversation is done

Printing a File

Windows enables you to print files from File Manager or Print Manager rather than starting the application, loading the file, and then issuing the print command. Both methods require the file extension to be associated with a program. *Your version of Print Manager may differ slightly from that shown in this section.*

To print a file from File Manager

1 Start File Manager.

2 Click the icon for the drive that contains the file you want to print.

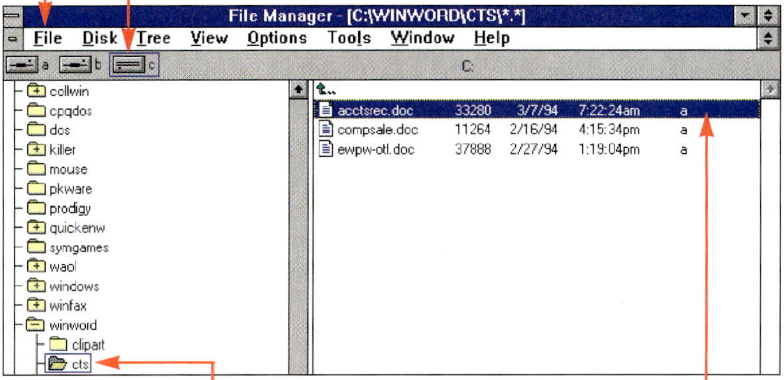

3 Click the directory that contains the file you want to print.

4 Click the file you want to print.

5 Choose File, Print.

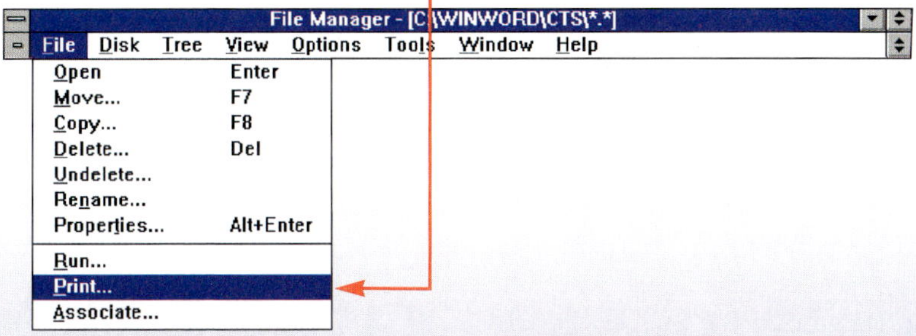

6 Choose OK to begin printing.

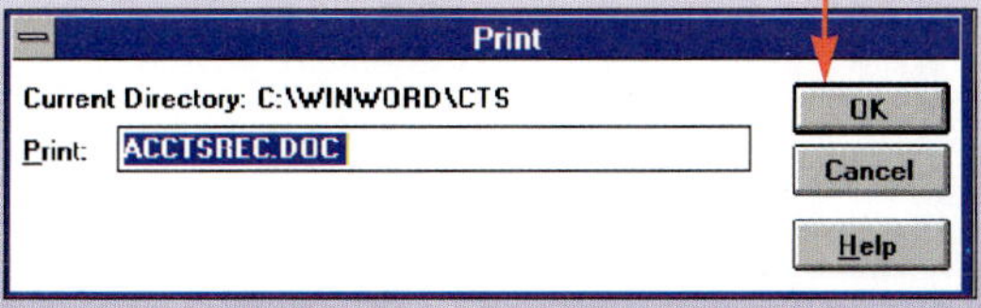

To print a file by dragging-and-dropping

1 Start File Manager and Print Manager; minimize Print Manager.

2 Click the icon for the drive that contains the file you want to print.

3 Click the directory that contains the file you want to print.

4 Click the file you want to print.

5 Drag the file icon to the Print Manager icon.

6 Release the mouse button to begin printing.

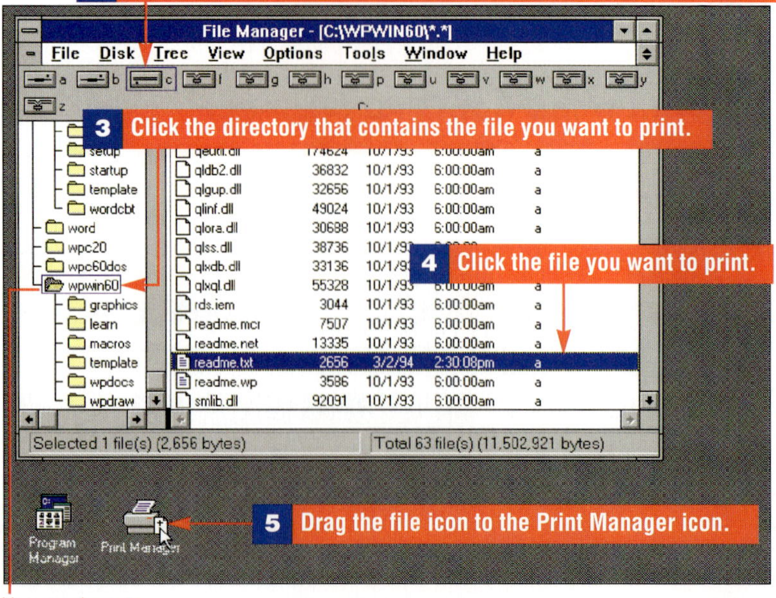

You may have to expand a directory

Pausing/Resuming a Print Job

You can pause a print job to load paper in the printer, answer the phone, and so on. When you are ready, just resume printing.

To pause a print job

1 Double-click the Print Manager icon.

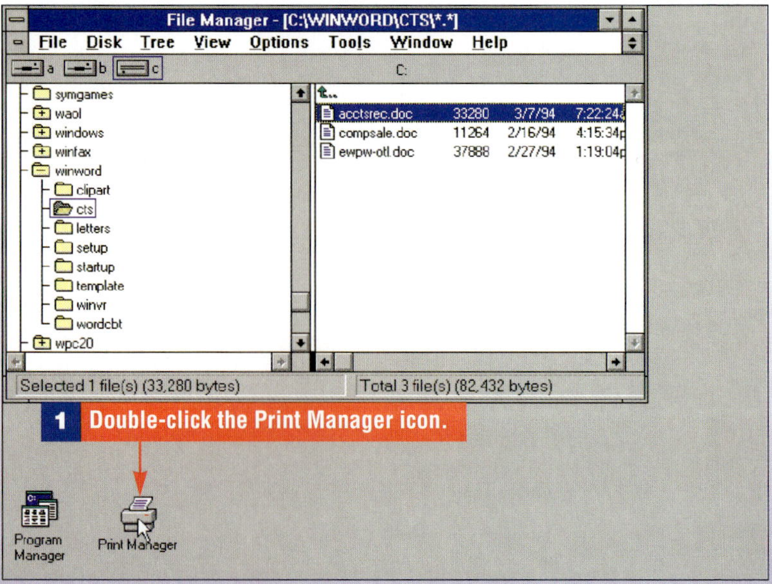

2 Click the printer you want to pause.

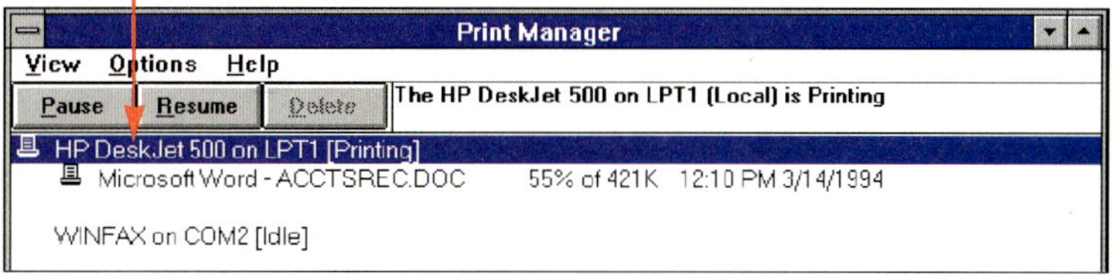

3 Click Pause to pause the printer.

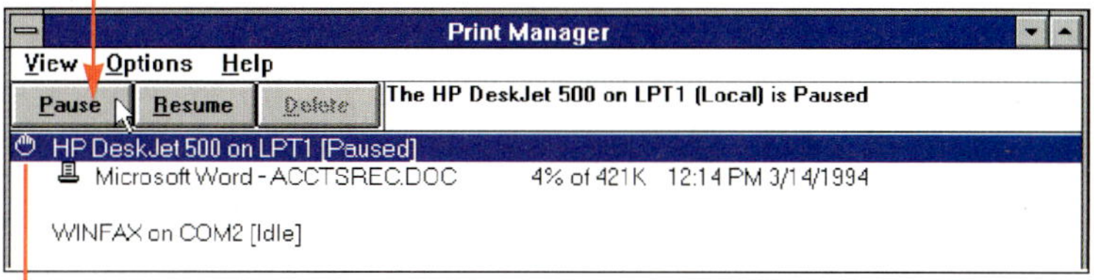

The hand icon indicates that the print job is paused

To resume a print job

1 From Print Manager, click the printer you want to resume.

2 Click Resume to resume printing.

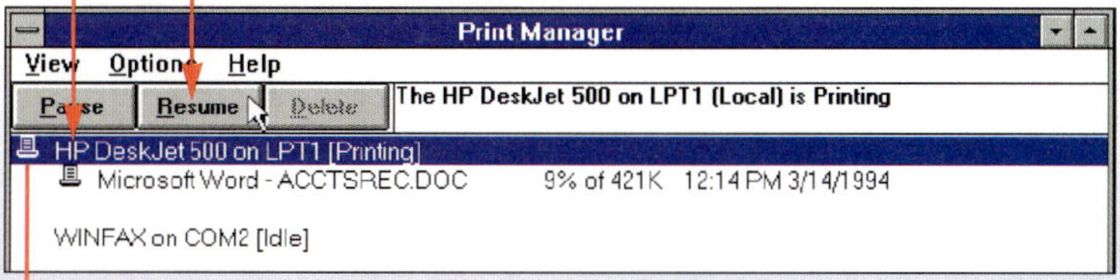

The hand icon is replaced by the printer icon

Deleting a Print Job

You can abandon a print job that is printing on the printer or is in line to be printed—for example, if you discover that you are printing the wrong file or using the wrong paper in the printer.

1 From Print Manager, click the print job you want to delete.

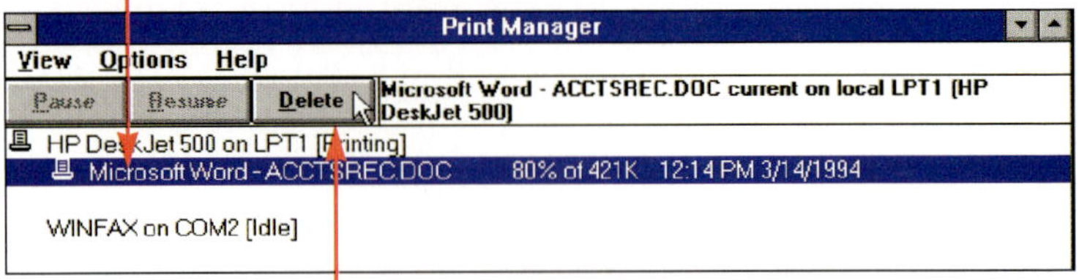

2 Click Delete to delete the print job.

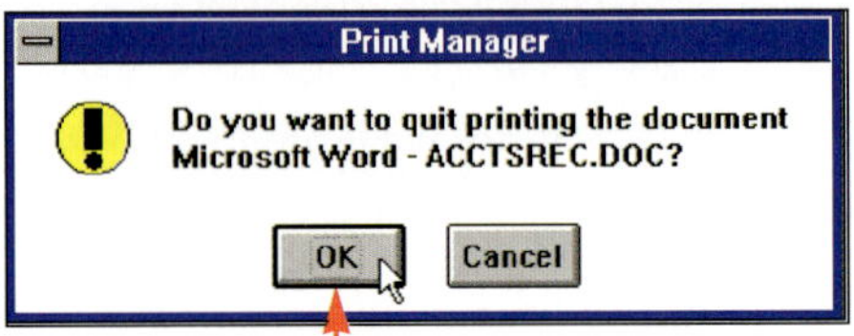

3 Choose OK to confirm that you want to delete the print job.

Setting the Print Priority

Print Manager's Priority feature determines how quickly a document prints. When you need greater processing speed for the application in the foreground, set print priority to low. If you need fast printing, set print priority to high.

1 From the Print Manager menu, choose Options.

2 Choose a priority.

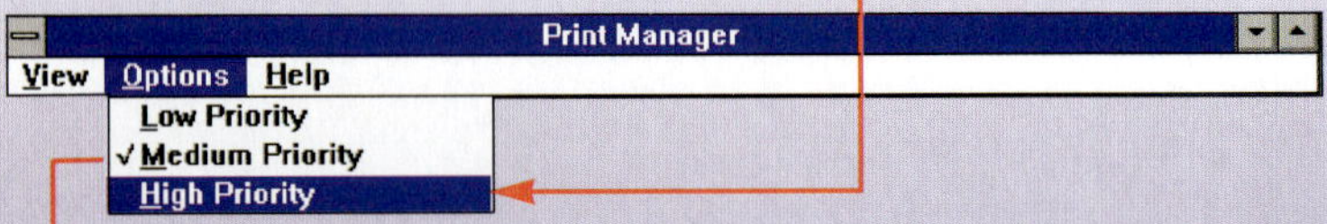

The check mark indicates the current priority

Selecting the Default Printer

You can assign the printer that Windows will use as the default printer. The default printer is the printer to which Windows will send information automatically when you print. Select the printer you use most often as the default printer.

1 From the Print Manager menu, choose Options, Printer Setup.

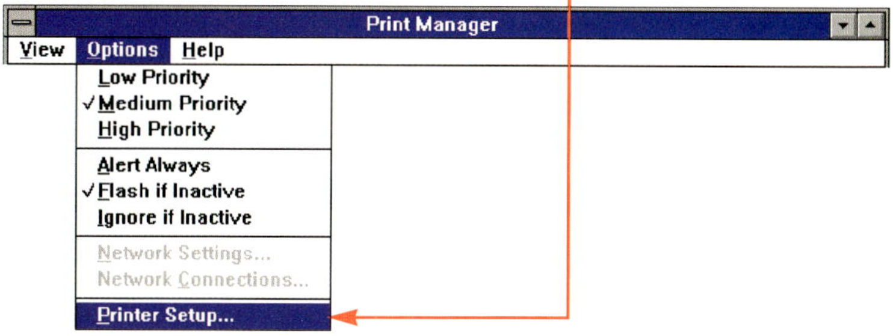

2 Click the printer you want.

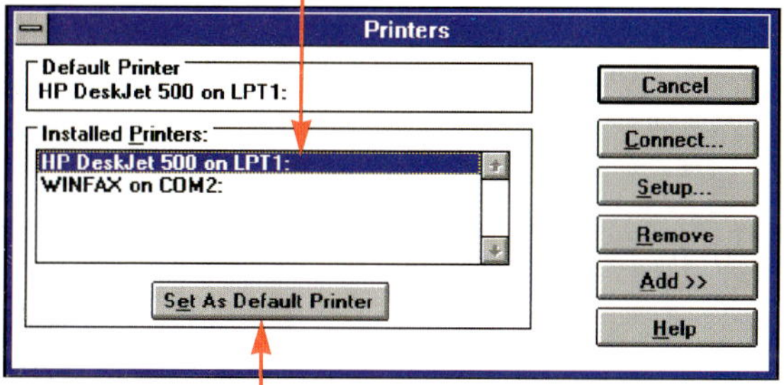

3 Click Set As Default Printer.

4 Click Close.

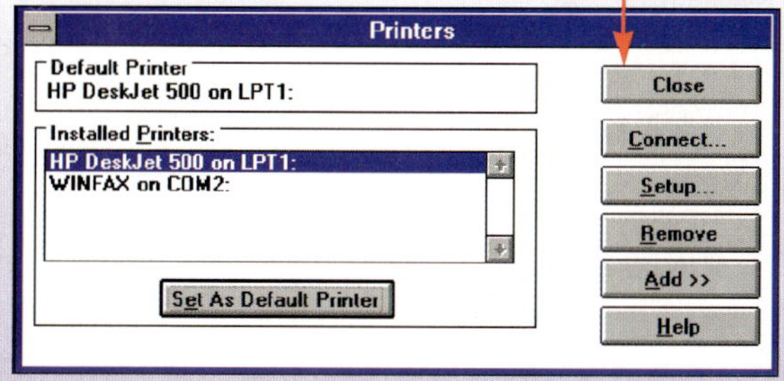

Adding Program Groups

A program group is a set of similar programs in a window. Each group contains program items (icons that represent the programs you can run from that window). When minimized, each program group is also represented by an icon.

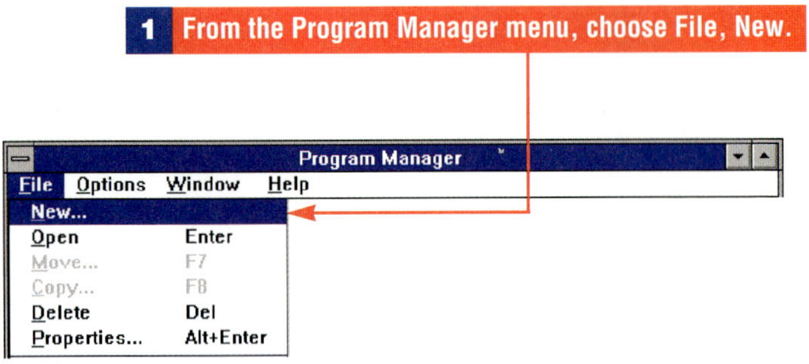

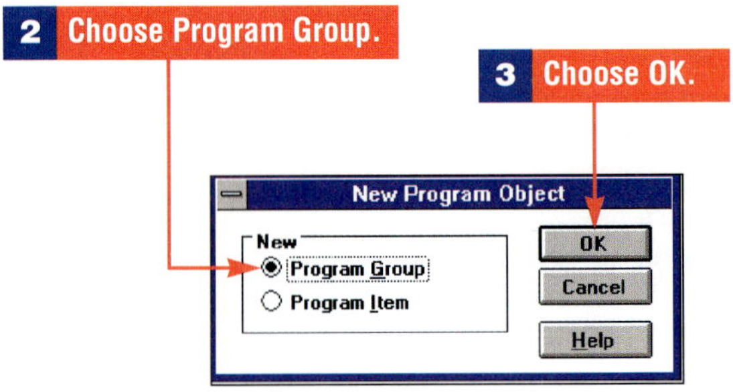

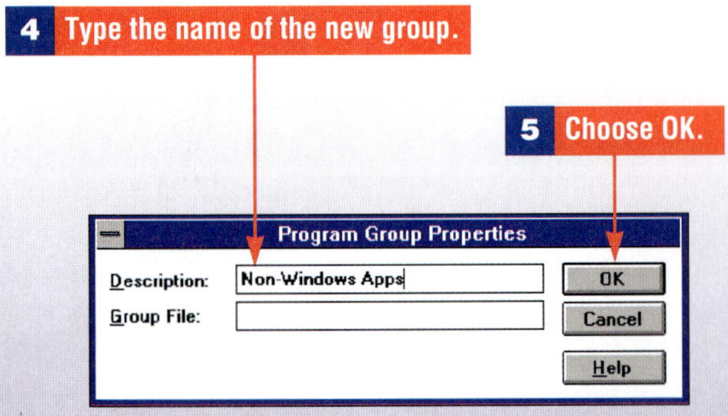

The new program group

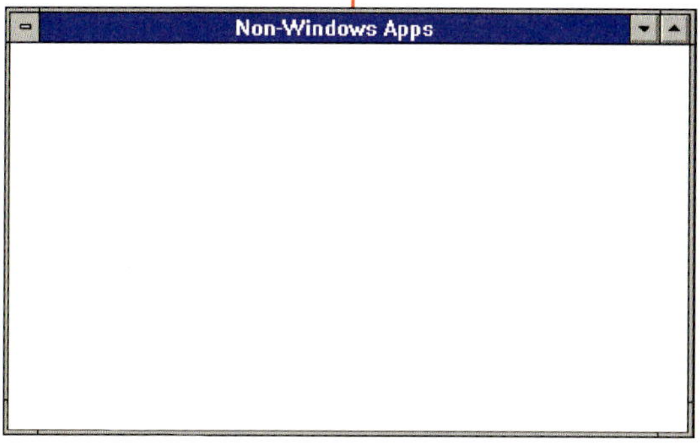

Deleting Program Groups

You can delete a program group and its associated icon from Program Manager when you no longer use the programs in that group. Deleting the group removes it from Windows but not from the disk.

1 Click the window you want to delete.

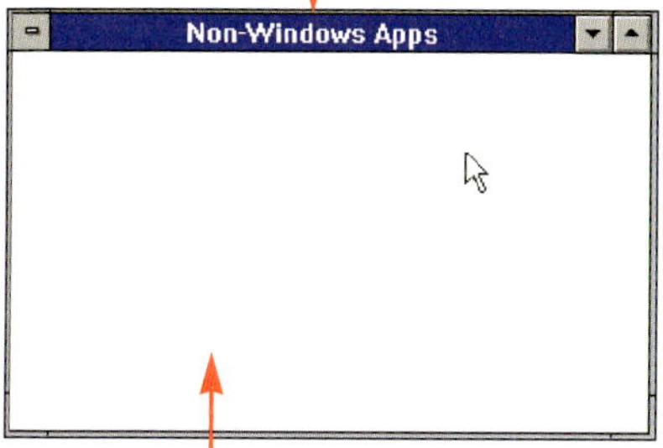

2 Delete all the program items.

3 Press Delete.

For details on deleting program items, see the section "To delete a program item"

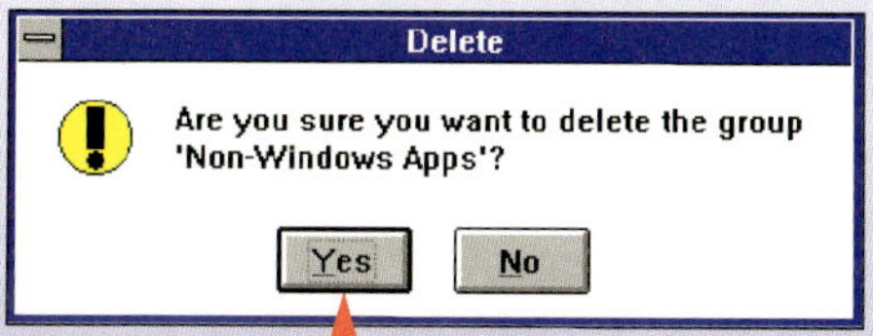

4 Choose Yes.

Adding Program Items

A program item is an icon for an application. You add program items to a program group so that you can start applications from those icons.

1 Click the window to which you want to add the program item.

2 Choose File, New.

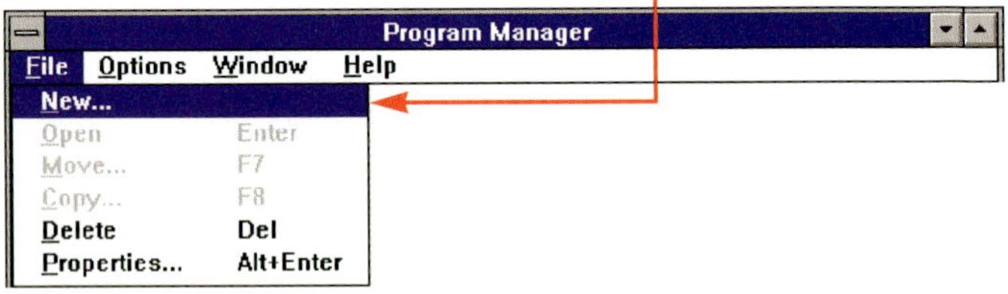

3 Choose Program Item.

4 Choose OK.

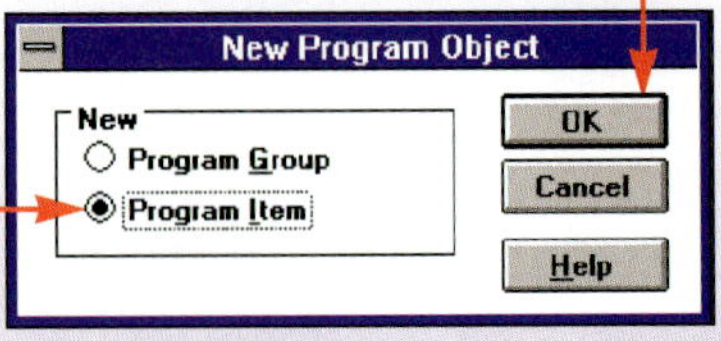

5 Type the name you want to appear under the icon.

Click Browse if you don't know the file name

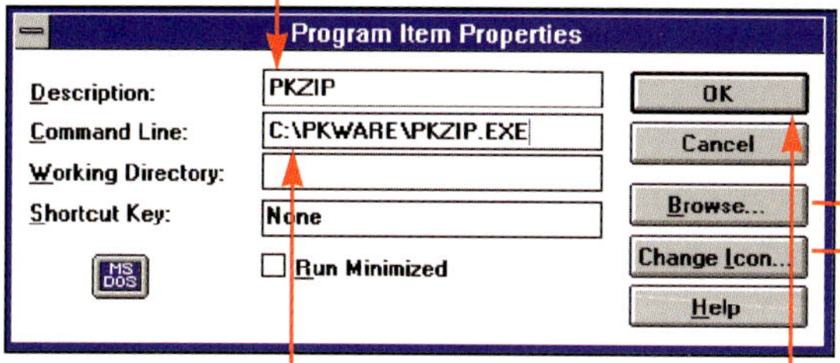

6 Type the path and file name that starts the program.

7 Choose OK.

Click Change Icon if you want to change the icon

The new program item

Deleting Program Items

You can remove a program item from a program group when you no longer use the application. Removing the icon doesn't delete the application's files from the disk.

1 Click the window containing the program item you want to delete.

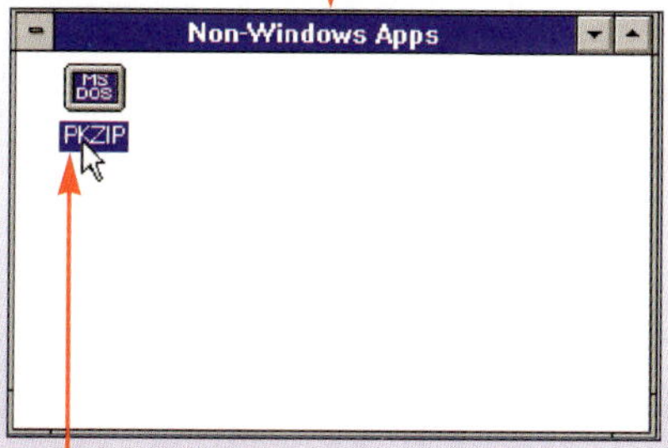

2 Click the program item.

3 Press Delete.

more ▶

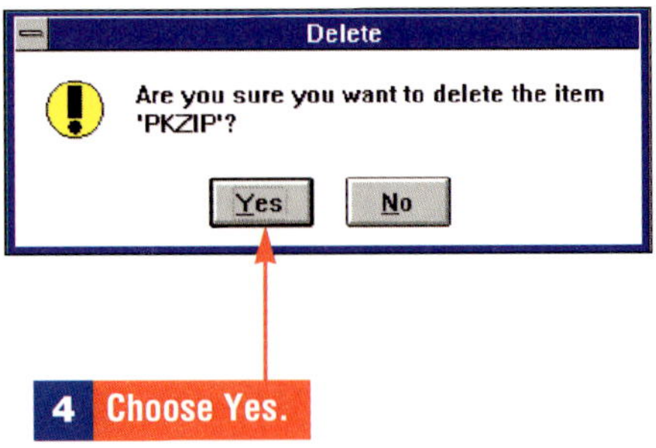

Moving Program Items

You can move a program item to a different program group. For example, you might move a database application's icon to a special group for applications you use every day.

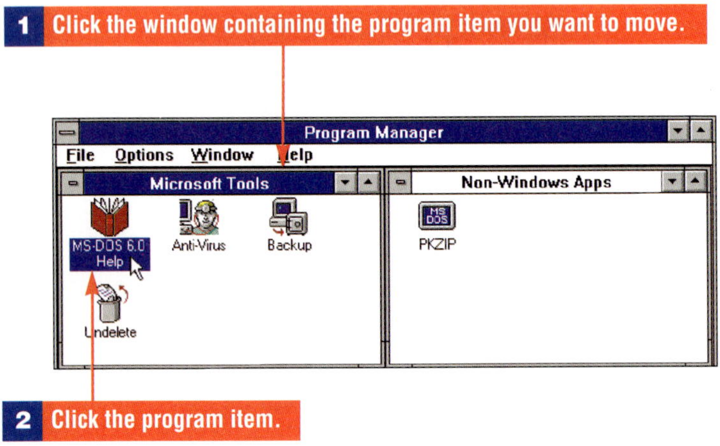

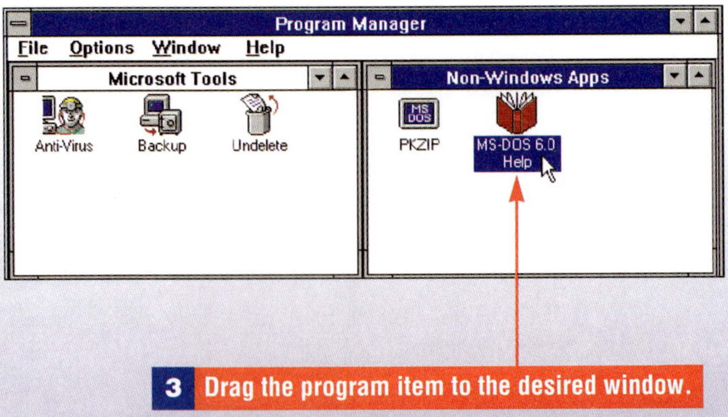

Setting Program Properties

The Properties feature enables you to specify the program item name, file name, and location on the disk, as well as change the icon used for that application.

1 Click the window containing the program item you want to change.

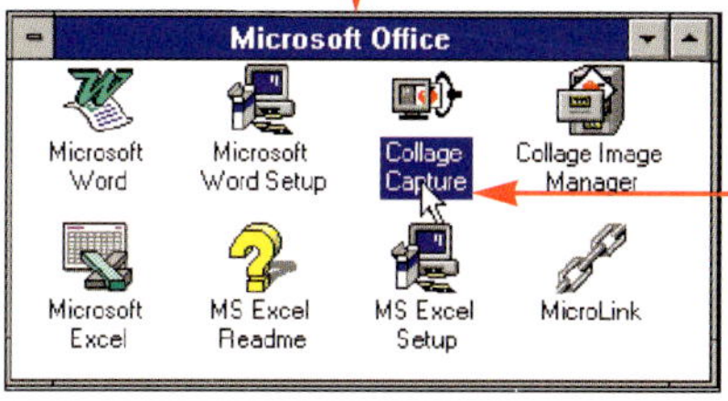

2 Click the program item.

3 Choose File, Properties.

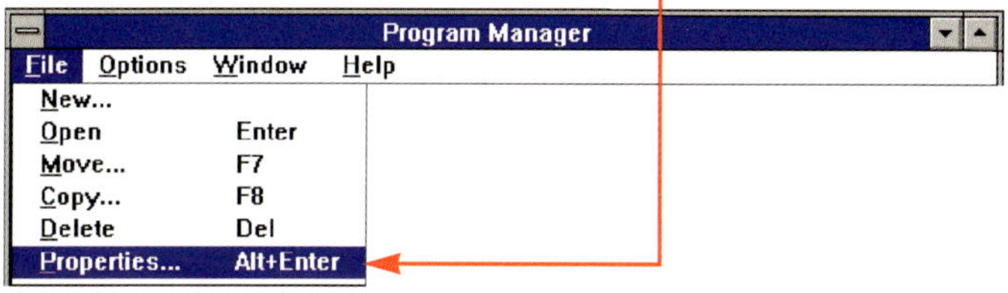

4 Change the properties as desired.

5 Choose Change Icon if you want a different icon.

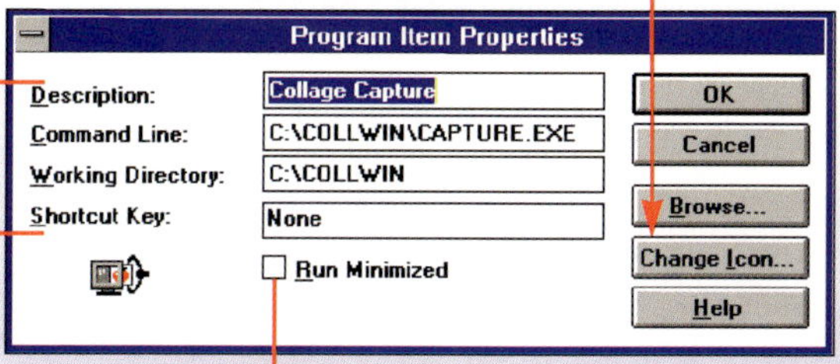

Select Run Minimized if you want the program to appear as an icon all the time

more ▶

6 Choose Browse to select an icon file.

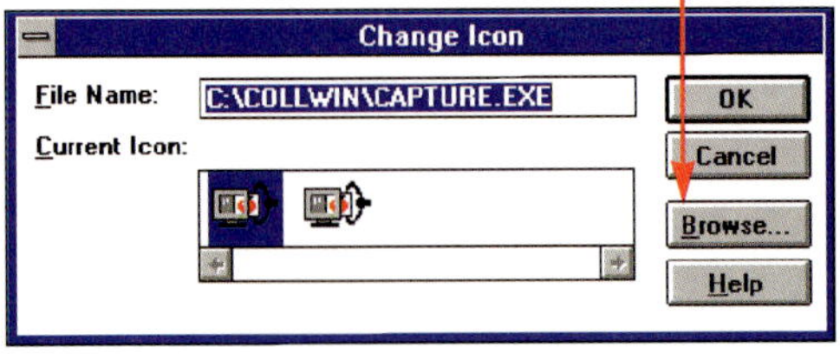

7 Select the directory containing the icon file (usually C:\WINDOWS).

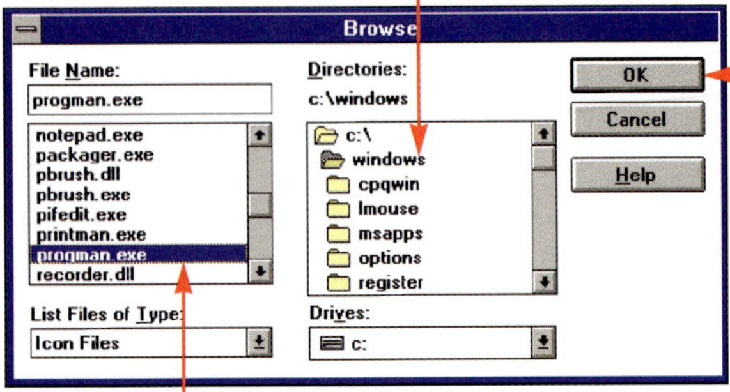

8 Choose progman.exe, moricons.dll, or another icon file.

9 Choose OK.

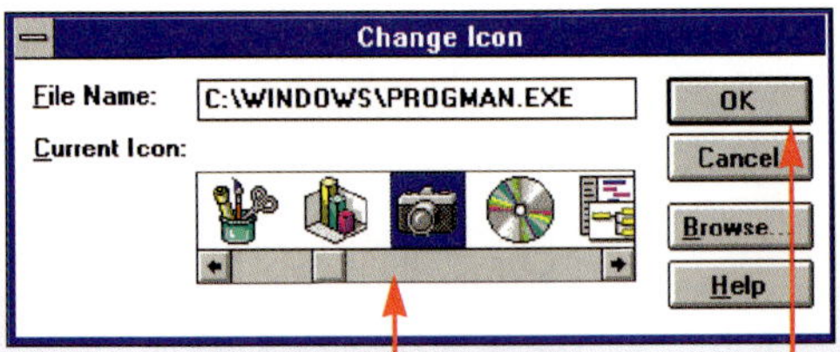

10 Scroll to see the icons in the file.

11 Select the icon you want.

12 Choose OK.

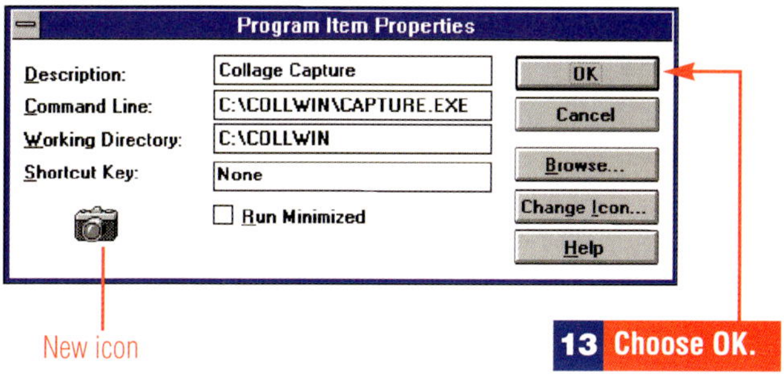

Starting Programs

You can start applications from Program Manager or File Manager. When you exit the program, you return to wherever you started the program—Program Manager or File Manager.

To start a program from Program Manager

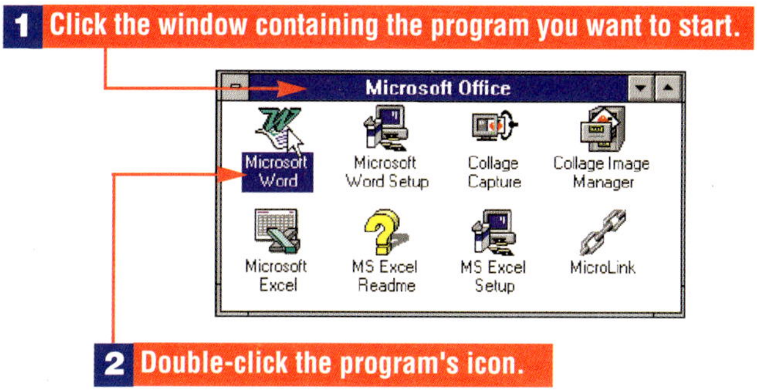

To start a program from File Manager

1 In File Manager, find the file or program you want to launch.

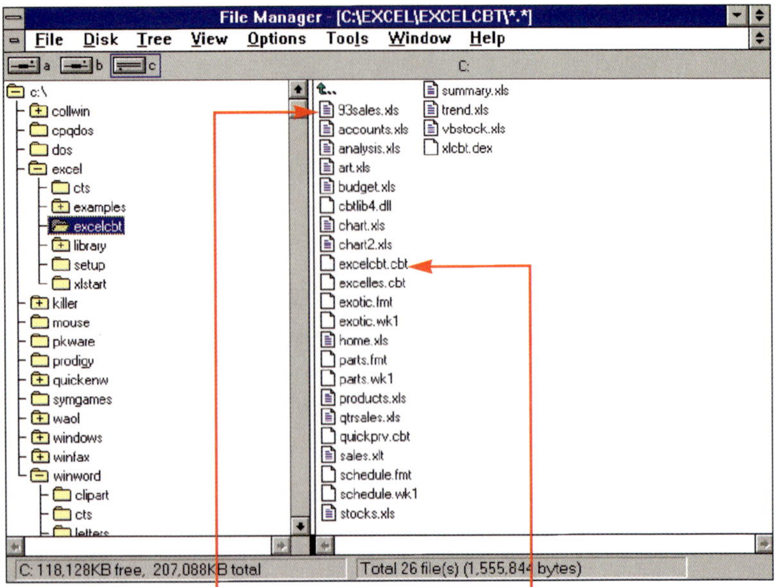

2 Double-click the icon for the file or program.

If the icon is empty, see the section "Associating Files" in "File Management"

Setting Up the StartUp Group

The StartUp group contains applications that Windows activates immediately on startup. Put accessories or applications in the StartUp group that you want to run as soon as Windows starts.

To place program items in the StartUp group

1 Open the window containing the applications you want.

2 Open or create the StartUp window.

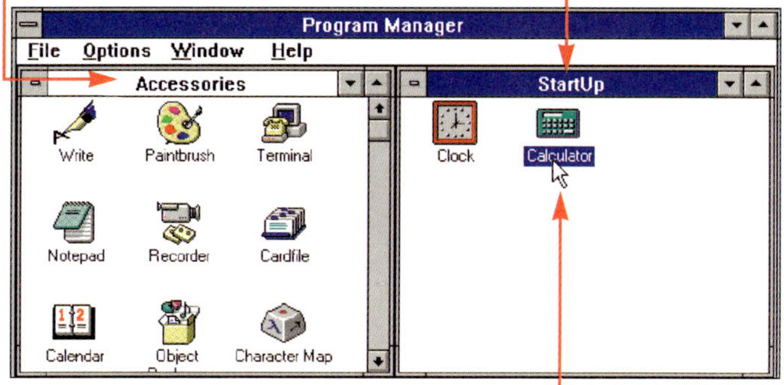

3 To move icons, drag the icons into the StartUp window.

To copy icons, hold down Ctrl while dragging

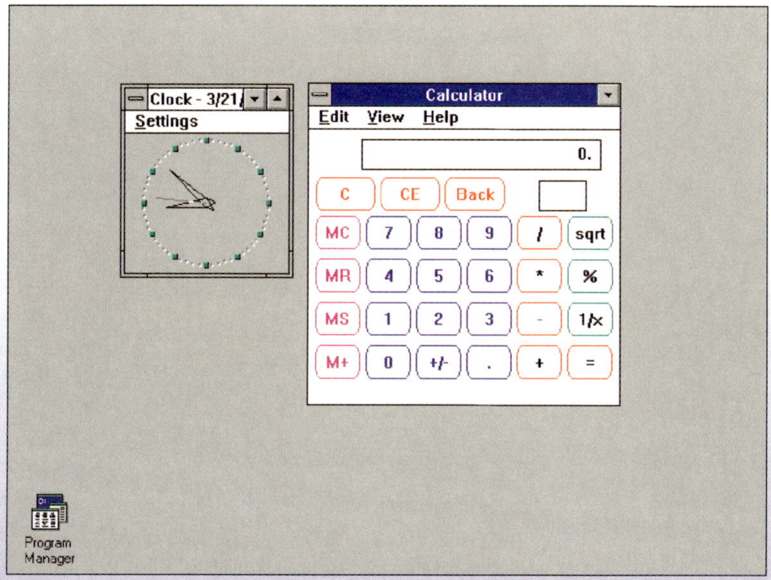

The next time you start Windows, the applications in the StartUp group run immediately

Changing System Settings

After Windows is installed, you can change the Windows system settings without reinstalling Windows. For example, you can change the display type if you get a new monitor or change the settings to add a mouse or a network setup.

To display system settings

1 Open the Main program group.

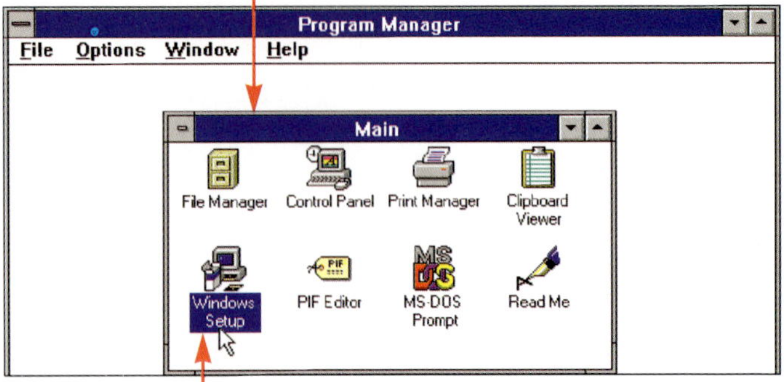

2 Double-click the Windows Setup icon.

3 Choose Options, Change System Settings.

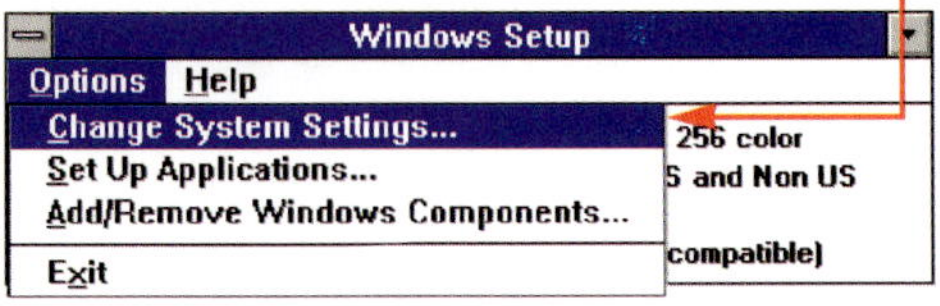

The current settings are shown in the dialog box

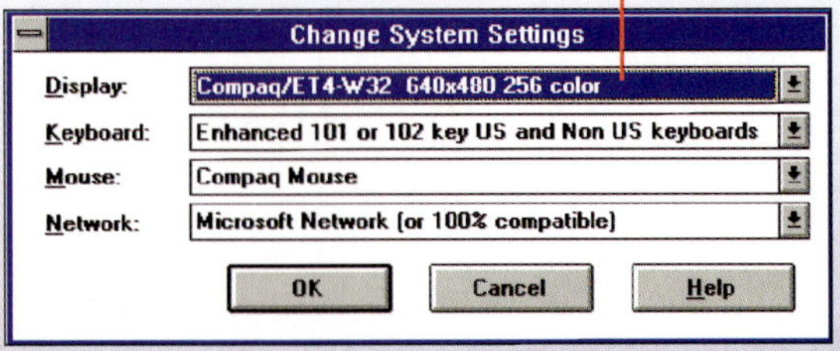

To change the display setting

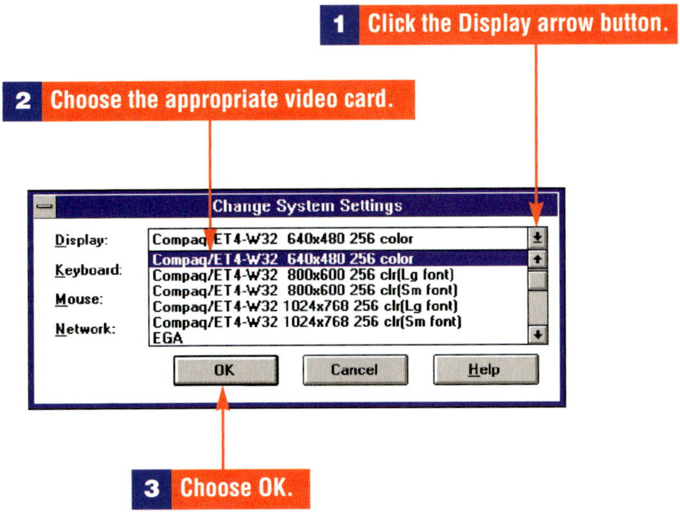

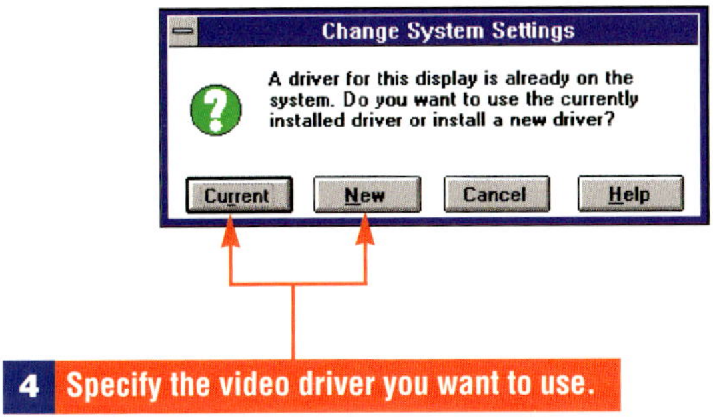

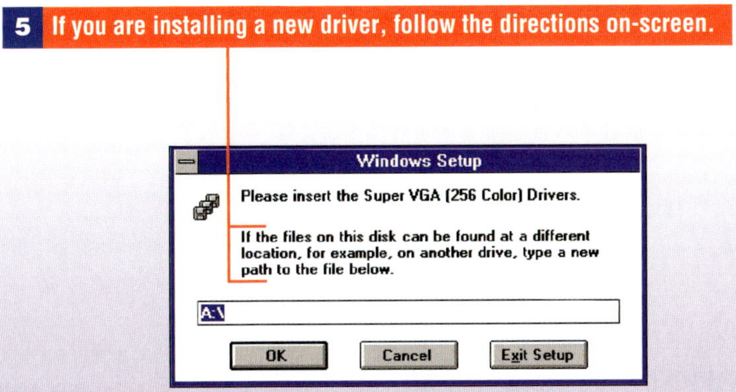

more ▶

6 Choose Restart Windows to use the new settings.

To change the keyboard setting

1 Click the Keyboard arrow button.

2 Choose the setting for your keyboard.

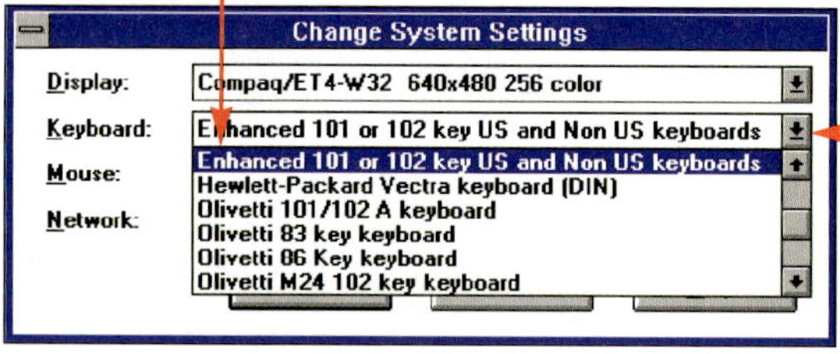

New keyboard setting

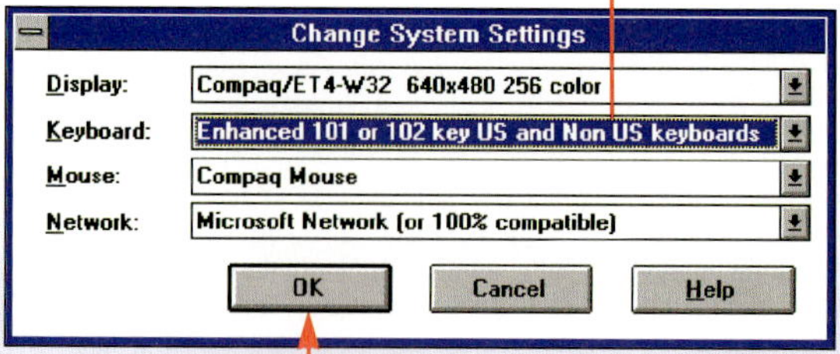

3 Choose OK.

4 If necessary, specify the location of the keyboard driver.

To change the mouse setting

1 Click the Mouse arrow button.

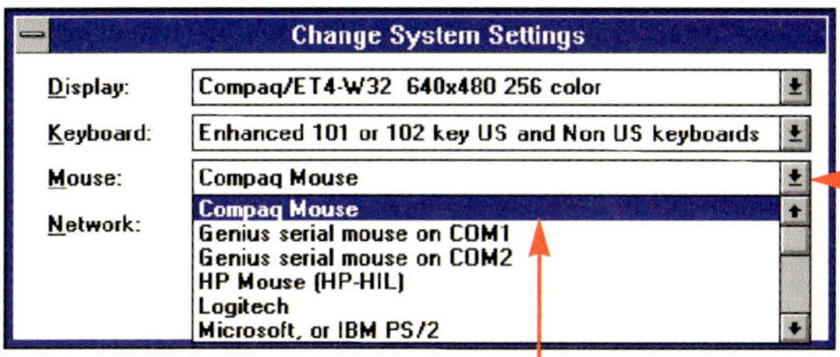

2 Choose the setting that matches your mouse.

New mouse setting

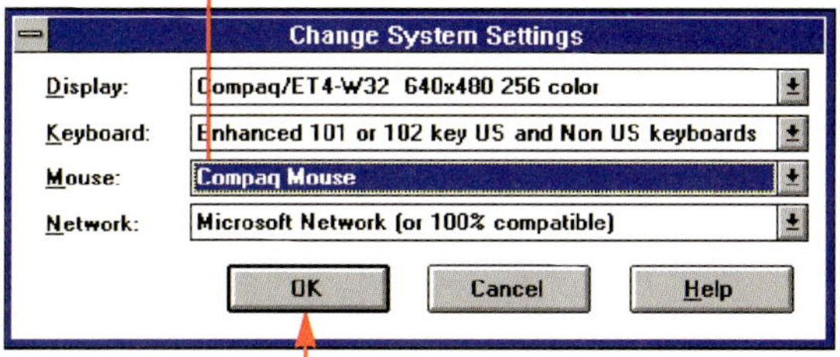

3 Choose OK.

4 Specify the mouse driver (follow the directions on-screen).

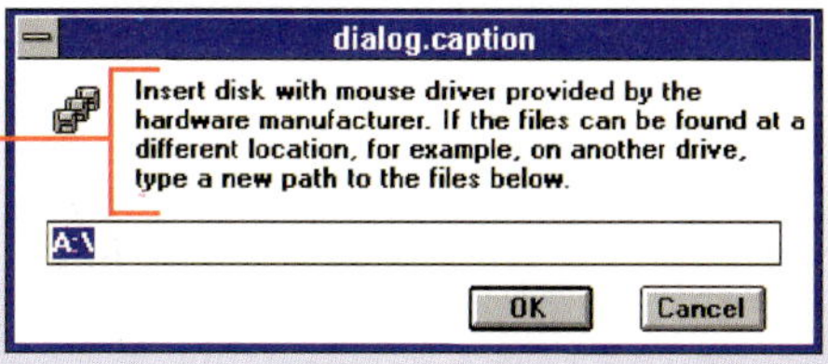

To change the network setting

1 Click the Network arrow button.

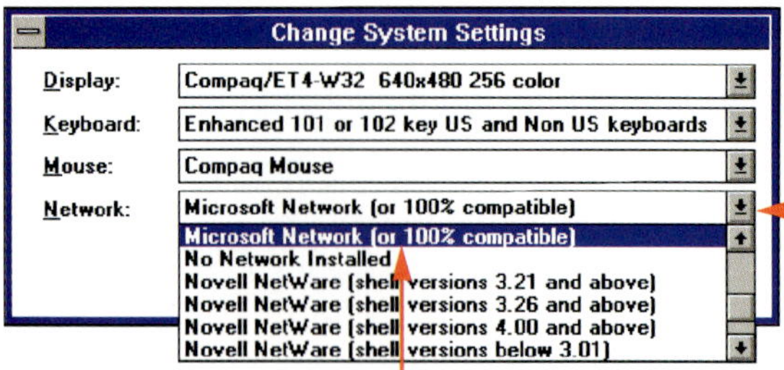

2 Choose the setting for the network you are using.

New network setting

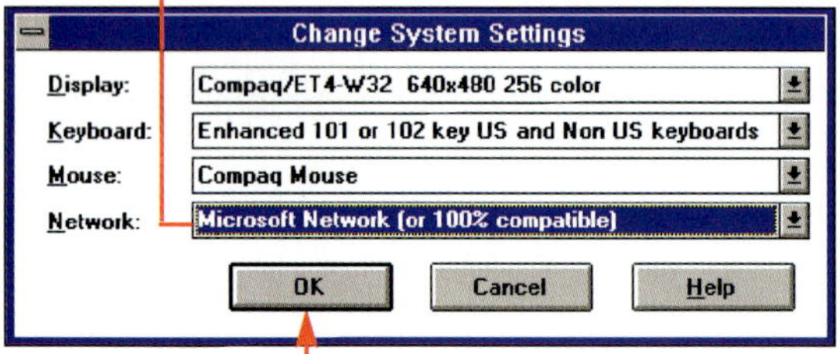

3 Choose OK.

4 If necessary, specify the network driver you are using.

To exit Windows Setup

1 Choose Options, Exit.

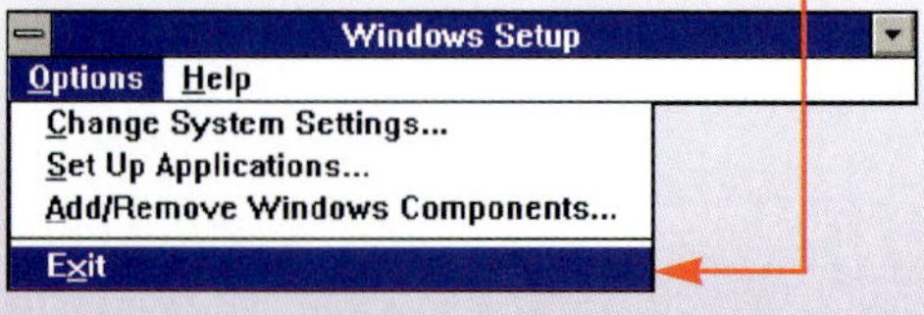

Setting Up Applications

The Set Up Applications feature enables you to install programs to run from Windows. After you install the program, Setup automatically creates an icon for a Windows program or a PIF for a non-Windows program.

To search for applications to install

1 From the Windows Setup menu, choose Options, Set Up Applications.

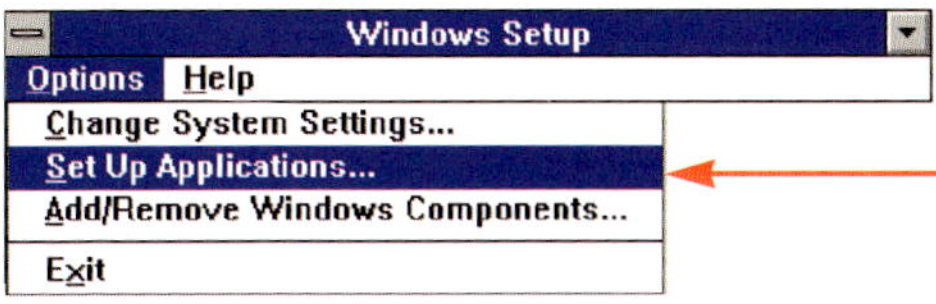

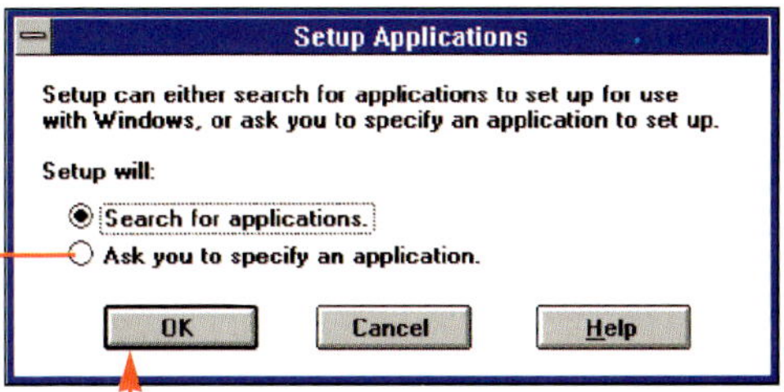

Use this option to set up a single application

2 Choose OK.

3 Click Path or the letter of the drive to search.

4 Choose Search Now.

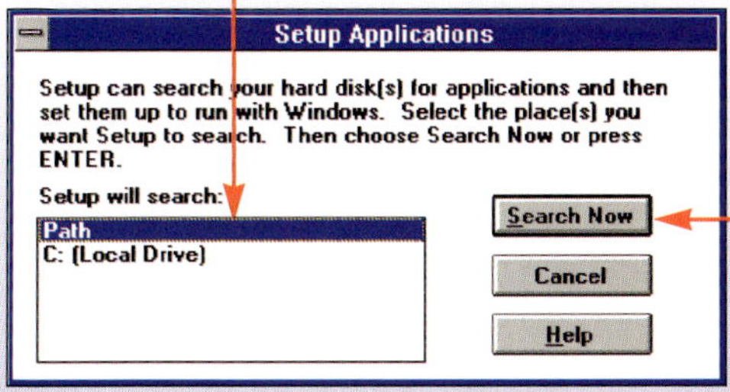

more ▶

5 Select the name of each application as it is found by Setup.

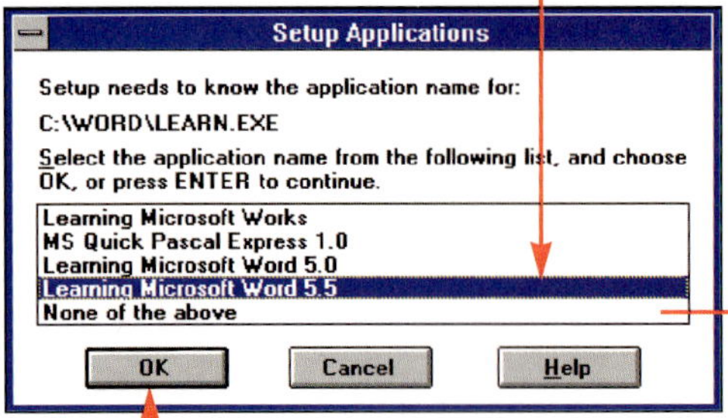

If the name is wrong, click None of the above

6 Choose OK.

7 Select the applications you want to run from Windows.

8 Choose Add.

9 Choose OK.

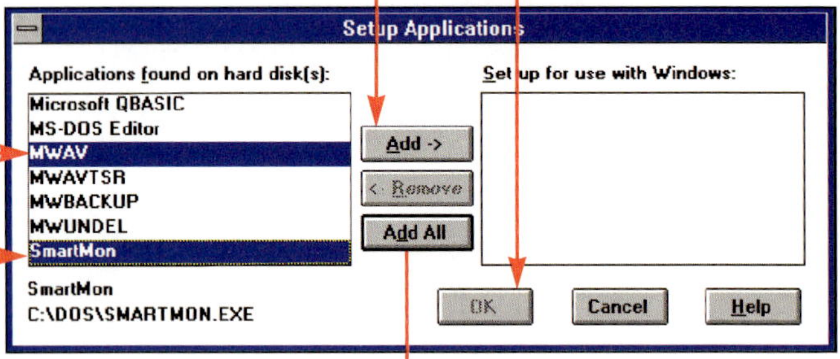

Choose Add All if you want to run all the applications from Windows

To install specific applications

1 From the Windows Setup menu, choose Options, Set Up Applications.

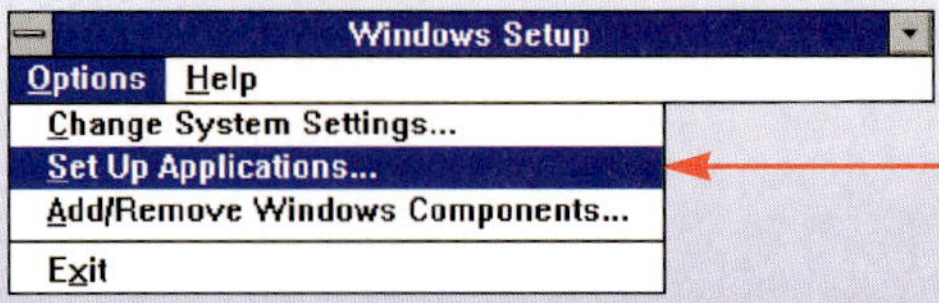

2 Choose Ask you to specify an application.

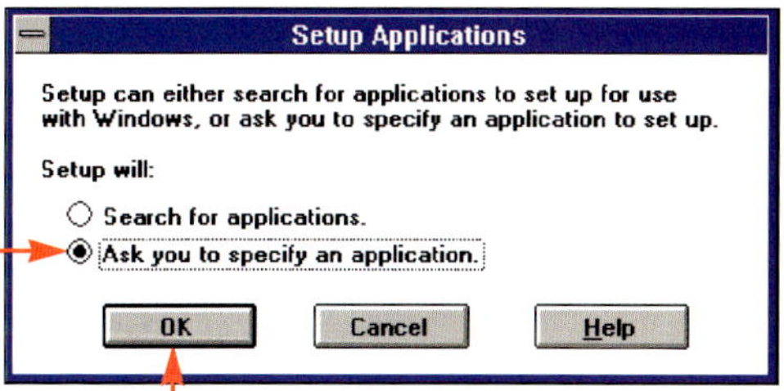

3 Choose OK.

4 Type the path and name of the application's start-up file.

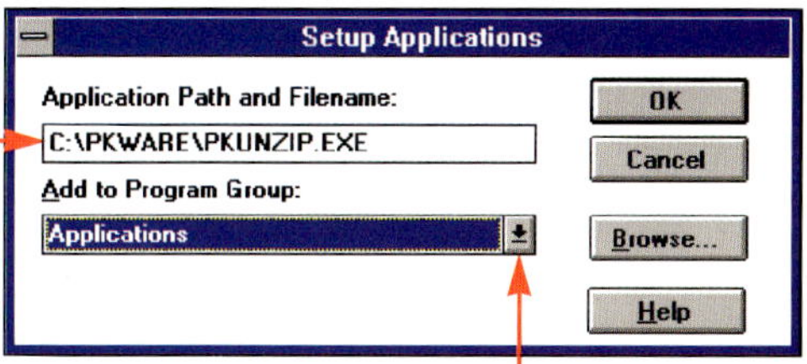

5 Click the Add to program group arrow button.

6 Select the program group where you want to add the application.

7 Choose OK.

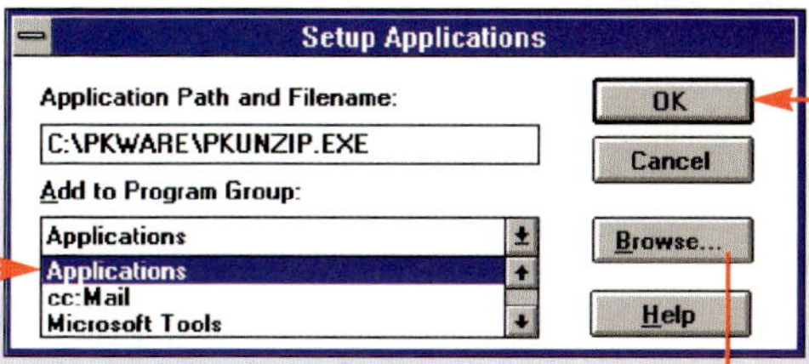

If you're not sure of the path and file name, choose Browse

Adding and Removing Windows Components

You can add or remove Windows components (such as games or screen savers) or specific files within a component. Adding files gives you more applications you can use; removing files regains valuable disk space.

To add or remove Windows components

1 Start Windows Setup.

2 Choose Options, Add/Remove Windows Components.

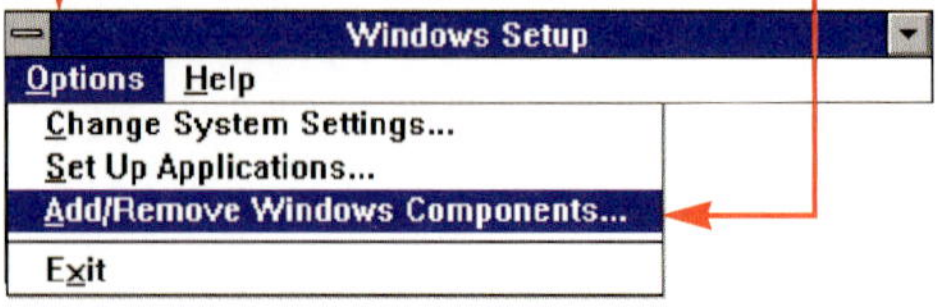

3 Click the check box to add or remove the files for the specified option.

4 Choose OK.

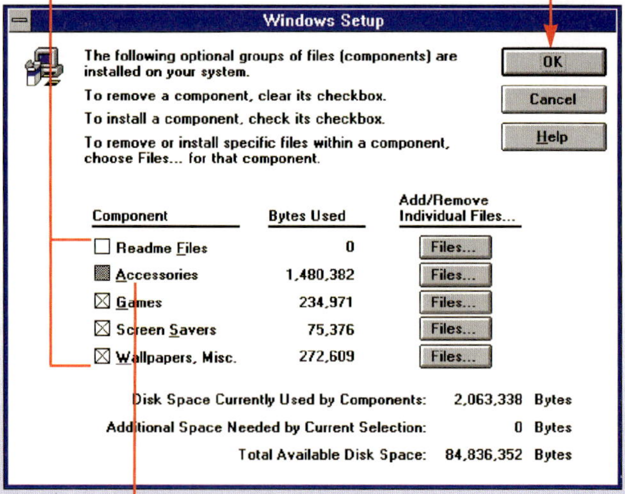

A shaded box indicates that some of the files for that option are already on disk

5 **If adding options, specify where to find the files.**

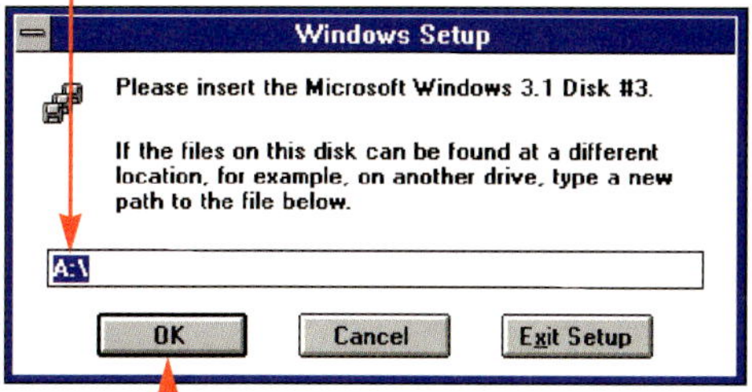

6 **Choose OK.**

7 **If removing options, choose Yes to remove each file.**

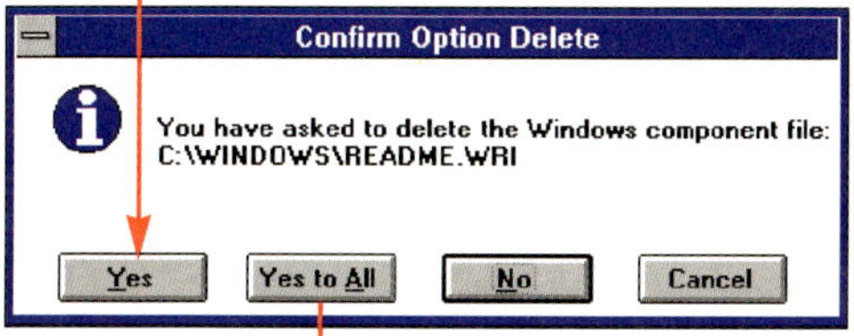

Choose Yes to All to remove all files

To add or remove specific Windows component files

1 Click the check box to add or remove the files for the specified option.

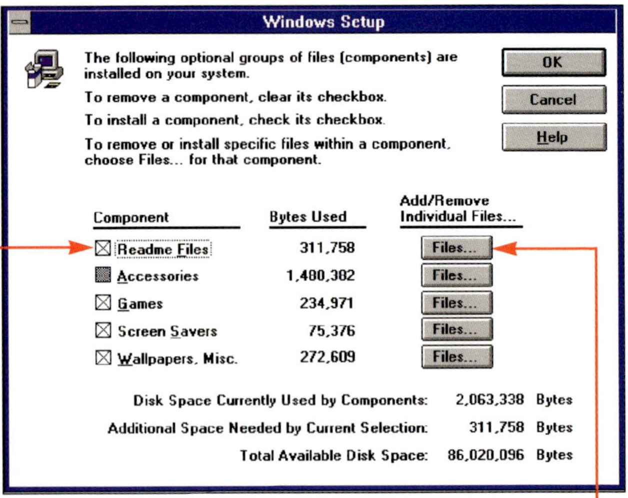

2 Click the component's Files button.

3 If adding files, click the files you want to load in the left box.

4 Choose Add.

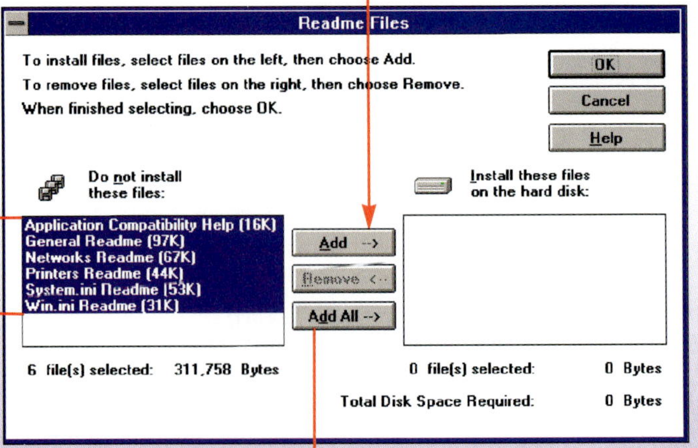

Choose Add All if you want to load all the files

5 If adding files, specify where to find the files.

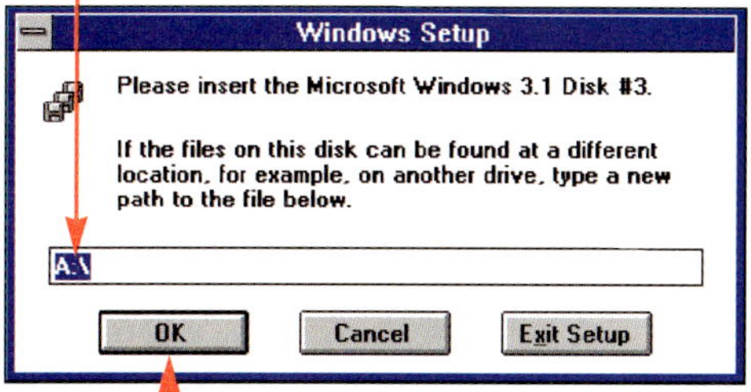

6 Choose OK.

7 If removing files, click the files you want to remove in the right box.

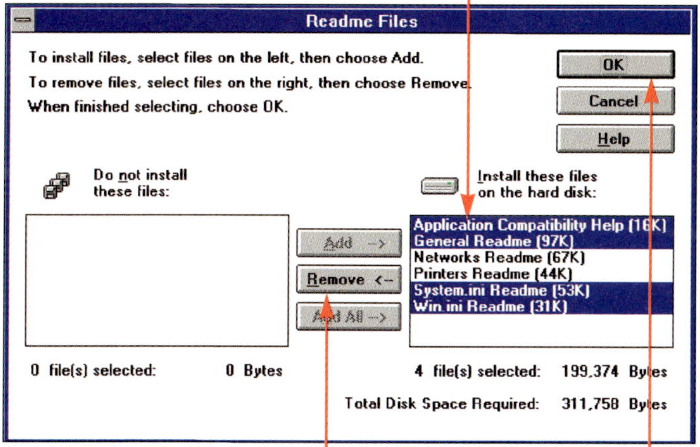

8 Choose Remove.

9 Choose OK.

10 If necessary, confirm that you want to remove the files.

Starting and Exiting Windows Accessories

Windows accessories are stored in the Accessories program group. This section covers the most popular Windows accessories: Write, Paintbrush, Cardfile, Calendar, Calculator, Clock, Media Player, Notepad. You start and exit most accessory programs in the same way.

1 From Program Manager, open the Accessories program group.

2 To start an accessory, double-click its icon.

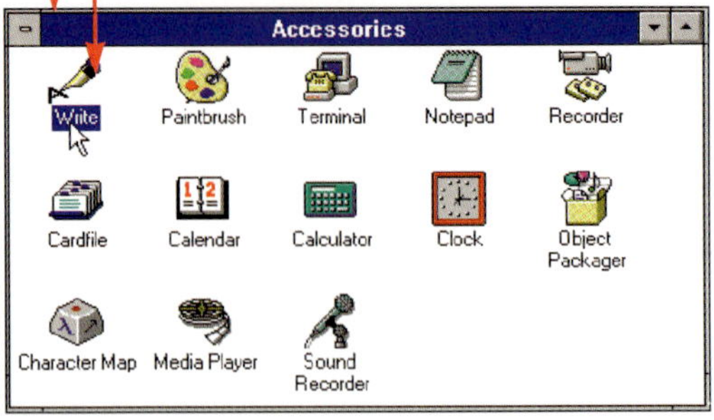

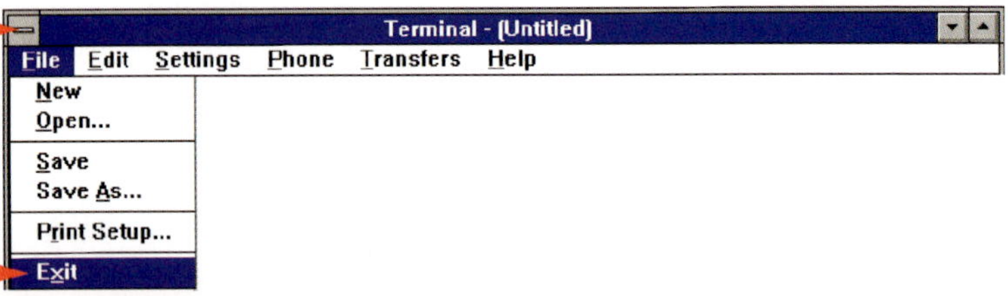

1 Choose File, Exit or double-click the Control menu box to exit.

Write

Write is a simple word processing program. You can create, save, open, edit, and print a document with Write.

To create a document

1 Type the desired text.

Text wraps to the next line automatically

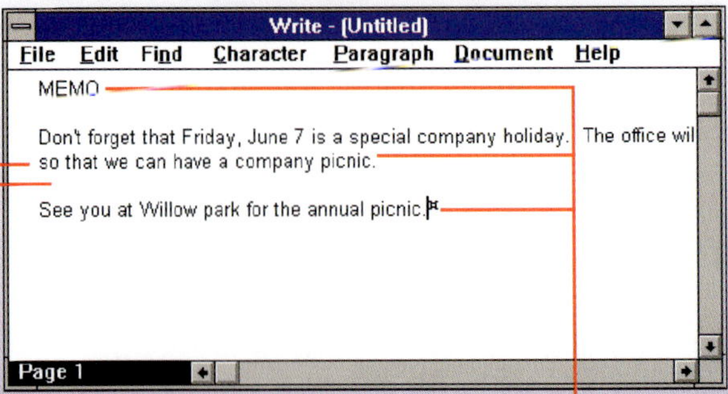

Press Enter to insert a blank line

Press Enter at the end of paragraphs and short lines

To save a document

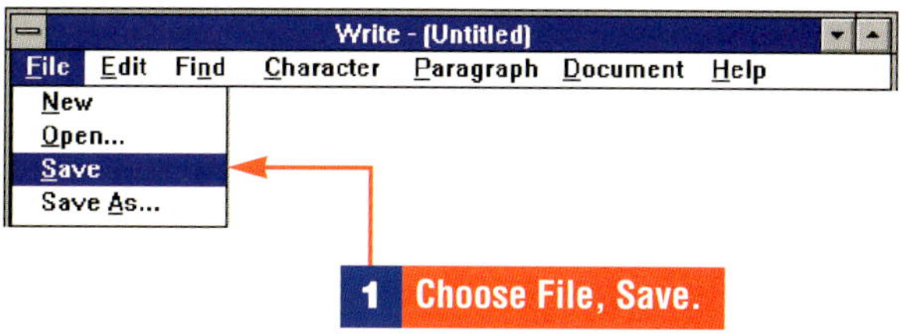

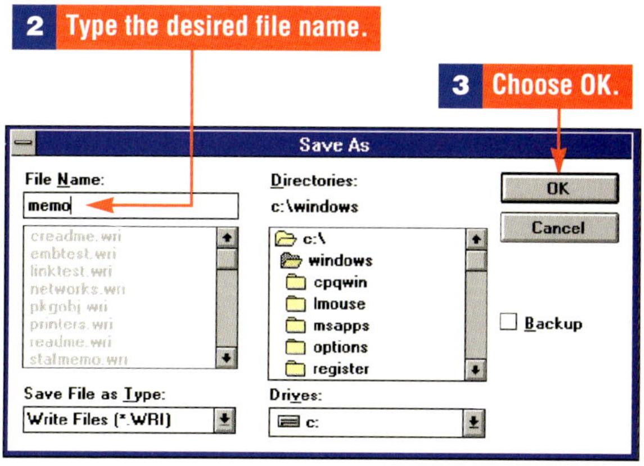

To open a saved document

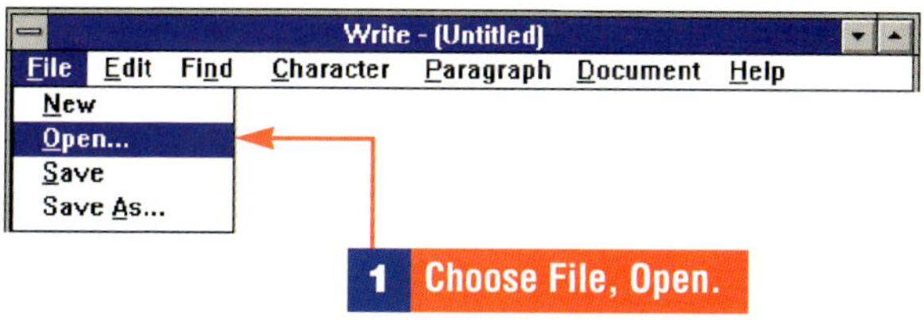

more ▶

2 Double-click the name of the file you want to open.

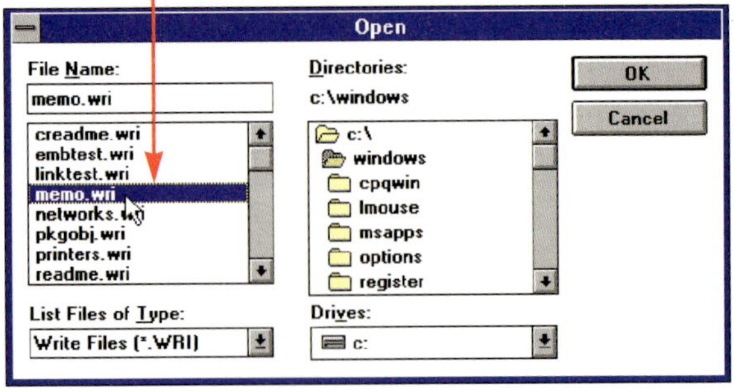

To edit a document

1 Click where you want to begin editing.

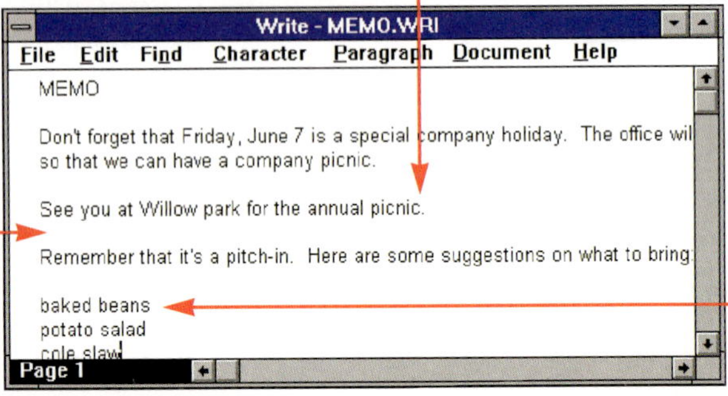

2 Press Enter twice if you want to end a paragraph and insert a blank line.

To delete text, select the text and press Delete

3 Type any new text.

To move and copy text

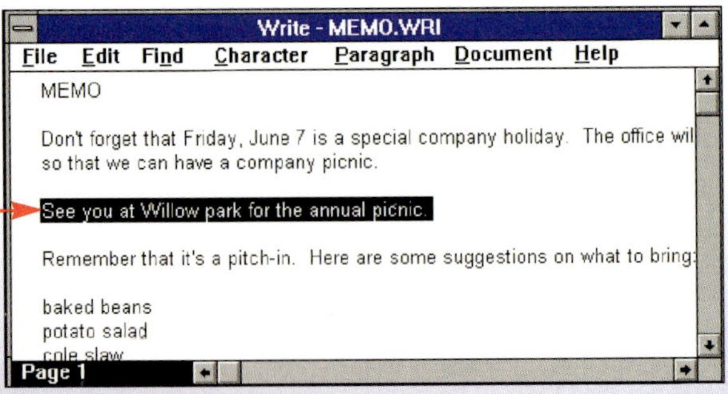

1 Select the text you want to move or copy.

2 Choose Edit, Cut to cut the text or Edit, Copy to copy it.

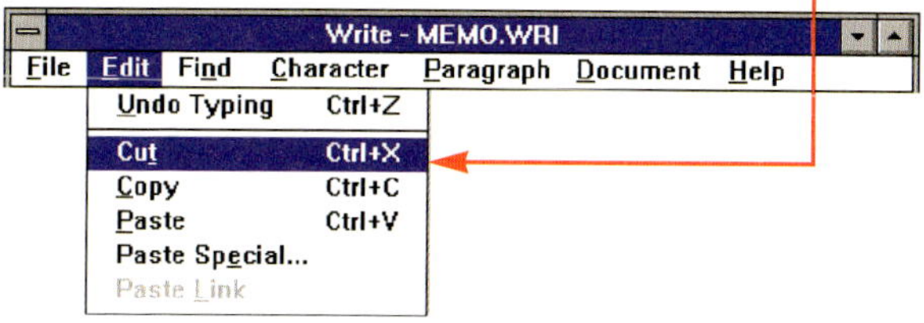

3 Move the insertion point to where you want the text.

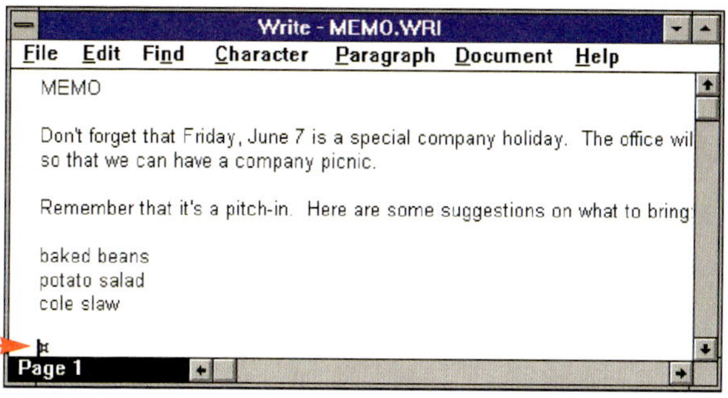

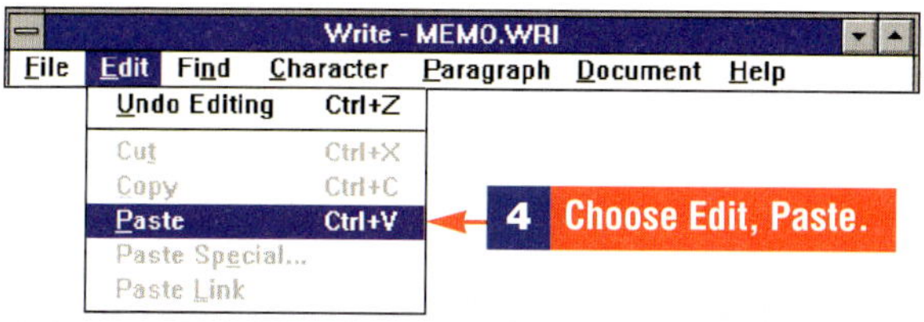

4 Choose Edit, Paste.

To print a document

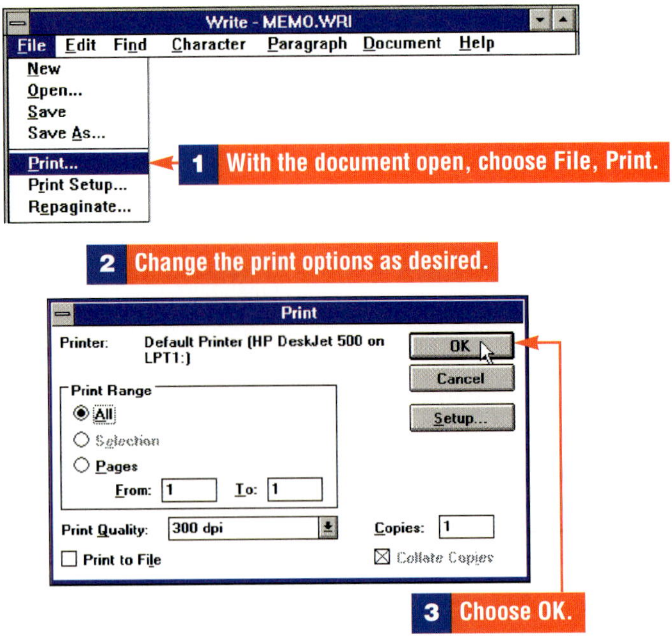

Paintbrush

With Paintbrush, you can create logos, icons, drawings, and other graphic illustrations for your programs or documents.

To create or edit a drawing

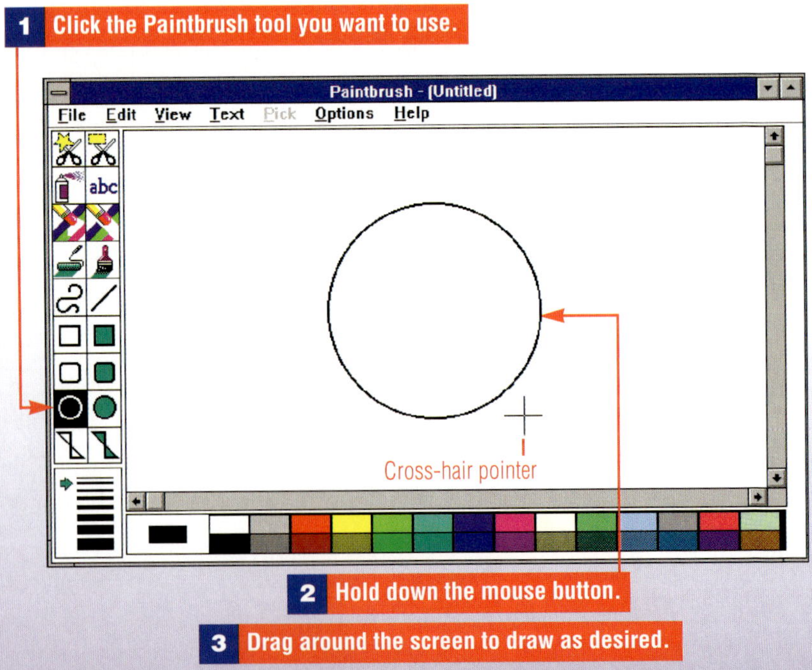

To add text, click the Text tool, place the insertion point, and then type the text

Paintbrush tools

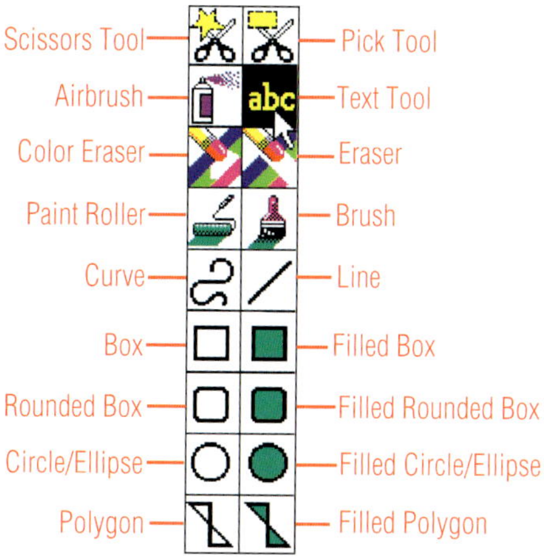

Tool	Usage
Scissors Tool	Cuts out parts of the drawing you don't want
Pick Tool	Selects parts of the drawing to copy or cut
Airbrush	Sprays color in a dotted pattern
Text Tool	Adds letters and characters
Color Eraser	Erases the foreground color, exposing color underneath
Eraser	Erases color, text, and lines
Paint Roller	Fills closed areas with color
Brush	Draws lines as you drag (to draw horizontal or vertical lines, hold down Shift while dragging)
Curve	Draws curved lines
Line	Draws straight lines
Box	Draws boxes with straight corners (hold down Shift while dragging to get squares)
Filled Box	Draws filled boxes with square corners
Rounded Box	Draws boxes with rounded corners
Filled Rounded Box	Draws filled boxes with rounded corners
Circle/Ellipse	Draws circles or ellipses (hold down Shift while dragging to get circles)
Filled Circle/Ellipse	Draws filled circles or ellipses
Polygon	Draws polygons from connected straight lines
Filled Polygon	Draws filled polygons

To change line styles or colors

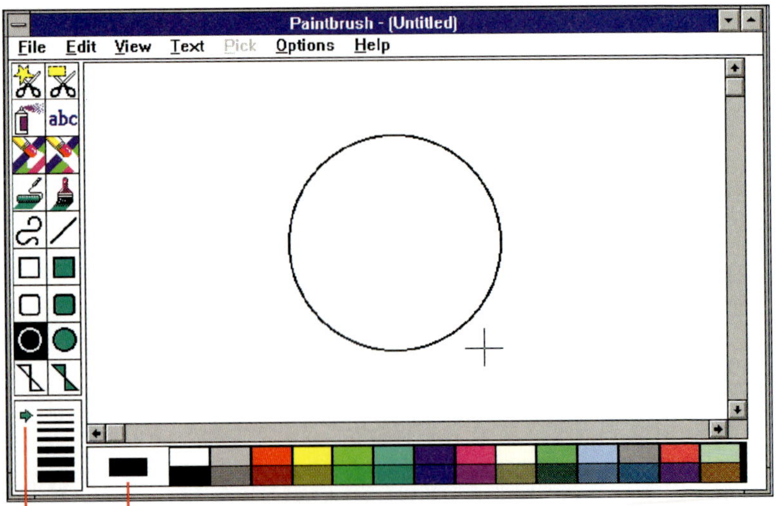

The current color appears in this box

An arrow points to the current line style

1 Click the line style or color you want to use.

To change text fonts

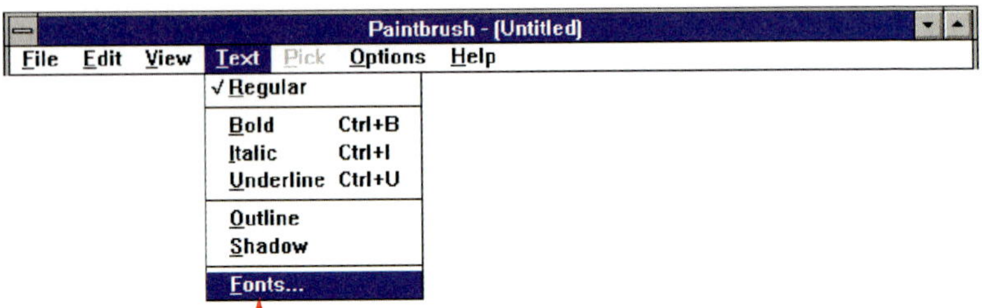

1 Choose Text, Fonts.

2 Click the font and font style you want to use.

3 Click the font size you want to use.

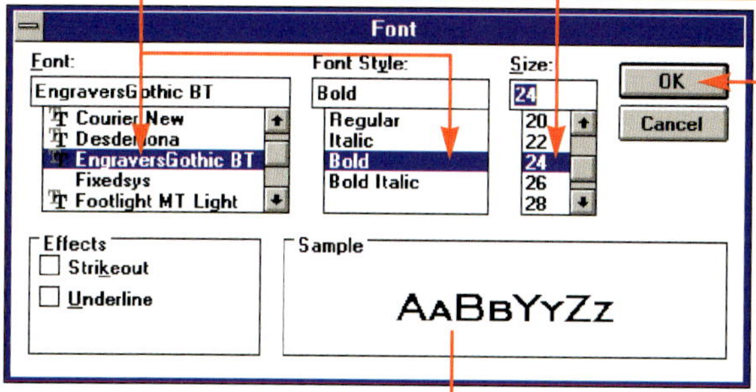

The sample changes as you change your selections

4 Choose OK.

To save a drawing

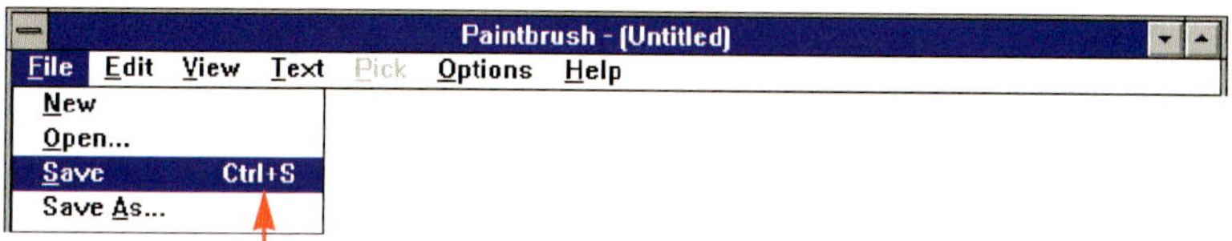

1 Choose File, Save.

For a quick save, press Ctrl+S

2 Type a file name.

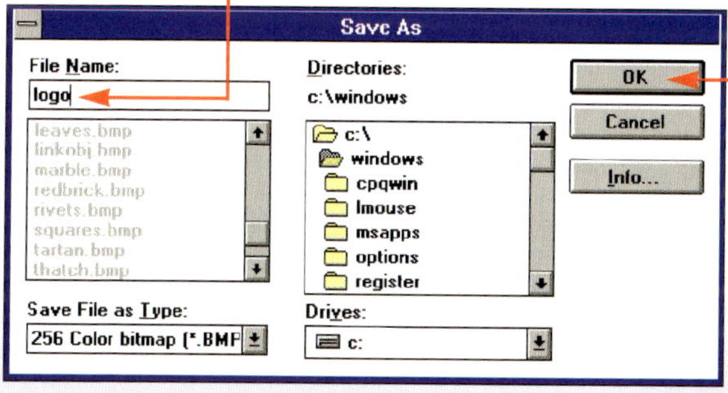

3 Choose OK.

This dialog box appears only the first time you save a drawing

Cardfile

Cardfile is a card-type database, like an electronic Rolodex. You can create a collection of cards; all the cards are stored together as one unit. You can also edit cards, add new cards, and print the cards.

To create a card file

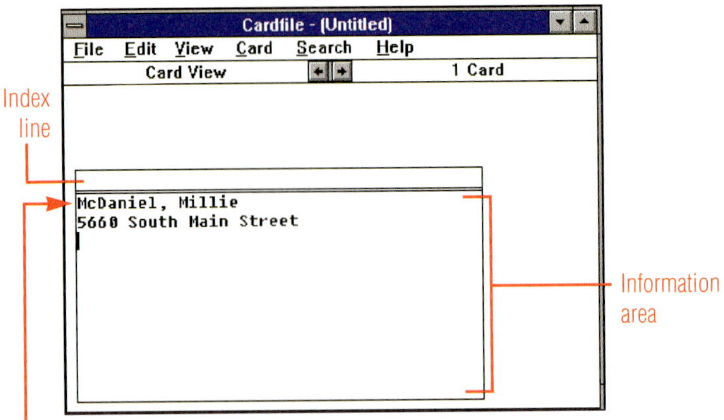

1 Type the text and press Enter for each line on the card.

2 Press F6 or double-click the index line (optional).

3 Type an index line for the card (optional).

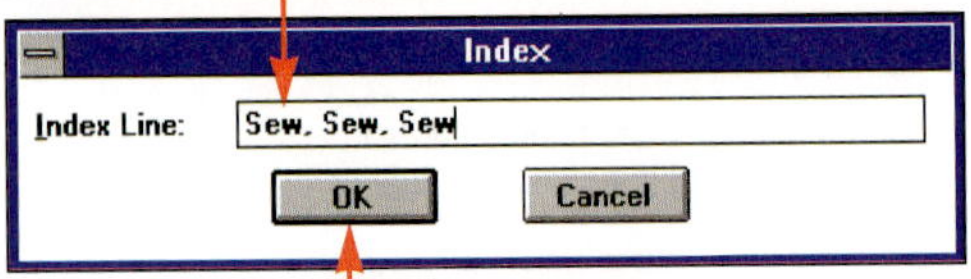

4 Choose OK.

Cardfile uses the index line entries to sort the cards

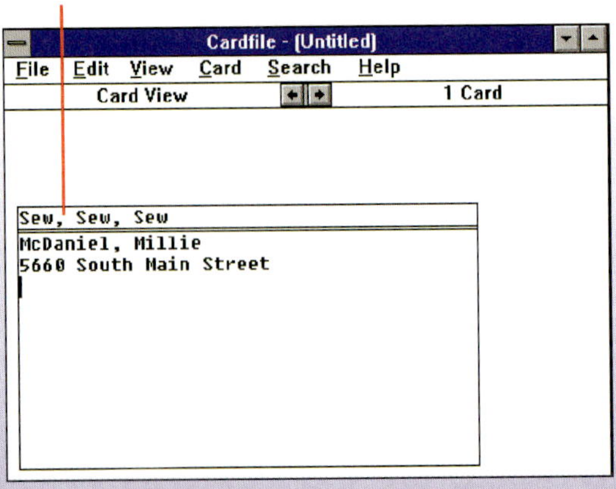

To save a card file

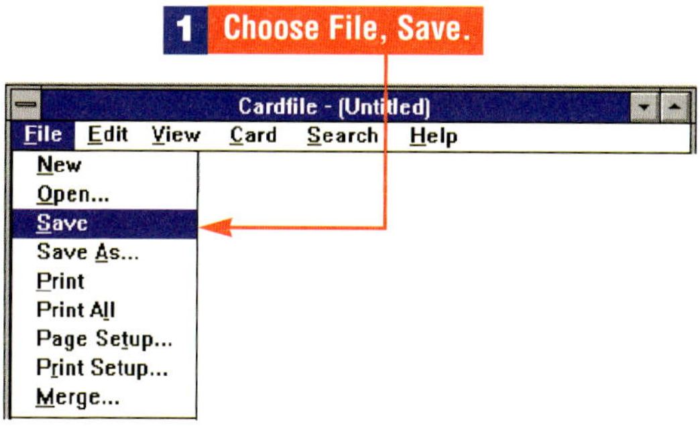

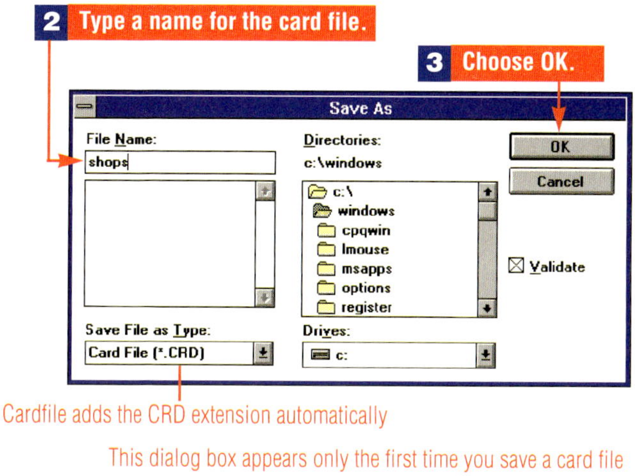

To open a card file

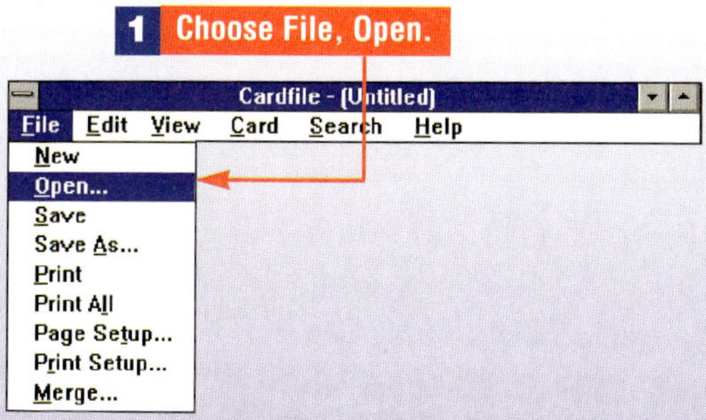

more ▶

2 Double-click the name of the card file you want.

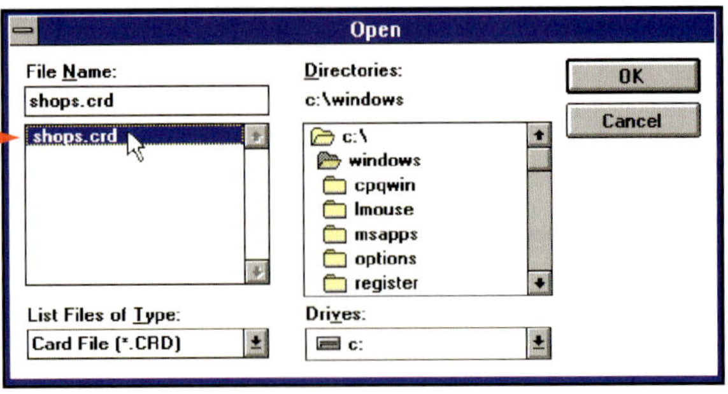

To add cards to a card file

1 With the card file open, press F7.

2 Type the text for the index line (optional).

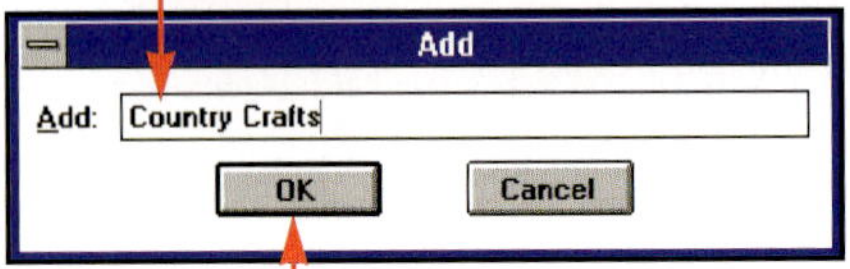

3 Choose OK.

4 Type the text of the card, pressing Enter after each line.

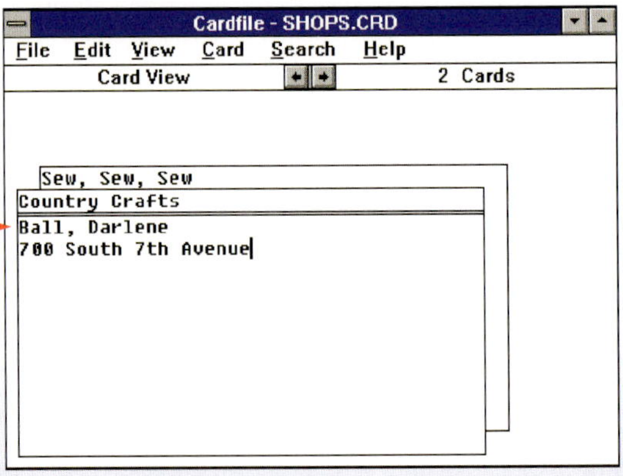

To find a card

1 Choose Search, Find.

If you know the index entry, press F4 and type the entry to find the card quickly

2 Type the text (from index or information area) you want to find.

3 Choose Find Next.

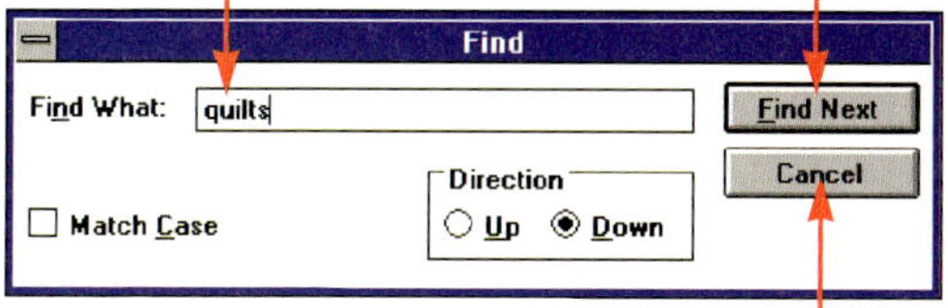

Choose Find Next again if Cardfile doesn't find the right card the first time

4 Choose Cancel to close the dialog box.

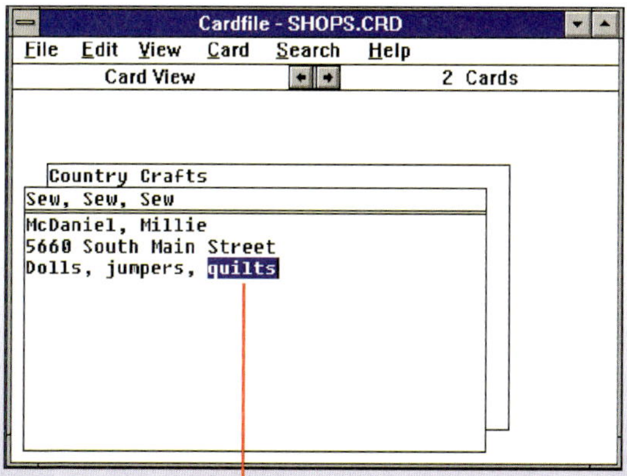

Cardfile moves to the card that matches the search text

To edit a card

1 Find the card in the card file.

2 Click where you want to add new text; then press Enter.

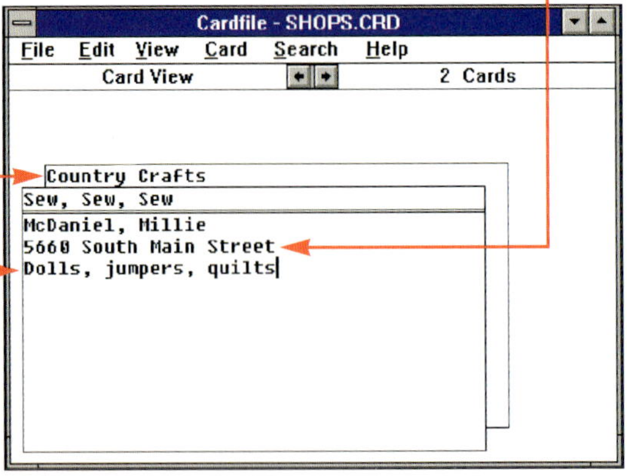

3 Type the new text.

To delete text, select the text and press Delete

To print cards

1 Choose File, Print All to print all cards.

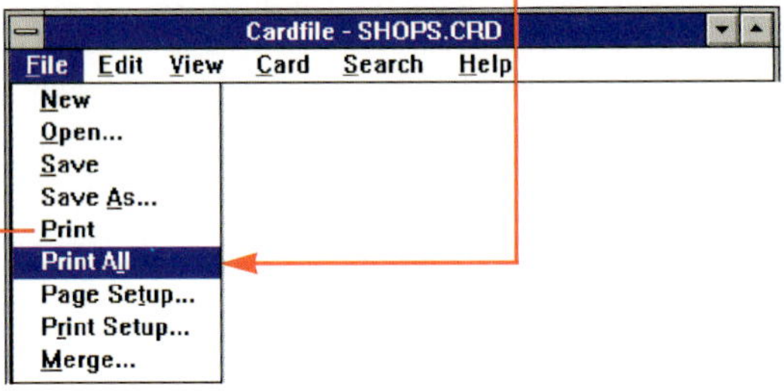

Choose File, Print to print only the current card

To delete a card

1 Find the card you want to delete.

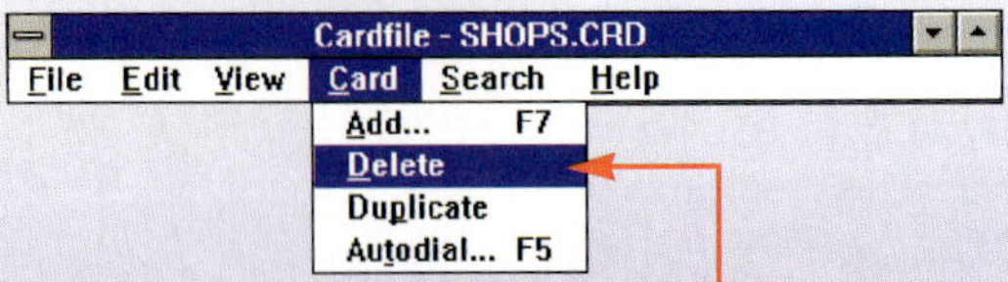

2 Choose Card, Delete.

3 Confirm the deletion by choosing OK.

Calendar

Calendar is an appointment-scheduler with a built-in alarm that you can use to remind you of important meetings, appointments, and so on.

To schedule an appointment

1 Click the right arrow button to scroll to the date you want.

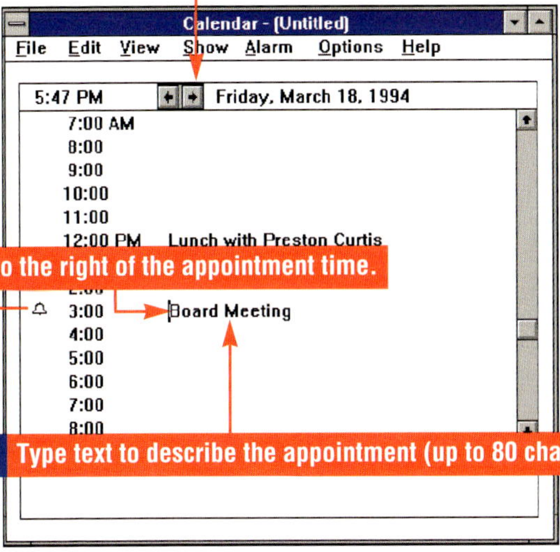

2 Click to the right of the appointment time.

3 Type text to describe the appointment (up to 80 characters).

4 Press F5 to set the alarm for that appointment (optional).

A bell appears next to the appointment time

To delete an appointment, select the appointment and press Delete

5 Choose File, Save to save the calendar file.

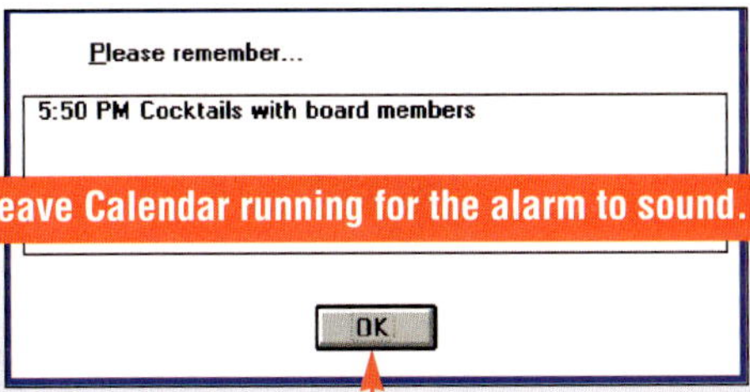

6 Leave Calendar running for the alarm to sound.

7 When the appointment reminder appears, choose OK to close the dialog box.

Calendar sounds an alarm at appointment time

Calculator

Calculator is a desktop calculator with scientific and financial functions. This utility works just like a pocket calculator, with one difference: you can use Calculator with the mouse or with the 10-key pad on your keyboard. To use the 10-key pad, be sure that Num Lock is turned on.

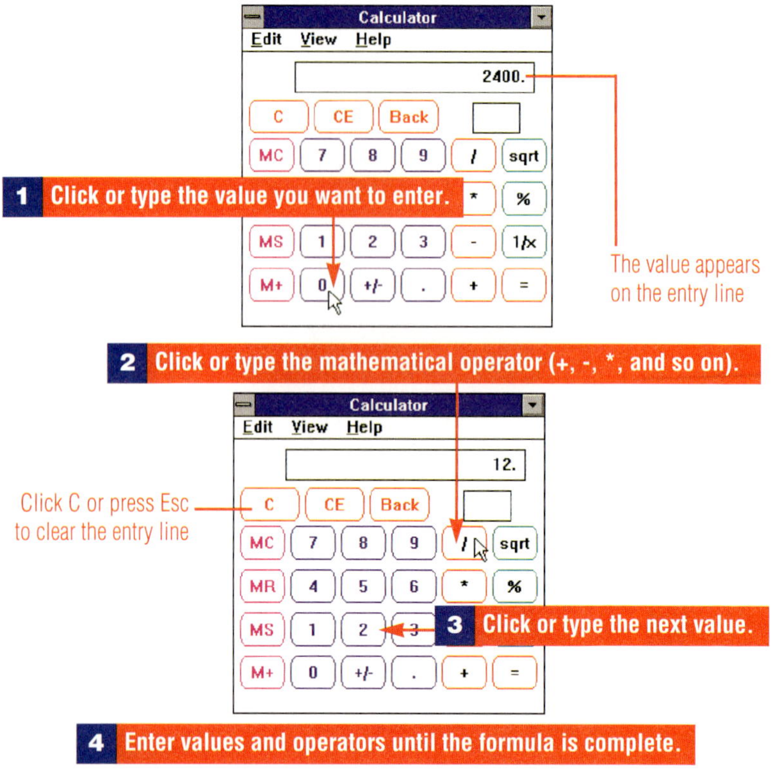

Clock

Clock is an on-screen analog or digital clock. You can customize the clock to display or not display the date, seconds, and so on, or to use a special font in the digital version. To change the clock format, choose Settings, Analog. To resize the clock, drag the border.

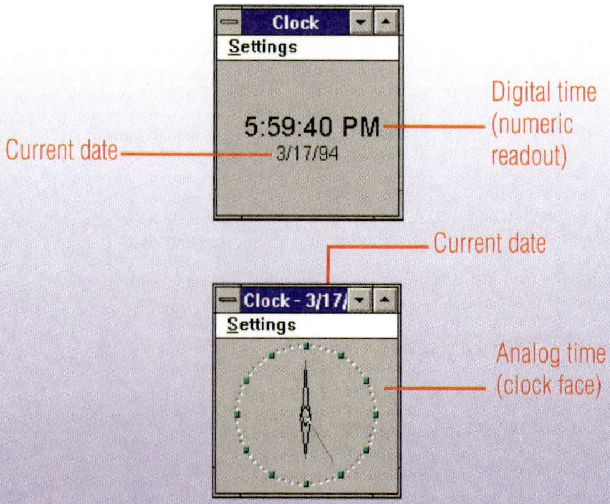

Media Player

Media Player is a program that enables you to control multimedia devices such as Windows-compatible multimedia voice, animated video files, and MIDI-based music files.

To operate Media Player

1 Choose Device and select the device you want to play.

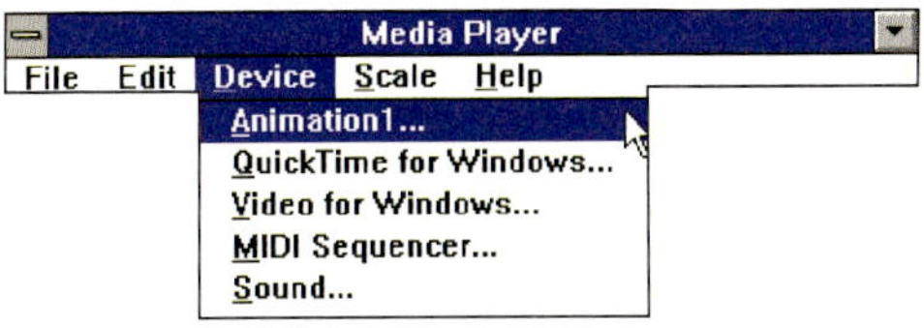

2 Choose File, Open to open the file you want to play.

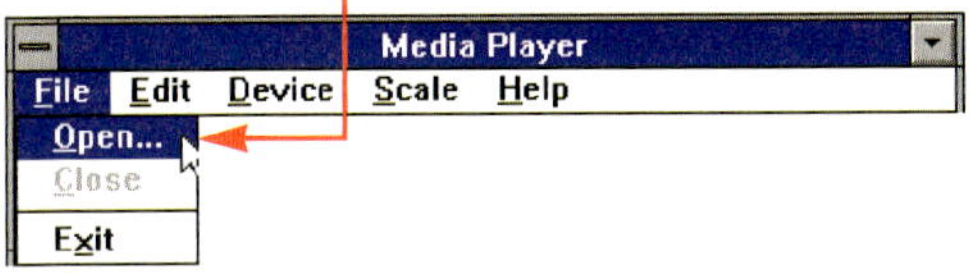

3 Choose the drive where the file is located.

4 Choose the directory that contains the file.

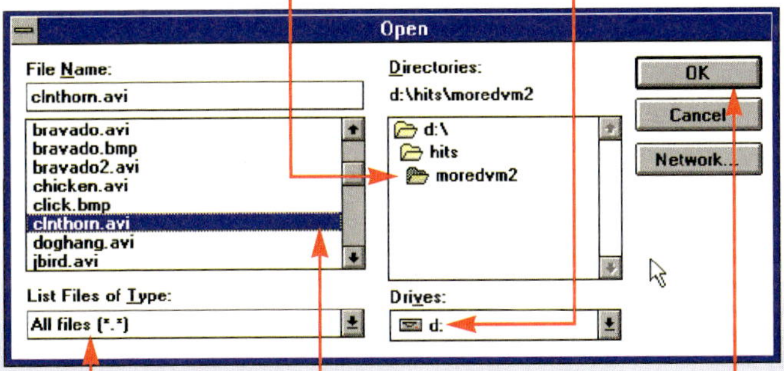

5 Specify the file type.

6 Select the file you want to open.

7 Choose OK.

To play a media file

1 Click the Play button to begin playing the file.

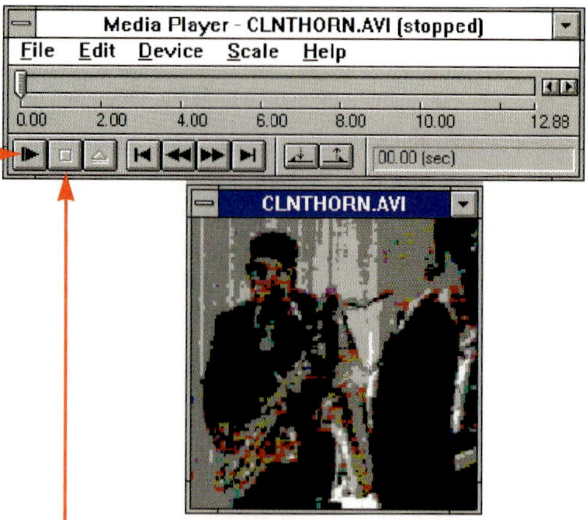

2 Click Stop to stop the file.

Click Pause to pause the file; click Pause or Play to restart

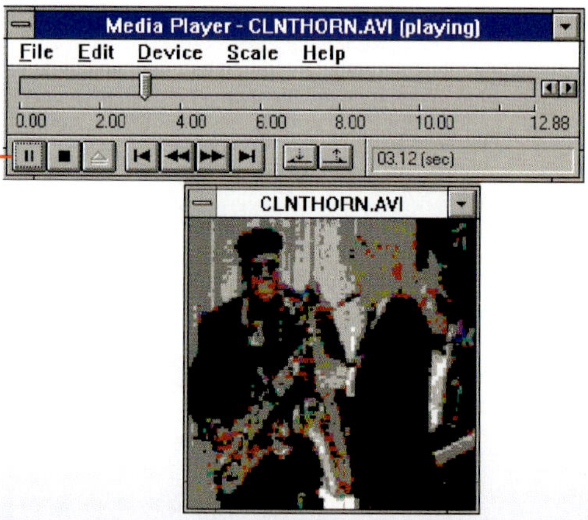

Click Eject to eject the file, if the device supports this action

Notepad

Notepad is a simple text editor, useful for recording reminder notes or creating and modifying ASCII files (such as batch files).

To create a note

1 Type the text for the note.

2 Press Enter to end each line.

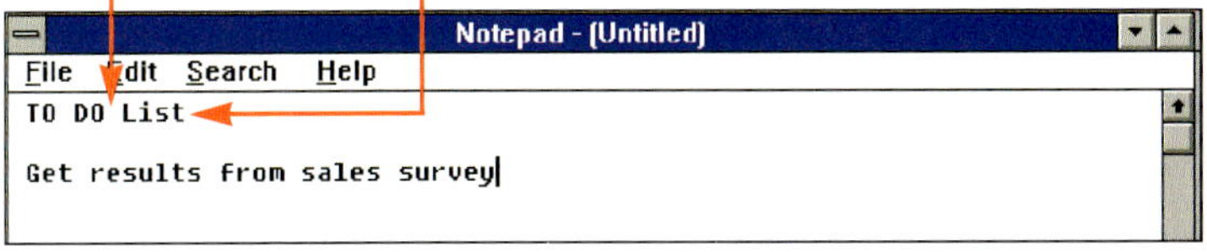

To save a note

1 Choose File, Save.

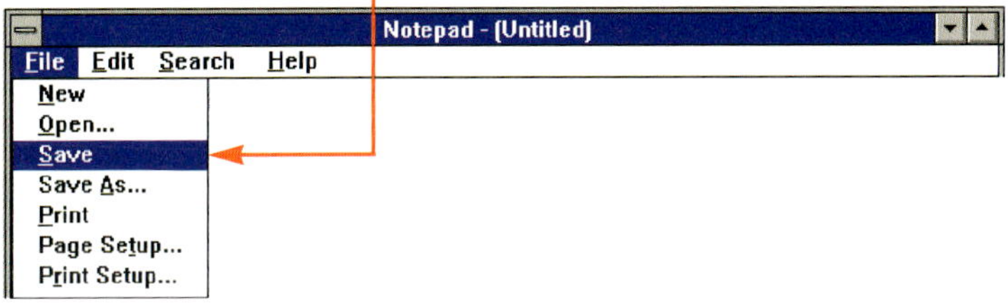

This dialog box appears only the first time you save a notepad

2 Type a file name for the notepad.

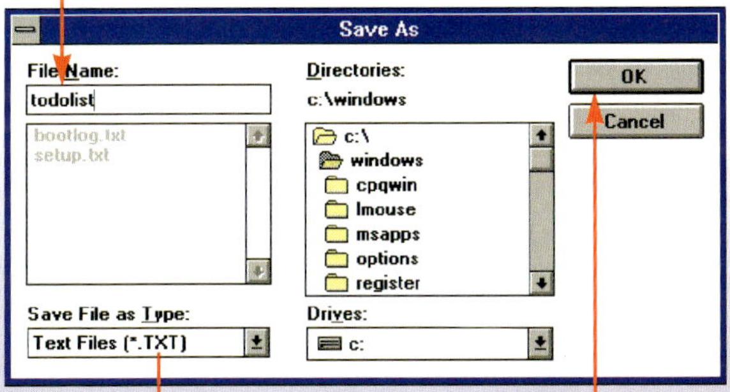

3 Choose OK.

Notepad supplies the TXT extension automatically

To edit a note

1 Choose File, Open.

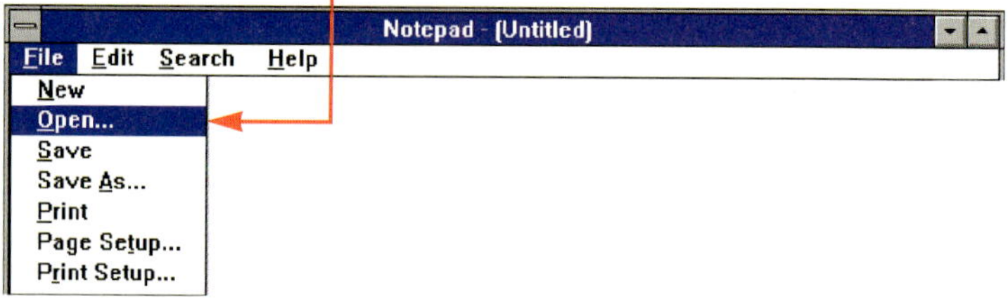

2 Double-click the name of the file you want to edit.

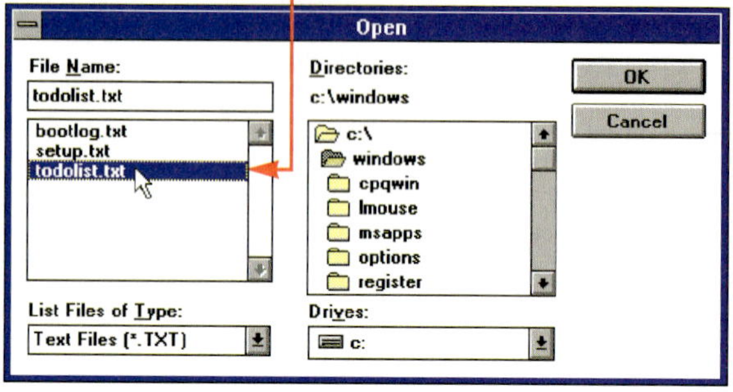

3 Type the new text as desired.

Press Enter to insert blank lines

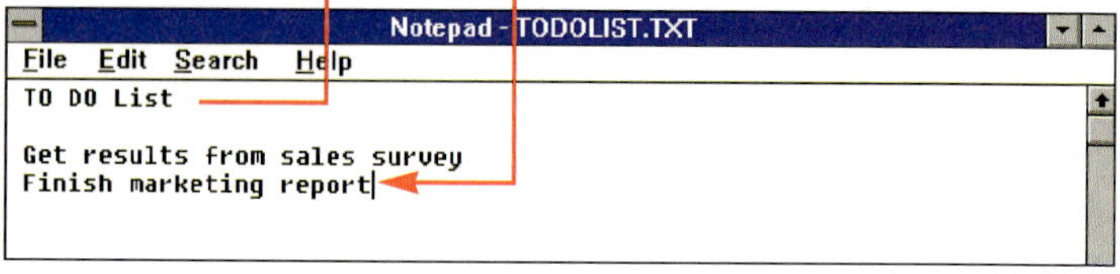

To delete existing text, highlight the text and press Delete

To print a note

1 With the note file open, choose File, Print.

The file prints immediately

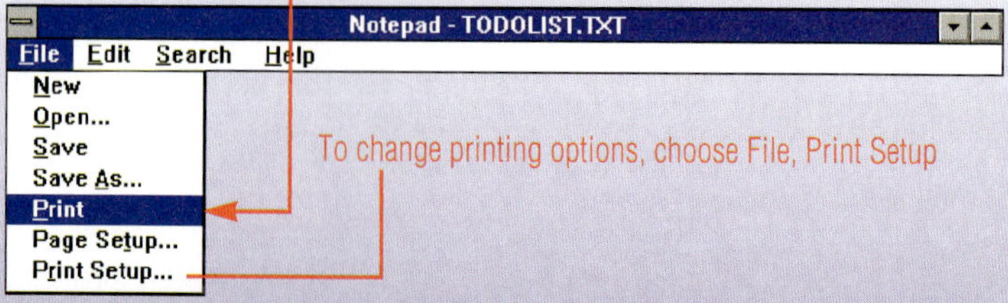

To change printing options, choose File, Print Setup

Index

F

G-H

I-J

K

L-M

T

U-V

W-Z